# ENVIRONMENTAL EXPRESSIVE THERAPIES

*Environmental Expressive Therapies* contributes to the emerging phenomenon of eco-arts therapy by highlighting the work that international expressive arts therapists have accomplished to establish a framework for incorporating nature as a partner in creative/expressive arts therapy practices. Each of the contributors explores a particular specialization and outlines the implementation of multi-professional and multi-modal "earth-based" creative/expressive interventions that practitioners can use in their daily work with patients with various clinical needs. Different forms of creative/expressive practices—such as creative writing, play therapy techniques, visual arts, expressive music, dramatic performances, and their combinations with wilderness and animal-assisted therapy—are included in order to maximize the spectrum of treatment options. *Environmental Expressive Therapies* represents a variety of practical approaches and tools for therapists to use to achieve multiple treatment goals and promote sustainable lifestyles for individuals, families, and communities.

**Alexander Kopytin, PhD**, is a psychiatrist, psychotherapist, professor in the psychotherapy department at Northwest Medical I. Mechnokov University, head of postgraduate training in art therapy at the Academy of Postgraduate Pedagogical Training at St. Petersburg, and chair of the Russian Art Therapy Association. He introduced group interactive art psychotherapy in 1996 and has since initiated, supported, and supervised numerous art therapy projects dealing with different clinical and non-clinical populations in Russia. Dr. Kopytin has also written and edited several books on art therapy and art psychotherapy.

**Madeline Rugh, PhD, ATR-BC,** is an assistant professor in psychology and visual art at St. Gregory's University in Shawnee, Oklahoma. Dr. Rugh has facilitated numerous workshops, both internationally and in the United States, on art therapy with disabled older adults, art therapy and spirituality, and art therapy and ecopsychology.

# ENVIRONMENTAL EXPRESSIVE THERAPIES

## Nature-Assisted Theory and Practice

*Edited by Alexander Kopytin and Madeline Rugh*

Routledge
Taylor & Francis Group
NEW YORK AND LONDON

First edition published 2017
by Routledge
605 Third Avenue, New York, NY 10017

and by Routledge
4 Park Square, Milton Park, Abingdon, Oxon OX14 4RN

*Routledge is an imprint of the Taylor & Francis Group, an informa business*



*Library of Congress Cataloging-in-Publication Data*
A catalog record for this book has been requested

ISBN: 978-1-138-23307-2 (hbk)
ISBN: 978-1-138-23308-9 (pbk)
ISBN: 978-1-315-31045-9 (ebk)

Typeset in Minion
by Apex CoVantage, LLC

# CONTENTS

# FIGURES

# FOREWORD

## Artistic Expression as a Force of Nature

*Shaun McNiff*

Alexander Kopytin and Madeline Rugh are once again taking a lead role in aligning the arts in therapy with nature. This anthology builds upon their *"Green Studio": Nature and the Arts in Therapy* (2016) and makes it clear that the time has come for a new paradigm of health and well-being, one that resonates closely with both creative expression and the whole of life. As the editors emphasize, the arts can be essential contributors to the growing movement toward "eco-therapeutic" thought and methods. Edith Cobb (1977/1993) was the first to name the creative imagination as an eco-system growing from childhood to then shape subsequent creative expression, and it is assuring to see these ideas maturing and expanding to worldwide practice in the arts, psychology, religion (Tucker, 2003), and other fields.

As we give respect and attention to our physical and natural environments, there is a corresponding effect on our selves. In caring for nature, we repair ourselves and ideally do a better job at this when the objective is not narrowly self-serving, when we view ourselves as caretakers of environments that sustain all of life. This way of thinking about well-being is distinctly different from the more self-centered perspectives that often permeate psychology with little recognition of the reciprocal influences between personal actions and environmental forces.

Eco-centric thought and methods restore lost relations with what this book calls "earth-based" values, principles that define the cosmologies of indigenous peoples throughout the world and inform the contemporary call for a "deep cultural therapy" (Berry, 1988, p. 206) that is needed to address the serious threats posed by the one-sided assumption that nature serves us. Peter London was one of the first in our arts therapy community to call attention to these issues in *Drawing Closer to Nature* (2003). In the spirit of

Thomas Berry, he spoke of how nature is "thick with interiority" (p. 69) and it "elevates us" (p. 75) when we care for it. Back to nature is back to reality. It is not a regressive atavism but rather a realization of the importance of being more attuned to what world traditions perceive as the vital and creative energy (*ch'i/ki/gi*, East Asia; *prana*, India; *mana*, Polynesia; *pneuma*, Greece) circulating through all forms of life, large and small (McNiff, 2016) and potentially contributing to a worldwide community of creation.

During the first decade of my work with the arts and therapy I looked beyond exclusive attachment to contemporary psychology to understand art healing. In researching the place of what we might call art medicine in world traditions, present and past (1979, 1981, 1992, 2004), I discovered transcultural elements such as the attribution of illness to soul loss and the person's alienation from physical and interpersonal environments. The art medicines generated by creative expression are innate aspects of nature. I have always felt that art healing, both present and past, happens within creative spaces that support the vital circulation of creative energy and its ability to transform difficulties into affirmations of life. My choice to work in groups and communities is an acknowledgment of how creative spaces act as nature's slipstreams supporting all participants in a communal effort to activate and access creative energy inside and outside of ourselves (McNiff, 2003). The physical and emotional aspects of the space work together as an ecosystem in generating creative forces that act upon people. I have always viewed my leadership role as one of cultivating and holding this creative environment and allowing it to do its work, which is much more than any one of us can do alone. In reality the creative space of the studio environment corresponds to the complex of inner spaces within each person. What we do outside has a reciprocal relationship on the inside and vice versa as with the larger web of eco-dynamics, which in my view offers the most empirical and supportive paradigm for creative expression, health, social relations, and care for the physical world.

As in nature, the creative space of artistic expression engages the whole spectrum of elements and forces—light and dark, positive and negative, gentle and tumultuous. Destruction can have its place too, as young children demonstrate when joyously making their play constructions fall apart before creating something new (McCarthy, 2012).

Everything large and small, visible and hidden, contributes to the process of total art expression (*Gesamtkunstwerk*) as in the ecosystems of nature. The sensory dimensions of artistic expression are arguably a necessity in realizing a more complete alignment with the creative processes of nature and restoring the soul loss resulting from alienation from the rigorous and sustained physical activity that has always connected us to our earthly origins and existence. The authors in this book offer many different ways of restoring healthy and creative contact with these eco-functions. And the editors create a slipstream effect generated by the creative space of the whole book, making it yet another ecosystem of vital and life-sustaining energy that will impact others.

Within the context of art and nature I am particularly attracted to connections with animals and their intelligences and sensibilities, relationships that have been incrementally lost through history. For example my surname from the Celtic, Mac-Cu-Duibh, son of a black dog, once had a close kinship with the animal realm, now erased through translation into English.

The wild animals and creatures of nature can help us preserve the most original and vital forces within our creative expression. Rather than simply attributing this wildness to bestial and feared elements that must be controlled, tamed, or extinguished, the arts can lead the way in helping us be more sensitive, agile, and resourceful humans. In our 1986 dialogue on art therapy James Hillman emphasized the instructive and numinous nature of animal experience:

> *The most important dreams for me are those with animals. I am not as interested in parents as in animals. I go after the animal. The animal knows what it wants; it has a nose, modes of protection; it is ecologically in the world.*
>
> (McNiff, 1986, p. 107)

What a difference this approach offers from the conventional psychological reductionism still prevalent today that reduces our artistic expressions of animals to base instincts and impulses.

*Environmental Expressive Therapies* offers a more realistic and life-affirming vision of how to create with all aspects of nature and become more resourceful partners. Rather than continuing efforts to subjugate the natural world, we respect and preserve it both inside ourselves and in the places we inhabit.

All of the eco-centric chapters of this book offer both a fresh and convincing paradigm for professional practice together with accessible ways of working that connect directly with nature. In my experience the latter emphasis on the practical engagement of natural surroundings and substances from nature invariably evokes archetypal and ritual dimensions that emerge from the context and possibly from the materials themselves. For example, in my studio groups, whenever we fashion objects from materials gathered from nature (sticks, grasses, stones, shells, etc.), I experience how these artifacts reliably generate shamanic, sacred, and ceremonial qualities. The same forces manifest themselves consistently in enactments engaging water and earth. It is as though the materials of nature hold these dimensions that act upon us when we work with them, attend to them, and contemplate their being. I keep emphasizing how we need to give more attention to systematically exploring and researching the various therapeutic aspects of the materials themselves (2004). The Chinese practices of *qigong* involving the five elements of water, wood, fire, earth, and metal present an important model carried through history, but as I have emphasized (2016), I am not as interested in becoming part of a particular system of practice but rather with how natural elements act upon us and generate art medicines.

As important as these methods of working directly with nature and natural materials are, I find it even more compelling to explore the way in which an eco-centric paradigm can inform all forms of creative expression and healing—inside and out, with natural materials and commercially produced art supplies, in nature spaces and in the most difficult of institutional settings where arts therapy practice often occurs.

In striving to help people everywhere participate confidently and get beyond common barriers to expression I have tried to show how artistic expression can be viewed as *a force of nature* that is as accessible as breath and elemental movement (2015). In getting started, a person does not have to do anything other than be present to what is happening in the immediate situation. I emphasize the movement basis of all expression and encourage the most elemental ways of moving as a way of entering the process of creation—repeating marks or gestures with painting and drawing. The same movement base applies to dance. With vocal improvisation we might repeat an elemental sound and do our best to stay with it and experience its qualities. Dramatic enactment often begins by stepping into a space witnessed by one or more persons and then being present to it. Art making can be like exercise or walking with an aesthetic attitude of openness, acceptance, and appreciation. If we perceive what we do like any other part of nature, the expression will happen naturally and with practice it will become more comfortable.

When art is approached as a basic human function, like breathing, there is no question about being able to do it. Over and over again I say, the simpler the deeper, with the test of efficacy determined by the ability to get started and then stay engaged, acting and being present in the most authentic way possible, moving naturally and trusting that the expressions and gestures have their own innate ways of perfecting themselves. Quality matters I say, but it is inseparable from a person's unique ways of acting in the present moment, of letting oneself truly be a basic force of nature where no one thing is ever the same and everything is unique to itself. If we act in this way, we will do something significant and make a contribution to nature while receiving the satisfaction it gives.

## References


Berry, T. (1988). *The dream of the earth*. San Francisco: Sierra Club Books.

Cobb, E. (1993). *The ecology of imagination in childhood*. Dallas: Spring. [First published (1977). New York: Columbia University Press.]

Kopytin, A., and Rugh, M. (Eds.). (2016). *"Green Studio": Nature and the arts in therapy*. Hauppauge, NY: Nova.
London, P. (2003). *Drawing closer to nature: Making art in dialogue with the natural world.* Boston: Shambhala.
McCarthy, D. (2012). *A manual of dynamic play therapy: Helping things fall apart, the paradox of play*. London and Philadelphia: Jessica Kingsley.
McNiff, S. (1979). From shamanism to art therapy. *Art Psychotherapy*, *6*(3), 155–161.
McNiff, S. (1981). The enduring shaman. In *The arts and psychotherapy* (pp. 3–28). Springfield, IL: Charles C. Thomas.
McNiff, S. (1986). A dialogue with James Hillman. *Art Therapy: Journal of the American Art Therapy Association*, *3*(3), 99–110.
McNiff, S. (1993). *Art as medicine: Creating a therapy of the imagination*. Boston: Shambhala.
McNiff, S. (2003). *Creating with others: The practice of imagination in art, life and the workplace*. Boston: Shambhala.
McNiff, S. (2004). *Art heals: How creativity cures the soul*. Boston: Shambhala.
McNiff, S. (2015). *Imagination in action: Secrets for unleashing creative expression*. Boston: Shambhala.
McNiff, S. (2016). *Ch'i* and artistic expression: An East Asian worldview that fits the creative process everywhere. *Creative Arts Education and Therapy: Frontiers in China—An International Academic Journal for Research and Practice*, *2*(2), 2016.
Tucker, M. E. (2003). *Worldly wonder: Religions enter their ecological phase*. Chicago: Open Court.

# INTRODUCTION

*Alexander Kopytin and Madeline Rugh*

Environmental or ecological expressive therapies (eco-arts therapies) establish a new, emerging approach to nature-based therapy. Nature-based expressive therapies are characterized by their original theoretical framework, which includes a paradigm and forms of therapy that bring the arts and nature together to provide beneficial effects both for human and nonhuman worlds. This new approach strives to achieve well-being and multiple treatment goals for individuals, families and communities and promote sustainable styles of life through people's involvement in expressive and creative activities in relation to environments in which they live.

Only in the last few years, due to the developing fields of community and social action expressive therapies, have professionals' interest in exploring new dimensions and meanings of the therapeutic environment included natural landscapes and materials. However most publications considering a therapeutic process from a more environmentally sensitive perspective have not developed a systemic platform integrating environmental and ecopsychology ideas and principles to a sufficient degree. This new book builds on the success of the editor's previous compilation, *Green Studio: Nature and the Arts in Therapy*, published by Nova Science. New authors and perspectives have been added as well as new material from previous writers. As a second effort, this book continues to embrace issues related to the phenomenon of environmental and ecological expressive therapies, building and deepening the case for recognition of the natural world in concepts of mental health and further enriching the application of expressive therapies to a nature-based understanding of wellness and health.

Ecological expressive therapies along with other scientific disciplines and therapeutic approaches related to concepts of ecology and the environment (such as environmental psychology, ecopsychology, eco-therapy, 'deep ecology' and ecohealth) reflect the increasing preoccupation of many people with reestablishing positive, sustainable ways of their relation to nature and their concern for negative changes in the biosphere related to human activity. These approaches represent a response, pressing psychological, social, educational and cultural issues in response to the global environmental crisis and encourage a shift in our orientation to the meaning and function of human relation to nature as a vital factor in health. They strive to embrace a wider scope of ideas and instruments related to diverse cultural backgrounds and professional specializations that provide multi-professional and multimodal integration and dialogue necessary to strengthen the ecological, nature-assisted expressive therapy position.

The spectrum of expressive therapies embraced in this movement is broad and includes either specialized therapeutic approaches using one particular expressive form such as art therapy, dramatherapy, music therapy and dance and movement therapy on the one hand, and those based on the integrative arts approach, expressive arts therapy, on the other hand. Other expressive therapeutic specializations like creative writing and play therapy, as well as original therapeutic methods integrating expressive arts and other nonverbal therapies, such as animal assisted therapy, horticultural therapy, wilderness journeys, adventure therapy, contemplative practices in nature and some others enrich this spectrum.

Ecological expressive therapies tend to constitute an increasingly significant part of the spectrum of contemporary eco-therapeutic methods characterized by the active stance in clients' relationship to nature. As we believe (Kopytin and Rugh, 2016, p. xii), the status of this new approach is, however, ambiguous. It is still unclear for most therapists whether it constitutes a new therapeutic model and even a paradigm with underlying philosophical or 'meta-psychological' assumptions together with distinctive forms of therapeutic interventions and an expert community that sustains the approach as a valid form of practice, or just a set of innovative, creative activities and ideas that can be implemented in the already established models of therapy. It is also unclear for most therapists whose professional identity and competences were established within the more traditional ideas and forms of practice that nature brings to the therapeutic process, and how it impacts therapeutic relations, clients' perception of themselves, expressive media used, quality and meaning of their creative endeavors and even goals of therapy.

Although most contemporary expressive therapies are rooted in the relational theories of therapeutic action, with their primary interest in human interpersonal relations, several strands of thought within expressive therapies and therapy at large exist that tend to give significance not only to clients' relations with a human world, but also with a wider context of their existence including natural and built environments and other forms of life, plant and animal worlds, local and planetary ecosystems. As we explained in our previous publication (Kopytin and Rugh, 2016, p. xii), this is more typical for holistic, depth-psychology, transpersonal, Gestalt schools of arts therapies, or for the bio-psycho-social approach paying more attention to the complex of environmental factors. These strands within expressive therapies together with the developing fields of ecological and environmental psychology, ecotherapy and ecohealth movements contribute to the establishing ecological, nature-based expressive therapies.

The role of environmental psychology and ecopsychology as providing a new perspective for expressive therapies and their new groundbreaking theoretical framework for practice should be emphasized. Environmental psychology is a field of study that examines the interrelationship between environments and human affect, cognition and behavior. The field has always been concerned with both built and natural environments, with early research emphasizing the former. However, as environmental sustainability issues became of greater concern to society in general, and the social sciences in particular, the field increased its focus on how humans affect, and are affected by, natural environments (De Young, 2013). In an effort to promote durable living on a finite planet, environmental psychology develops, and empirically validates, practical intervention strategies.

Like environmental psychology, the ecopsychology field is also broad-based and includes a number of special therapeutic approaches embraced in the ecotherapy spectrum enhancing people–environment interactions and personal well-being. Ecopsychology can be seen as a worldview and diverse social movement that recognizes a synergy between human mental health and well-being and the health and ecological integrity of the natural environment. This is a perennial idea that has gained new currency and a sense of urgency in the modern environmental movement, particularly in its 'deep ecology' wing.

The mission of ecopsychology, as proposed by Roszak (1992), is to validate that an emotional connection to nature is normal and healthy, and to make the environmental movement more effective by appealing to positive ecological bonds rather than promoting conservation based on messages of fear or shame. 'Ecotherapy' is a therapeutic strand linked to ecopsychology, 'an umbrella term for nature-based methods of physical and psychological healing' (Buzzell and Chalquist, 2009, p. 18) embracing different therapeutic interventions for addressing ecopsychology's concern with transforming humans' relationships with nature.

Both environmental psychology and ecopsychology maintain a rich network of researchers and practitioners who share the goals of creating durable behavior change at multiple levels, promoting an environmental ethic and maintaining harmonious human–nature relationships. Today the fields of environmental psychology, conservation psychology and ecopsychology are helping society to form an affirmative response to emerging environmental and natural resource constraints. This is a grand challenge because the response must plan for, motivate and maintain environmental stewardship behavior through a period of significant energy and resource descent.

The book includes highlights of the work that expressive therapists from different parts of the globe have accomplished over the last several years to meet these challenges and establish a new platform and instruments for environmentally sensitive therapeutic practices. The book has been edited to provide practitioners not only with the new theoretical perspectives, but with methods and tools that can help them to incorporate nature into their daily work with different populations and patients, their varied needs and clinical and psychosocial issues. A considerable part of the book focuses on the variability of expressive and instrumental forms that can be applied in the context of the nature-based therapies: expressive music, dramatic performances and rituals, dance and movement, visual arts, narratives and creative writing, play therapy techniques and multimedia events. It represents a variety of practical approaches and tools used with different populations, such as children and adolescents, families, adults and senior people, and in various institutional contexts including clinical, educational, social and community-based settings.

Publication of this book signifies a new step forward that helps to develop and integrate a real ecotherapy platform in expressive therapies. It represents the pressing psychological, social, educational and cultural issues surrounding the recent development in the field of expressive therapies and therapeutic approaches in general in response to the global environmental crisis. It is important to recognize the book as a part of this movement that encourages a shift or transformation in our orientation to the meaning and role arts and creative function of the human psyche in our connection to nature. It embraces a wider scope of ideas and instruments to demonstrate the vibrant quality of this approach characterized by a considerable number of contributors with their diverse cultural backgrounds and professional specializations that provide multi-professional and multi-modal integration and dialogue necessary to strengthen this growing field of ecological expressive therapies.

## References

Buzzell, L., and Chalquist, C. (2009). *Ecotherapy: Healing with nature in mind.* San Francisco: Sierra Club Books.

De Young, R. (2013). Environmental psychology overview. In S. R. Klein and A. H. Huffman (Eds.), *Green organizations: Driving change with IO psychology* (pp. 17–33). New York: Routledge.
Kopytin, A., and Rugh, M. (2016). Introduction. In A. Kopytin and M. Rugh (Eds.), *Green Studio: Nature and the arts in therapy* (pp. 7–18). New York: Nova Publishers.
Roszak, T. (1992). *The voice of the earth*. New York: Simon & Schuster.

# PART I

# The Emerging Paradigm and Theoretical Constructs of Environmental and Ecological Expressive Therapies

# 1

# NATURE-ASSISTED ART THERAPY

## Technique or Transformation?

*Madeline Rugh*

### Introduction

> *At a time of planet-wide environmental crisis, it seems both outrageous and irresponsible that so few mental health clinicians connect the epidemics of mental distress in industrial societies with the devastating impact of our suicidal destruction of our own habitat and eco-cidal elimination of whole species that used to share the Earth with us. Many therapy clients also don't realize that the grief and fear they struggle with may be natural responses to the death of so many living beings and the ongoing distress of earth, air, and ocean life all around us. Because we are not being informed about links between mental health symptoms caused by the way we live and the accelerating inner and outer devastation, we remain mystified about why we feel so much pain.*
>
> (Buzzell and Chalquist, 2009, p. 19)

Harsh words, yes. Hard to hear, yes. Time to hear? YES! This chapter seeks to facilitate a direct look at how we as Western people and especially we as mental health clinicians participate in our ongoing environmental devastation and subsequent denial. I am addressing our behavior not to cause guilt, remorse or despair but to free the way to bring our considerable gifts to the service of person—planet healing. There are two major characteristics of Western culture especially related to therapy that have contributed to our current environmental crisis and continue to affect our ability to respond. The two characteristics are:

1. The notion of an isolated, independent ego, our "split" consciousness and general perception of the world (split consciousness refers to our

preference for dualistic awareness where the body and mind are split, the person and nature are split, spirit and material are split, etc.).
2. The dominance of the left hemisphere and hyper-rationality and objectivity of positivist science.

The reason for exploring our nature/human split in this way is to suggest there is a need for radical transformation and to encourage a deeper examination of those aspects of psychology and therapeutic practice that may inadvertently be supporting the very mindset that is destroying the biosphere. There exists a plethora of excellent books and articles exploring the topic of this chapter from many different disciplines. This writing cannot do justice to the abundance of ideas available; rather, it seeks to briefly synthesize a few basic examples from the literature to alert the reader to the possibility that something deeper and greater is at stake in "nature-assisted art therapy," which requires more than "using" nature as another technique. It points to the necessity of a complete transformation of the fragmented Western consciousness starting with our own.

## Who Needs Healing?

> *To turn our dangerous situation around fully . . . we must heal the underlying sickness—our relationship with the planet, our worldview. This means literally changing how we perceive the world around us, and that requires the alteration of our consciousness.*
>
> (Devereux, 1996, p. 17)

Many years ago I was hired as an art therapist to help a group of staff members who routinely worked on intense deadlines, to "de-stress." I spent several sessions with approximately eight professional grant writers and evaluators who happily and readily participated in my arts-based interventions. However, as we came near the end of our time together it became apparent that the main cause of the intense stress had much more to do with the person who hired me, the head of the department. This person enjoyed the adrenaline rush and drama of working right up to the deadline and so did not help manage the workload effectively or provide adequate support. This made me very uncomfortable, as I realized that my work with the staff to ease their stress meant I was merely helping them to accommodate to a "sick" system.

> *The healers of mind and spirit, too, are caught up in efforts to enable their patients to fit comfortably and drowsily into an insane world careening toward the abyss. Ahead loom destabilization of climate, the loss of one-third of the species presently on Earth, and the ongoing destruction of whole ecologies. Such things are not just problems or accidents but*

> *symptoms of a deep mental derangement that can be cured only by a correspondingly deep healing.*
>
> (Orr, in Buzzell and Chalquist, 2009, p. 15)

This is basically the perspective I take on nature-assisted art therapy. The focus must be a transformative one that includes the very structures of psychology upon which we form our healing practices and upon which our culture, as currently envisioned, was also formed. So it is that "using nature as a mere tool for human healing perpetuates the very self-world splits responsible for both our ecologically resonant maladies and a deteriorating biosphere" (Buzzell and Chalquist, 2009, p. 20).

As persons responsible for assisting with healing and helping, the healing of our dysfunctional worldview, the "alienated consciousness" could not be more critical and represents a different orientation to our usual understanding of "therapy." It finds its resonance with the idea of cultural healing that is seldom, if ever, part of the training in therapy.

Suzi Gablik, in her book *The Re-enchantment of Art* (1991), admonishes artists to take up the cause of "cultural healing," or worldview transformation. I agree with this wholeheartedly but also feel that art therapists hold an especially valuable key in this regard. Art therapy has as its focus bringing the arts to bear on human life in the ancient way, through the ritual of art making in the service of healing and wholeness. However, as has been stated, therapists including art therapists largely operate from a Western worldview that leaves them (us) serving traditional psychological constructs that do not recognize the deeper or wider dimensions of "Self" or soul (transpersonal psychology, depth psychology, some expressions of cognitive behavioral therapy [CBT], and ecopsychology being notable exceptions) and the recognition of an ecological aspect to our identity.

There is then a powerful and unavoidable spiritual dimension to this terrain. At the time of this writing, Pope Francis issued his encyclical, placing care for the environment (our "common home") at the center of his spiritual leadership. This is a radical and unprecedented direction set by a spiritual leader of his magnitude. He states that we need to "hear the cry of the earth and the cry of the poor." In a materialist/consumer culture, these are two cries we really don't want to hear. When looking at our worldview, of who and what we think we are as human beings existing within a living planet of diverse life forms, we can no longer afford to abandon or shun the spiritual dimension and the numinous qualities of nature.

Our ecological crisis is a crisis of imagination, challenging our limited ways of seeing and calling forward much ancient wisdom that we abandoned in our search for security and control through a science based on hyper-rationality and objectivity and secularism. As Aristotle stated so long ago, "the soul never thinks without an image" (Aristotle, *On the Soul*, 4th century bc from Arnheim, 1969, p. 12). The expressive arts therapies, then, should be or could be at the forefront of facilitating this radical shift in awareness and perception. And psychology, as so many have recently stated, championed particularly by James Hillman, needs to return to its original meaning, the study of the soul.

It should be clear then, that I am not advocating for merely adding nature to our therapeutic strategies; rather, I am advocating first and foremost for a deep shift within ourselves and a challenge to the very structures of our training. The many practices and suggestions for implementing nature-assisted art therapy are all very valuable, but it is my contention that these suggestions, to be most effective, need to be situated within a transformative vision. Depth psychologist Mary Watkins makes the following critical observations in this regard:

> *Reliance on unquestioned traditional structures, especially in the face of issues for which those structures are inadequate as currently practiced and imagined. The issues for which traditional psychotherapy seems unprepared are the now all too familiar environmental ones . . . the rapid extinction of animals and plants, the depletion of soils, toxicities in air and water. Most traditional psychological theories operate in the absence of acknowledgment of our interdependence on the natural world and have formulated their theories of human health as if the natural environment were a backdrop to our dramas. This, of course, was not true of Indigenous people but reflects a profound disconnect peculiar to Western consciousness.*
>
> (Watkins, in Buzzell and Chalquist, 2009, p. 224)

## Ego, Self and Soul

Our conditioned reliance on psychological systems that do not include the natural world in human development and that are based on the notion that we are a disconnected isolated ego is part of the construct that supports Western violence toward nature, which we as therapists can change, indeed must change. Furthermore, we cannot talk about an expanded notion of self or ego or reconnecting with nature (inner nature and outer nature) without also addressing the spiritual dimension.

Most world religions and wisdom traditions recognize that there is a distinction between the "small self"—the ego—and the soul. One is seated in the "head" and the other in the "heart." For example, Franciscan priest Father Richard Rohr (2003), referring to the writings of Father Thomas Merton, identifies two aspects of self: the "false self" (ego), which is not the "bad" self except when it is seen as the ONLY self, such is the case in the Western personality and culture. Whereas the "true self" can be understood as the eternal soul or spirit. The false self is concerned with appearances and popularity, is fearful and seeks security through acquisition of things, property, cars and money (for example), which clearly links this conception of "self" with our economic orientation of consumerism and materialism. The false self is overly identified with work, with its reputation and with things it owns. The false self is easily offended and often defensive. It is bored, isolated, and lonely, seeking distraction and entertainment. It needs to be "right" and therefore needs and seeks out someone or something else to be "wrong."

Living in the world as though this were all we are and where the only thing that matters is our acquisition of things, money and reputation that we must then protect at all costs, is a life of "not-enough," of competition for resources, of winning and never losing. This life does not make sense, it isn't even LIFE!

On the other hand, the "true self," or Self with a capital "S" (from Jungian or depth psychology), can be understood as the Soul, the divine life-force in every person AND in every sentient being and natural form. The Soul or true self resides in communion and connection within the soul of the natural world or anima mundi. When we live with an awareness of this deeper aspect of being and learn to listen to the voice of the soul as expressed in imagery, then the soul works more easily with our personality, our false self, and gives it depth, equanimity, meaning and joy. "Nature is not matter only, she is spirit" (Mazis, 2006, p. 14).

## Health From a Planetary View

In his book, *The Great Work* (1999), Father Thomas Berry and Sister Miriam McGillis have brought the writings of Jesuit priest Father Teilhard de Chardin to this matter. In a synthesis of the biological sciences and spiritual principles they identified three aspects of ecological integrity the planet requires to support its natural healing functions, such as maintaining the life-sustaining ratio of oxygen to carbon dioxide in our protective atmosphere. Those three aspects are (1) maintaining diversity; (2) individuality and subjectivity; and (3) communion. Our culture currently violates all three of these biological/spiritual necessities for planetary wellness. Clearly, diversity is violated when we suppress the voice of other people and ideas, or when we grow food with massive single-crop factory farming methods; these are violations of the first principle. Individuality and subjectivity refers to the awareness that each living being needs to be itself in order to serve its function in the interconnected web of life. It does NOT mean individualism as we currently understand that word, which is another word for our isolated ego where "individualism refers to the supposed right of an individual to act alone, in disregard of other individuals" (Berry, 2000, p. 32). More remarkably, each life form (including rocks and rivers) has an inner spirit, that is subjectivity. So every life has a deep inner direction and purpose that needs to be recognized and honored.

Furthermore, subjectivity supports the third element, communion. This inner subjectivity, or soulfulness, supports communication, communion and thus deep connection. In this, we as Western people have not only forgotten how to listen, but stand in profound resistance to the very idea of communion that will be discussed shortly. Recent research from the Heartmath Institute (Buhner, 2004) clearly indicates that our heart is an organ of perception, not a mere pump. In this role, the heart is continually sending information out from us and receiving information back from the more-than-human realm. Cultivating awareness of the heart in this expanded role will be critical to reconnecting with nature in a transformative way. "The universe is a communion of subjects, not a collection of objects" (Berry, 1999, p. 16).

Depth psychologist Robert Romanyshyn applies this understanding of subjectivity and communion to another critical aspect of Western psychological conceptual terrain, the nature of the unconscious. Romanyshyn suggests that we need to reimagine the meaning of consciousness and unconsciousness in the following way.

> *The notion of the unconscious in depth psychology is too limiting. It is an anthropomorphic prejudice inescapably yoked to a definition of ego consciousness as neurotic. It is the product of cultural-historical cir cumstances which have led to planetary crises and which we can no longer afford. From the point of view of greenness . . . we need to reimagine the unconscious as another frequency of range of consciousness. In effect, we need to re-tune the frequency of our ego consciousness so that we might begin to respond to the other vibrations of consciousness which compose all creation. Our symptoms, our dreams, our imaginal musings are not the products of our unconscious. Indeed, we say that we think of it this way only because the range of our ego consciousness has been so limited. On the contrary, symptoms, dreams, and imaginal moments of inspiration are the consciousness of the world. What we call the unconscious is the many faceted consciousness of creation.*
>
> (Romanyshyn, 1997, pp. 168–169)

Romanyshyn's description of consciousness is highly provocative and extremely useful in looking at what core beliefs and assumptions we need to attend to as therapists in order to connect up with the natural world in a transformative versus technique-oriented way. For example, even if we were to work from his idea as a kind of "hypothesis," a "what if this were true," how might our therapeutic practices shift? How might our perception of the beings and forms of nature shift? In addition the word "frequency" is significant here. It suggests another path to transformation that would involve practicing intentional shifts in consciousness. More open states of mind are not uncommon during the art-making process that we may have relegated to creative "flow," not recognizing the deeper significance or potential with regard to the "ego" and to communion with the natural world, which is part of our inner world (so-called unconscious). Other consciousness shifting methods include prayer, mediation, mindfulness, walking, contemplative movement and music, and so forth. Paul Devereux (1996) indicates that our usual and accepted state of consciousness in the West is "mono-phasic," meaning it accepts only one narrow band of information coming from the world (inner and outer worlds, I might add). Our mono-phasic predisposition is also related to the dominance of the left hemisphere and "objectivity" of science, which will be addressed shortly.

## The Disconnected and Isolated Ego

Probably one of the most radical ideas I have read about the ego and Western consciousness comes from Jungian psychologist Jerome Bernstein in his book, *The Borderland* (2005). Dr. Bernstein describes the following intriguing idea. He speculates that the Western ego developed in its current and now pathological form in the story of the "garden of Eden," the story of the fall, of becoming "self-conscious." Becoming aware of our nakedness represents not the story of the first creation, but the first creation of the state of consciousness that no longer experiences itself in unity (called the participation mystique) with all life. In other words, the garden represents an earlier type of awareness of oneness, where we were part of the natural world in a way that we could not reflect upon it. The "fall" of becoming self-conscious was a necessary step to creating the sense of separation from the world so that we might (eventually) come to love and express wonder at the incredible beauty and unimaginable depth of the cosmos that we can only do when we experience the world as "Other." Paradoxically, when this otherness is considered sacred and embraced in a state of wonder and awe, the sense of oneness returns. This makes me think that our current ego-based malaise could be temporary if we were to fully recognize this possibility. But at the moment and for the last several hundred years that separate awareness has mistaken itself as the only "real" state of being and calcified into the fearful, isolated, false self we recognize as the Western ego threatened by the wild wonder of creation and seeking to control it.

> *A hubristic western ego does not see itself as a part of a codependent system coevolving with the rest of the ecosystem, it sees itself instead as controlling the entire process and is caught in a power complex. It is unconscious of seeing itself as a superior operator not beholden to the same natural laws as a co-evolutionary partner—at its own peril.*
>
> (Bernstein, 2005, p. 52)

Bernstein further explains:

> *The western ego is highly resistant to anything that aims at changing its self-definition and outward orientation and has an abhorrence of the irrational, trans-rational and unconscious, particularly nature and the collective unconscious which are perceived to be anathema to its very being.*
>
> (Bernstein, 2005, p. 52)

Bernstein believes that the borderland personality or trans-rational ego (rather than irrational) is an adaptive shift in the Western ego that is showing up now to support our survival and the survival of all species on the planet. Borderland personalities experience the world as a sacred "Other," often hearing the voice of animals and plants, not as pathology, not as anthropomorphism or projection, but the activation of the healing principle of communion (as previously described by Thomas Berry) for which we are designed. The borderland kind of awareness is still part of the consciousness or mind of indigenous people and might be thought of as the return of our own "indigenous" mind coming forward after thousands of years of suppression. I was especially attracted to Bernstein's hypothesis because I am a borderland person. My earliest childhood memories involve experiencing the natural world as something like Winnicott's "holding environment," as Mother. My whole life has been supported and guided by this profound sense of being loved and cared for by more than human beings. This brings us to our next area of concern, theories of human development.

## Human Development Sans Nature

> *Very little in my culture taught me that my existence depends on the existence of earth.*
>
> (Griffin, 1995, p. 75)

The role of the natural world in theories of human development is basically non-existent, with the focus being entirely on the relationship with other humans and society. "Developmental psychological theories of attachment (for example) do not make adequate space for the role of nature even as a significant other, let alone as a primary caregiver, as is the case with some borderland individuals" (Bernstein, 2005, p. 115). Certainly, as I have stated, this was the case for me as I have very early memories of being loved and held by the natural world—the wind and the trees in particular.

Indigenous people across cultures and time have recognized and maintained beautiful person–planet rituals, clearly placing the human in relationship with natural world. For example, Anita Barrows, developmental psychologist, describes a general practice of naming a child in relation to a totemic animal who accompanies the child throughout their life and forms the vital link between that child and nature. The Hopi have powerful rituals for the newborn.

> *At dawn, the infant is carried to the east and presented to the rising sun, while the mother says, "This is your child." The Hopi's dependence on nature is acknowledged and the infant joins not only the human community, but the community of Earth.*
>
> (Barrows, in Roszak et al., 1995, p. 102)

Many Native American tribal cultures share this awareness of belonging to the Earth, of interconnectedness and interdependence, through the concept "Mitakuye Oyasin," a Lakota Sioux phrase meaning everything is my relative, or, all my relations.

James Hillman (1996), depth psychologist, describes another way of looking at the limits of developmental psychology as currently practiced. His theory is called the Parental Fallacy, challenging traditional psychology with its obsession regarding the role of the parents in the outcome of the child's life. He suggests there is something more beyond the nature/nurture debate that guides each one of us, the Soul, the guiding spirit or Daimon. Paul Shepard clearly articulates what is meant here when he states that "despite the many distortions culture heaps upon each newborn generation, *there is a secret person undamaged in every individual waiting to reconnect with nature*" (in Roszak et al., 1995, p. 101). That is not to say that parents are not influential but to allow for the possibility of something more mysterious and invisible. Western history (our own wisdom tradition) has an ancient Aristotelian word for this process called entelechy (Whitmont, 1993, p. 55), which means an inner directed movement within all life forms toward wholeness no matter what happens from the outside. Once again, the lack of attention to the soulful potential has rendered our therapeutic efforts shallow, contributing to a dangerous inflation of the Western ego's "power complex," Bernstein's reference to our psychological hubris in relation to the living world. Furthermore, Hillman's Parental Fallacy includes the natural world in a significant way.

> *Being shaped so fatally by the parental world means having lost the larger world-parents, and also the world at large as parent. For the world too shapes us, nurtures us, teaches us. If today our civilization is turning toward the environment to stave off ecological disaster, the first step of this rapproachment with nature is to cross the threshold of the parental house into the home of the world. We are parented by everything around us—if "parenting" means watching, instructing, encouraging and admonishing. . . . The more I believe my nature comes from my parents,*

> *the less open I am to the ruling influences around me. The less the surrounding world is felt to be intimately important to my story. Yet even biographies begin by locating the subject in a place; the self starts off amid the smells of a geography. The moment the angel enters a life it enters an environment. We are ecological from day one. The parental fallacy is deadly to individual self awareness, and it is killing the world.*
>
> (Hillman, 1996, pp. 86–87)

## Positive Science, Objectivity and the Dominance of the Left Hemisphere

> *The intuitive mind is a sacred gift and the rational mind is a faithful servant. We have created a society that honors the servant and has forgotten the gift.*
>
> —Albert Einstein

I am not advocating for the rejection of science—the careful, thoughtful and methodical exploration of our world—rather I am questioning an obsession with a particular viewpoint that dominates our scientific culture referred to as "positivist." It is the science of "objectivity" whose primary assumption is that we can be totally "objective" in our observations and perceptions. This belief in "objectivity" is based on the notion that we are separate from the world and can manipulate, measure, and use the world in any way we see fit. Susan Griffin states that, "very young I was taught that science was objective and that subjective response had no value in describing reality" (Griffin, 1995, p. 15). Understanding the world scientifically serves two primary functions: prediction and control. Psychology as a science proudly subscribes to this function in its research methods. The notion of valuing and honoring only objective consciousness (although this idea has been thoroughly challenged by quantum physics) represents hyper-rational and linear thinking *to the exclusion of all other ways of knowing*. And it has become a deep part of a disconnected Western state of mind and the Western ego.

The epigraph by Einstein at the beginning of this section reflects recent research by psychiatrist Iain McGilchrist regarding hemispheric differences. The title of McGilchrist's book is *The Master and His Emissary* (2012). The title is based on an ancient Middle Eastern story about an emissary taking over the role of his master, usurping the master's power. Based on McGilchrist's research, the Master is the (intuitive) right hemisphere, the Emissary (faithful servant) is the left hemisphere. That Western people have this out of order *and* have created a whole way of being in the world based on this dis-order *and* are exporting this distortion globally is our crisis and our responsibility to address.

McGilchrist's work indicates that the differences in hemispheres are not accurately portrayed by the usual split of emotion versus reason, language versus visual. Instead, both hemispheres are involved in emotion, reason, language and visual processing. What he did discover is much more incredible: the left and right hemispheres represent two *radically different worldviews*. This is extremely relevant to our environmental crisis, as it is a crisis in large measure, produced and supported by the overdominance of a left hemisphere worldview. This is very complex material, so, at the risk of being oversimplistic I would like to give the reader a "feel" for the terrain.

The *right hemisphere* sees a world in a way that favors the broad, open, alert, contextualized, metaphorical, embodied living world. It is interested in individuality not just categories of things. It embraces change, evolving, and interconnectedness. It is comfortable with mystery, paradox and wonder. The right hemisphere can use the left hemisphere's preferred style of awareness *but the reverse is not true.*

The *left hemisphere* sees the world in a way that favors focused, narrow, detailed attention. It works only with what is already known, that which is fixed, static and concrete. It can only deal with what is already expected, thus the need for prediction and control. Its emphasis is on parts and not the whole, on precision, on the technical and mechanical. It manipulates for self-serving and self-protective reasons often expressed as paranoia. It readily cuts off what does not fit with its view and is therefore a self-consistent, closed system. It loves perfection and produces emptiness. It likes to focus on material things, technology, quantifiable things and repeatable things. Sound familiar?

From a left hemisphere worldview, the phrase "I'll believe it when I see it" is actually "I see what I already believe." This has profound implications for communication and connection with the more-than-human realm. In fact, it is not possible to connect with or listen to the voice of the sacred "Other" without the full participation of the right hemisphere. According to McGilchrist, Western culture and the isolated ego—which *is* the left hemisphere's voice!—is actively suppressing the right hemisphere, now threatening the collapse of our home, our living biosphere.

Many of the training programs for art therapists have shifted to an emphasis in graduate research that is clearly "positivist" or left hemispheric in nature, often leaving behind the very discipline that sets them apart: art. Iain McGilchrist states that in dealing with the closed system of the left hemisphere (he refers to it as a hall of mirrors, only reflecting back endlessly what we already know) there are areas of weakness by which we might "escape."

> *These points of weakness in the self-enclosed system are three rather important, indissolubly interlinked, aspects of human existence: the body, the soul and art (which relies on the body and soul coming together). Although the left hemisphere plays a part in realizing each of these realms of experience, the right hemisphere plays the crucial grounding role in each of them: the "lived" body, the spiritual sense, and the experience of*

> *emotional resonance and aesthetic appreciation are all principally right-hemisphere mediated. What is more they each have an immediacy which bypasses the rational and the explicitness of language, and therefore leads directly to territory potentially outside of the left hemisphere's sphere of control. These areas therefore present a serious challenge to its dominion, and they have evoked a determined response from the left hemisphere of our age.*
>
> (McGilchrist, 2012, p. 438)

This statement clearly describes what we already know about the healing quality of art therapy, its capacity to bypass the thinking mind, here recognized as the dominant and domineering left hemisphere. The arts also aid in the synthesis and proper relationship of the hemispheres—giving the right hemisphere its role as master and the left the role of faithful servant when we need to discuss or analyze something we have made. It seems to me that recognizing this deeper, more profound meaning of our work in the expressive arts is critical to courageously moving toward the required shift in consciousness.

The role of science, the dominance of the left hemisphere and the role of the isolated Western ego consciousness is summarized in the following quote by Vine Deloria Jr., Native American scholar, theologian, historian and activist:

> *I think the primary difference between the western and indigenous ways of life is that Indians experience and relate to a living universe, whereas western people, especially scientists, reduce all things, living or not to objects. The implications of this are immense. If you see the world around you as a collection of objects for you to manipulate and exploit you will inevitably destroy the world while attempting to control it. Not only that but by perceiving the world as lifeless you rob yourself of the richness, beauty, and wisdom to be found by participating in its larger design. In order to maintain the fiction that the world is dead—and that those who believe it to be alive has succumbed to primitive superstition—science must reject any interpretation of the natural world that implies sentience or an ability to communicate on the part of nonhumans.*
>
> (DeLoria, in Bernstein, 2005, p. 35)

## Conclusion

No one individual can say how we should imagine and draw forward this transformative vision. Contemplating or reflecting on and actively exploring the ideas presented of the true self and false self, the guiding inner subjectivity of soul or entelechy the Daimon, recognizing the earth as "holding environment" and the potential of the Parental Fallacy, the role of the heart in perception, and the incredible thought that the unconscious is the consciousness of all life, provides a foothold for cultivating an authentic relationship to outer nature that is our inner nature.

Finally, Thomas Berry, following the observations of Teilhard de Chardin, makes the incredible assertion that we human beings are the awakening of the consciousness of the Earth herself, now capable of reflecting on her beauty and wonder. This is an idea worth savoring and a clear expression of what is meant by the ecological self. "Here, in its human mode, the universe reflects on and celebrates itself in a unique mode of conscious self-awareness" (Berry, 1999, p. 56). If we can situate the many wonderful exercises and practices shared in this book and others into a context for transformation, we will begin to address the shift in consciousness required for healing ourselves and protecting the myriad of lives that compose the Earth and our more-than-human world. "Our challenge is to create . . . a new sense of what it is to be human. It is to transcend . . . our species isolation, to enter into the larger community of living species" (Berry, 2015, p. 42).

## Note

For persons interested in more detailed suggestions for the development of skills in listening, communion and connection, they are part of another publication soon to be released by the author titled *Nature-Assisted Art Therapy: Everybody Speaks Blue Sky*.

## References

Arnheim, R. (1969). *Visual thinking*. Berkeley: University of California Press.

Barrows, A. (1995). The ecopsychology of child development. In T. Roszak, M. E. Gomes, and A. D. Kanner (Eds.), *Ecopsychology: Restoring the earth, healing the mind* (pp. 100–110). San Francisco: Sierra Club Books.

Bernstein, J. S. (2005). *Living in the borderland: The evolution of consciousness and the challenge of healing trauma*. New York: Routledge.

Berry, T. (1999). *The great work: Our way into the future*. New York: Bell Tower.

Berry, T. (2015). *The dream of the earth*. New York: Counterpoint.

Berry, W. (2000, Spring). Life is a miracle. *Orion Magazine: Nature, Culture and Place*. Great Barrington, MA Orion Society and the Myrin Institute.

Buhner, S. H. (2004). *Secret teachings of plants: The intelligence of the heart in direct perception of nature*. Rochester, VT: Bear.

Buzzell, L., and Chalquist, C. (2009). *Ecotherapy: Healing with nature in mind*. San Francisco: Sierra Club Books.

Childre, D., Martin, H., Rozman, D., and McCray, R. (2016). *Heart intelligence: Connecting with the intuitive guidance of the heart*. Lexington, KY: Waterfront Press.

Deloria, V., Jr., in Bernstein, J. S. (2005). *Living in the borderland: The evolution of consciousness and the challenge of healing trauma*. New York: Routledge.

Devereux, P. (1996). *Re-visioning the earth: A guide to opening the healing channels between mind and nature.* Rockefeller Center, NY: Fireside.
Gablik, S. (1991). *The re-enchantment of art.* New York: Thames and Hudson.
Griffin, S. (1995). *The Eros of everyday life: Essays on ecology, gender and society.* New York: Doubleday Books.
Hillman, J. (1996). *The soul's code.* New York: Random House.
Mazis, G. A. (2006, Fall). Psyche and nature: Tower and nature, Yin and Yang, archetype and Earth. In *Psyche & Nature: A Journal of Archetype and Culture.* Part 1 of 2. New Orleans, LA: Spring.
McGilchrist, I. (2012). *The master and his emissary: The divided brain and the making of the Western world.* New Haven and London: Yale University Press.
Rohr, R. (2003). *Everything belongs: The gift of contemplative prayer.* New York: Crossroad.
Romanyshyn, R. D. (1997). Egos, angels, and the colors of nature. In D. Fideler (Ed.), *Alexandria: The order and beauty of nature* (pp. 162–172). Grand Rapids, MI: Phanes Press.
Whitmont, E. C. (1993). *The alchemy of healing: psyche and soma.* Berkeley, CA: North Atlantic Books.

# 2

# ENVIRONMENTAL AND ECOLOGICAL EXPRESSIVE THERAPIES

## The Emerging Conceptual Framework for Practice

*Alexander Kopytin*

### The Role of the Arts in Providing Meaningful and Mutually Supporting Human Connection to Nature

Artists have always been inspired by the beauty and mystery of nature. Some of them even emphasized the decisive role of nature in their creative endeavors and reflected the close bonds of mutual dependence that human beings have with their environments. Such expressions of Leonardo da Vinci as "Nature alone is the master of true genius" or "Nature is the source of all true knowledge" could be recalled.

Landscape painters often revealed high sensitivity to nature and an exceptional ability to feel and render the vital quality of their relation to nature through art even before environmental issues become evident. Vincent van Gogh, whose art is abundant with poetic and visionary landscapes, reveals the pivotal role of nature for creative endeavors in his letters. In one of his letters to his brother Theo (Wasmes, June 1879), he explains:

> *I know no better definition of the word* art *than this, "Art is man added to nature," nature, reality, truth, but with a meaning, with an interpretation, with a character that the artist brings out and to which he gives expression, which he sets free, which he unravels, releases, elucidates.*

In another letter (The Hague, Sunday, September 3, 1882) he even explained his creative method based on his relatedness to nature when he wrote:

> *I'm glad that I've never learned how to paint . . . I don't know myself how I paint. I sit with a white board before the spot that strikes me—I look at what's before my eyes—I say to myself, this white board must*

> *become something—I come back, dissatisfied—I put it aside, and after I've rested a little, feeling a kind of fear, I take a look at it—then I'm still dissatisfied—because I have that marvelous nature too much in mind for me to be satisfied—but still, I see in my work an echo of what struck me, I see that nature has told me something, has spoken to me and that I've written it down in shorthand. In my shorthand there may be words that are indecipherable—errors or gaps—yet something remains of what the wood or the beach or the figure said—and it isn't a tame or conventional language which doesn't stem from nature itself but from a studied manner or a system. Herewith also a scratch from the dunes. Standing there were small bushes whose leaves are white on one side and dark green on the other, and which constantly move and sparkle. Behind them dark wood.*

Some expressive arts therapists emphasize the key role of the arts in connecting people to their living environments. As Peter London (London, 2004) puts it, making art is a perfect vehicle for recovering our lost sense of unity with nature. When we draw closer to nature through art, we simultaneously draw closer to our Selves and thereby enjoy a richer, more authentic creativity and deeper, fuller life.

One of the pioneers of American art therapy, Elinor Ulman, articulated the notion that *art* is "a means to discover both the self and the world and to establish a relation between the two" (Ulman, 1961, p. 12). She also called art "the meeting ground between the inner and outer world" (Ulman, 1971, p. 94). Not knowing about ecological expressive arts therapies that had yet to be developed, Ulman—who had studied Chinese painting and landscape design as well as art and therapy—had intuitively identified the profound link between the arts, nature, and finding the self.

When asked by a group of graduate students to name her favorite artists, another pioneer of art therapy, Judith Rubin, first hesitated but then realized that it was actually quite simple: "Mother Nature." A well-known expert of art therapy, artist Shaun McNiff, believes that creativity is a defining quality of the human spirit, a force of nature; the mainstream of imagination is accessible to all (McNiff, 2015).

Doing arts, as other forms of creative activity, can be not only a means of meaningful interaction with people, the human world, but of relating to the environment at large and more-than-human too. Creative acts can involve the embedment in the ecosystem and attunement to various environmental phenomena and forms of life by which certain aspects of human experience, in particular, those related to our biological history as closely interwoven with the more-than-human world, could be actualized and brought to the conscious mind, to provide health and well-being and support our perception of ourselves as "ecological subjects," our *eco-identity*.

The visual and performing arts as well as other forms of organized and meaningful human expression existed in human history long before civilized human mind came to an understanding of creative acts as a form of prevailingly individualistic activity. The wider, environmental perception of the arts can be found both in many world traditions especially in those characterized "by ideas about the interconnectedness of all things, perpetual movement, impermanence, and how small and humble acts generate larger changes in the world" (McNiff, 2015, p. 12). Such perception of the arts is also implied in contemporary environmental movement and represents the perennial need of human beings to keep their intrinsic connection with the natural world around.

Considerable similarity between modern environmental and ecopsychological understanding of the arts and world traditions, with their practices of collective expressions as a means to establish human connection with the environment, can be found. Both contemporary ecotherapy and world traditions can be characterized in their perception of the arts as implying the vital function of supporting healthy bonds with nature. According to such perception of the arts, natural environments and forms can be highly attractive to humans not only due to their practical value, but also to their aesthetic, cognitive and spiritual meaning and their ability to support well-being, vitality and coping ability in human beings.

One of the examples of such function of the arts could be intentionally erected massive stone structures, like the medicine wheels of the indigenous peoples of North America, or the prehistoric stonework of Europe, Africa, South America, Celtic menhirs, Mayan stelae, and the great standing stones of Easter Island in the Pacific—all marking sacred ritual sites related to human need to use their vital connection to the environment.

Contemporary environmental artists, especially those involved in the eco-art movement, often tend to use the whole environment as a living matrix to reveal and emphasize implied harmonious life forms. The field of environmental arts has developed alongside an increasing awareness of ecological matters and the rise of the environmental movement since the 1960s. However "once an area of interest for a relatively small group of people, art that addresses environmental issues has in the last five years become part of the artistic mainstream" (Brown, 2014, p. 6).

Due to the development of environmental psychology and ecopsychology the new perspective on our understanding of the role of arts in human history as a healing tool and a powerful means to provide adaptation and development of human resources has been opened. Holistic therapies, the "green movement" and postmodern environmental or ecological art help to expand our perception of the arts as an expression of the human need to reestablish healthy bonds with the environment.

"Private Moon" (2003–Present) is an environmental project by Russian artist Leonid Tishkov, which can be an eloquent illustration of the arts in their service of supporting human bonds to nature. The artist and his illuminated "private" moon have since traveled all around world—Russia, New Zealand, the Arctic, Japan, China, France, Italy, the United States and more. Leonid Tishkov explained the part of his project called "Journey of the Private Moon in the Arctic" (2010) in the following way:

> *Miracles can happen in this realm: the moon comes down from the heavens, glistening polar bears walk on ice floats, white clouds bathe in the sea together with blue whales and delicate icebergs float in the sky. The snow there emits light and the melting glacier calls out to us, humans, whispering "I am still alive." My private moon helps turn our earth into a magical space, which must be preserved as the supreme treasure.*
>
> (Text by Leonid Tishkov, www.privatemoon.ru)

The arts possess their own means of solving the problems facing the planet. In many cases, the artist's role is not, however, to provide definitive answers to these problems.

> *Unlike the scientist, who must follow established scientific methods, the artist is free to question and redefine anything or everything at any stage, to be wide-ranging and open to all possibilities. . . . As a result, artistic projects are able to withstand a far higher level of risk than typical scientific experiments, which often come with expectations of tangible results or even profit for their funders. They can engage local communities and garner broad support in ways that science alone can rarely do. They can offer tools for reflection, discussion, awareness and action that lead to new ways of thinking about and of being in the world. And they can bring about real change—sometimes deliberately, sometimes unintentionally—that has lasting benefit, whether to the few or to the many.*
>
> (Brown, 2014, p. 8)

A spectrum of engagement with nature through the arts is wide and embraces different positions from objective observer to active interventionalist in order to provide positive effects on the environment and our behavior. Environmental psychology helps to expand our understanding of the arts as a representation and dynamic form of the constructive interplay between human beings and their surroundings. One of the important concepts of environmental psychology that can help to support ecotherapeutic application of the arts is that humans are engaged and purposeful in their relation to the environment (De Young, 2013). Although

> *there is still much to be learned about human-environment interaction. . . . the reasonable person model, and the related tools of small experiments and adaptive muddling, provide a context for creating interventions*

> *that bring out the best in people. . . . This framing recognizes humans as active, purposive beings, not as mere recipients of the information patterns generated by environments or experts.*
>
> (De Young, 2013, p. 32)

Environmental activity with the use of arts can be one of characteristics of humans as active, purposive beings who according to Levine's concept of *poiesis* (Levine, 2011) possess

> *the basic capacity . . . to shape their worlds. The human being is distinct from other creatures in that it is not pre-adapted to a particular environment. Instead it has the ability to build radically different worlds suitable (or not) to life in a wide diversity of surroundings. In building its world, the human shapes the environment, and as it does so, it shapes itself. World building is self-building.*
>
> (Levine, 2011, pp. 23–24)

## Functions of the Arts That Can Be Relevant for Ecotherapy Goals

### *The Arts as a Meaningful Action Leading to the Changed Perception of the Natural Environment*

Study of the cultural history of humankind helps us to recognize that doing arts brings new meaning to human relations with nature and thus helps to reach environmental psychology and ecotherapy goals to promote a different attitude toward nature, the so-called intrinsic standpoint (Berger, 2009b, p. 64); raise consciousness of our place in the natural world and our interdependence; encourage people to transcend their own personal problems and develop a sense of being part of a bigger whole, thus allowing the spiritual awareness of a relationship with the natural world; develop the self-directed need to be caring and preserve and respect natural world and develop lifestyles that will aid this position (Clinebell, 1996). Doing arts with and in nature also helps to reach such goals of ecotherapy as to facilitate healing and accomplish well-being as an inner state of wellness, including a physical, mental and emotional state of consonance that exists in a healthy environment and is based on a harmonious connection with that ecology (Burns, 1998).

According to environmental psychology, meaningful action is the opportunity to make a useful contribution to a genuine problem. It may involve being effective at a large scale (e.g., the choice of livelihood, a lifelong struggle for environmental justice or food security), but perhaps more often it involves actions at a more modest level (e.g., participating in a stewardship activity, community involvement, voting). The meaningfulness experienced is less about the scale of the effort and more about deriving a sense of making a difference, being listened to and respected, and feeling that we have a secure place within our social group. Reasonable behavior is more likely when people feel that they are needed and that their participation matters. A number of studies indicate that doing something judged worthwhile or making a difference in the long run are primary motives underlying voluntary environmental stewardship behavior (Grese, Kaplan, Ryan, and Buxton, 2000). In these studies the notion of meaningful action emerged as one of the most significant sources of satisfaction.

Arts in nature and with nature can be an effective form of experimenting with meaningful environmental action that uses citizens' capacity and wish to bring coherence and beauty into their living space. De Young (2013, p. 17) writes that

> *to increase the probability of success, we must encourage experiments on a multitude of options. Citizen and environmental experts alike should constantly tinker with new institutional forms, metaphors, norms and principles. Perhaps most importantly, we must each become behavioral entrepreneurs, exploring new behaviors and new ways to combine old behaviors. Perhaps a behavioral aesthetics is possible, a way to live our daily lives as a work of art as we adapt-in-place. We may be facing a materially simpler life but it may be possible to live with beauty.*

One of the significant effects of doing arts with and in nature is that arts give natural landscapes and objects some kind of "distinctive meaning, relevance and status" (Sontag, 1990, p. 28). Doing arts as a form of environmental activity can help people to recognize *the meaningfulness and beauty* of nature even if they initially didn't recognize such qualities. Creative environmental acts can be understood from an ethological perspective, as a "behavior of art" related to one's ability to "make-special" (Dissanayake, 2002) where natural phenomena, such as objects, processes and whole ecosystems, "green spaces" can assume specialness and be celebrated.

Following this idea we can recognize that if the person is focused even on the most depressed, sad and colorless environment and starts looking beneath the superficial exterior of things or places using arts, she/he will often see some spark of life, unique, individual aspects that characterize those objects or places. However, defensive reactions and selectivity of perception are also possible as a reflection of conscious or unconscious attempts on the part of the person to avoid confrontation with some "ugly," "dark" or "traumatized" sides of nature.

### *The Arts as an Authentic Expression of Human Positive Connection to and Care for Nature*

From the viewpoint of environmental and ecopsychology, the human inclination to do arts as a form of environmental practice supporting physical, emotional and spiritual bonds with nature, can be considered as an expression of the human instinct of mutually supportive relationships with nature and healthy resonance with many living forms abundant in the natural world. This inclination can be explained from the perspective of the *biophilia hypothesis*, which postulates a pervasive attraction that draws people to nature with its different mineral, plant and organic forms as a representation of healthy and contained life with its cycles of transformation. The *biophilia hypothesis* is also based on the presumption that our relation with these natural forms can be mutually healing and go beyond their practical value as mineral resources and often enable to perceive them as emotionally compelling symbols.

Formulated by Wilson in 1984 (Wilson, 1984, 1993) and then elaborated by Kellert and Wilson (Kellert, 1993), the biophilia hypothesis is described as the "innately emotional affiliation of human beings to other living organisms" (Kellert, 1993, p. 31). Kellert (1993) presumed that it is a "human dependence on nature that extends far beyond the simple issues of material and physical sustenance to encompass as well the human craving for aesthetic, intellectual, cognitive, and even spiritual meaning and satisfaction" (p. 18).

Doing arts with nature and in nature can be an authentic expression of human care for nature that doesn't require specific talents and professional competences related to the arts. This necessarily requires, however, "turning ourselves inside out, with the heart as the site of reconnection" (Chalquist, 2007) in order to be able to dissolve through "the art of biophilia" (Kopytin, 2016) the psychological barriers that characterize the history of our progressive alienation from the land and fuel the environmental crisis.

The arts can be an expression of healing metaphysics based on human positive connection to and care for nature, because

> *we have not lost, and cannot lose, the genuine impulse. It awaits only an authentic expression. The task is not to start by recapturing the theme of a reconciliation with the earth in all of its metaphysical subtlety, but with something much more direct and simple that will yield its own healing metaphysics.*
>
> (Shepard, 1995, p. 40)

## *The Arts Help People to Feel in Control of the Environment and Participate in Its Management and Restoration*

Because the goal of ecotherapy is to facilitate people's interaction with the environment in order to achieve not only health-promoting effects on an individual level (the micro level), but also public and environmental health outcomes (the macro level), the arts can be used to promote clients' active position in their relationship with the environment and develop their perception of themselves as those who are able to exert a certain amount of influence on it. Environmental psychology supports the idea of *participation* and strives to enhance citizen involvement in environmental design, management and restoration efforts. Environmental, nature-based arts can support achieving these goals. This can be a result of people's better understanding of environmental issues and their relation to personal and community agendas.

Being involved in environmental expressive/creative activities, doing arts in nature and with nature, people can "personalize" and appropriate the environment. This can also be a significant factor of their feeling safe and in control of the space. For Dissanayake (2002), "human beings seem to have a natural tendency to make sense of their environment, to find or impose upon it a pattern of order and hence comprehensibility" (pp. 113–114).

The controlling function of the arts can be especially important in ecotherapy activities, when the client perceives the environment as lacking control (which is natural for most outdoor activities) and evoking anxiety. Being able to leave certain personal markers through doing arts in the environment can help the people feel more safety and control of the situation. The arts mediate one's interaction with the space and help to provide equilibrium between the dynamic quality of the natural environment and more static nature of artworks.

Burls (2007) chose to use the term "contemporary ecotherapy" in order to emphasize forms of ecotherapy "in action." She referred to research into the therapeutic and restorative benefits of contact with nature that has generally looked at three main areas of contact: viewing nature; being in the presence of nearby nature; or active participation and involvement with nature. Although all three of these aspects are embraced in ecotherapy, the strongest component of what she calls "contemporary ecotherapy" is in the active participation. This has so far been described as gardening, farming, trekking, walking, horse riding, adventure therapy and some other activities. Environmental arts belong to the same category of contemporary ecotherapy activities.

The active stance in clients' relationship to nature is the main characteristics of "contemporary ecotherapy" (Burls, 2007), and a significant factor of mutuality can support collective behavioral change. According to Halpern and Bates (2004), behavioral interventions tend to be more successful where there is an equal relationship between the influencer and the influenced and where both parties stand to gain from the outcome (p. 25). In public mental health, such mutuality can be seen in the relationships between practitioners and service users, where the latter assume greater responsibility.

For Burls (2007),

> *In ecotherapeutic approaches, there seems to be a further level of mutuality: the role of the influencer is adopted by people who would normally be classed as the influenced. In benefiting from personal lifestyle changes and associated recovery, the service users help to develop a framework for*

> *reciprocity towards the environment and the community. In doing so, the community is influenced to care for and respect the environment and, in addition, to see their local green spaces as a source of health and well-being.*
> (p. 35)

## *The Arts as a Form of Ecological Personalization*

Our perception of the constructive human interaction with the natural environment through the arts can be enriched by a concept such as *personalization* of space/environment (Gregory, Fried, and Slowik, 2013; Heimets, 1994) as related to psychosocial aspects expressed through territoriality as well as through people's need to maintain a sense of belonging, ownership and control over their space. Personalization can also be understood as a human behavior aimed at bringing about distinctive features of an individual to the environment. Personalization provides people with a greater sense of ownership and control over the space, and helps to establish and maintain a sense of individuality (identity). As a result of personalization of the space, not only existing ego-structures can be brought forward and expressed in the environment, but further development of the personality and appropriation of new, positive characteristics of their identity, Eco-Identity, in particular, become possible. Environmental arts can be understood as an *ecological form of personalization* based on the sustainable and supportive human interaction with the natural world.

As far as the use of the arts in ecotherapy practices is concerned, acts of ecological personalization usually imply the perception of the environment not only as a physical and biological realm, but as a "potential space" in which symbol formation can take place. Such "potential green space" becomes a container of symbolic forms from which different meanings and knowledge of the psyche and human and more-than-human world can be derived. Nature serves as a mirror that is able to reflect physical and mental phenomena and processes experienced by an artist (a client participating in ecotherapy sessions) shaping these phenomena and processes through expressive forms.

"Green Studio" (Kopytin, 2016) is an ecotherapy "potential space," a special creative environment where various expressive acts take place, and it enables relating between the inner processes of the human body and psyche and the outer processes of the natural environment. The natural environment with its metaphors can enable people to "express the inexpressible" and sometimes help them to depict what words are unable to convey, irrespective of a person's language, background or beliefs (Linden and Grut, 2002, p. 16).

Personalization of the landscape through the arts usually means that people leave certain physical, personalized marks of their presence in the environment. Moreover, projecting certain personal or group qualities onto the environment and establishing some meaningful inner bond with it can be characterized as powerful psychological mechanism to personalize the space even without leaving any physical markers of one's presence in the environment. Some of the ways to personalize the environment through expressive ecotherapy activity could be building "homes" in nature (Berger, 2009a), creating environmental art, designing, creating and maintaining "green spaces" such as gardens, performing personal and group rituals, dance and movement practices, taking pictures of the natural environment and object, and so forth.

Creative personalization of the environment implies symbolic or ritual acts through which certain exchange of information, energy and matter between human beings and the environment through organized symbolic forms of the arts can take place. Through acts of creative personalization of the environment, people select objects or scenery and combine them in some cohesive constructions (like parks and other environmental creations), frame and mark them, create their narratives and internalize certain parts of the environment as significant inner markers of their identity.

As far as therapeutic and rehabilitative practice with the use of environmental and ecological expressive arts therapies is concerned, acts of creative personalization based on a client's interaction with space can not only promote an environmental ethic, harmonious human–nature relationship and more active participatory position in people's relationship with the world around, but also support self-esteem and empowerment and help to overcome feelings of helplessness and lack of privacy.

### *The Arts Facilitate Narrative Activity Based on Clients' Interaction With the Environment*

Narrative-construction can be one of several effective ways to assist with appropriation and personalization of the environment. When people create and tell stories that concern their relationship with the environment, they have rich possibilities to discover and maintain their individual or group identity, formulate complex earth-based meanings and bring their intentions and the sense of a goal into the narrative. Narrative activity as a significant part and a result of environmental arts-based activities can be an expression of the important thesis of environmental psychology that humans are engaged and purposeful (De Young, 2013). Creating narratives as a part of arts, therapeutic nature-based activities can activate these inherent qualities in people.

Different special assignments—visual journaling, in particular—can be used to facilitate narrative activity. This can be an album of sketches, a collection of found natural objects, or photographs, a storyboard with a series of drawings illustrating one's walkabouts in nature made throughout or between sessions. Significant memories and biographical meanings can be revealed, for instance, when the client is visiting and interacting with the environment and natural objects related to her/his biography and identity formation.

Narratives can reflect some micro- or macro-events that took place in the process of a walkabout or just being in nature. These micro- or macro-events could be natural processes observed by the client and related to her/his inner reactions. One of the effects of such activities can be story-making that helps with a sense of cohesiveness in a client's perception of her/his experience of relationship with nature.

Narrative-construction can be applied in ecotherapy practices, when people either spontaneously, or as a response to some natural places, objects or events, as well as some environmental photos or sketches create stories through which their experience of nature can be literally or metaphorically expressed. People can be encouraged to keep environmental diaries or art journals illustrating their personal stories, or some cultural and archetypal themes. Narrative activity gives clients more time and possibilities to focus and reflect on micro- or macro-events confronted throughout their walkabouts or certain periods of their life. Clients can be encouraged to present their narratives together with a series of found objects, or drawings and photographs made during their outdoor journeys.

### *Doing Environmental Arts Supports Mindfulness and a Sense of Physical Presence in the Environment*

Doing environmental arts can be a means of connecting symbolic forms of the arts and language to the immediate physical experience of the natural world (the life process). Some environmental arts-based activities can be considered as a way to develop somatic awareness and embodied sense of self in one's relation to the environment. This effect is more obvious as a result of environmental arts-based activities that balance time between mindfulness and creative expression, when emphasis is placed on meditative journeys or path-working (walkabouts) as a form of mini-pilgrimages in the "green area" accompanied or followed with participants' involvement in doing arts (drawing, taking photographs, making environmental constructions, botanical arrangements, etc.). Other expressive forms such as dance and movement, ritual, music improvisation and narrative-construction in order to express and integrate complex experiences can expand the scope of expressive/creative arts therapeutic techniques.

Embodiment effects can be easily facilitated through mindful horticultural activities, or meditative journeys in search for certain areas or objects in the environment, followed with taking photographs or drawing the scenery or with creating environmental art constructions like "green mandalas" or "homes in nature" and so forth. Through such assignments participants become physically more active and feel more embedment in the environment. Often, the projective nature of the arts enables one's identification with natural objects and environments on a physical level and projecting one's perception of the body or its parts onto natural processes and environments. Through this process symbolization of somatic phenomena and processes is possible.

Mindfulness-based arts therapeutic techniques can be integrated into ecotherapy practices. In this way body-mind-environment focused activities can support the goals of ecotherapy by fostering reconnection and returning to experiencing ourselves in the here and now as embodied beings. This requires attention to physical sensations in their relation to mind states evoked by one's presence and interaction with the environment. It should be emphasized that the curative powers of nature are enhanced by the degree of mindfulness and mental focus one brings to these interactions (Louv, 2005). Participants can immerse in "quiet fascination" (Kaplan, 1995, p. 103) and a state of presence in the environment throughout different parts of the session.

Participants can be encouraged to use different arts and instrumental media like photography to explore experiential awareness and practice mindful attention by documenting responses to sensory stimuli. For instance, participants can be asked to take pictures of what they move toward as pleasant and to also photograph what they experience as unpleasant as it was used in new mindfulness-based art therapy intervention (Peterson, 2013), which can be an example of a palliative environmental program.

Whichever particular expressive arts are being used, participants can be encouraged to immerse themselves in a kind of meditation with their absorption in physical and emotional processes on the one hand, and being attentive to the environmental stimuli on the other hand. They can walk or act mindfully, keeping a sense of their presence in the environment with immediate experience here and now, appreciating their physical contact with the natural objects and sensory qualities of the "green space" with its "field effects."

Mindfulness-based environmental expressive arts therapies programs can include an introduction with mindfulness instruction and emphasis on the role of attention in health. Warming-up activities involving breathing and relaxation and exploratory walkabouts in certain environments can be introduced as helping to provide deeper effects.

It is difficult to say whether through any arts-based activities (for instance, through taking photographs of the environment and objects) participants bring meaning in the environment, or meaning implied in the environment "finds" them. It is possible to explain the process of finding significant and meaningful objects and scenery during mindful and creative exploration of the environment with the use of Gibson's theory of affordances. According to his theory (Gibson, 1986), what clients notice and identify as relevant for them in the environment often depend on what they are looking for. As active motivated agents, clients do not passively receive environmental information. Instead, they extract and "create" meanings from and for the environment depending on their grasp of what they need. As Gibson (1986) observed, affordances are as much a part of the environment as they are of behavior.

There are many valuable functions implied in doing arts as far as ecotherapy goals are concerned. The *focusing function*, in particular, is more evident when people take photographs or draw (Kopytin, 2004), or take as a found object what they find most interesting or meaningful or move toward as pleasant. It helps clients/participants to find latent, previously hidden meanings and actualize and integrate experience related to photographs, drawings or found objects and the mindful process, when they are involved in such activities.

Other important functions that support therapeutic goals include *reflecting the dynamics of external (environmental) changes in their relation to inner dynamics of clients* (Kopytin, 2004). Arts enable us to see and recognize changes in the environment as a result of natural processes, or human interventions, including those made by citizen participation in the design, management and restoration of the environment/"green spaces." Arts can also help to *contain and organize, frame and reframe* people's powerful and sometimes ambiguous reactions and experiences evoked by their interaction with the environment.

## Basic Theoretical Assumptions of Environmental and Ecological Expressive Arts Therapies (Eco-arts Therapies)

Environmental or ecological expressive arts therapies (eco-arts therapies) mean something more than just a set of innovative creative activities and ideas that can be implemented in the already established expressive/creative arts therapeutic approaches. It is a new set of empirical forms of therapeutic and health-promoting work supported by a constellation of theoretical, "meta-psychological" ideas that have a certain distinctive quality. Environmental or ecological expressive therapies (eco-arts therapies) strive to bring the arts and nature together to provide beneficial effects both for human and nonhuman worlds.

Together with environmental psychology, ecopsychology, ecohealth, deep ecology and some other established scientific fields or forms of social activism, ecotherapy and eco-arts therapies belong to the *environmentalist movement*. This movement challenges the basic foundations of the current civilization and can even be considered as related to the paradigm shift, because the paradigm, in Kuhn's (Kuhn, 1962) view, is not simply the theory, but the entire worldview in which it exists, and all of the implications that come with it. This is based on features of the landscape of knowledge that scientists can identify around them. A significant aspect of the environmental movement is concerned with a radical change in personal beliefs, complex systems or organizations, replacing the former way of thinking or organizing with a radically different way of thinking or organizing the structure of social life and human psychology.

According to Brown (1995),

> *ecopsychology addresses the problem of effective communication with the general public, that will have to meet the demands of the environmental revolution. However, the issue it raises amounts to more than a matter of public relations and personal therapy. There is an underlying philosophical issue. It has to do with our understanding of human nature, or, if you will, the nature of the soul.*
>
> (p. xiv)

He also emphasized that it brings a new perspective on our understanding of health and pathology and ways how personal and collective insanity could be cured, because

> *at its most ambitious, ecopsychology seeks to redefine sanity within an environmental context. It contends that seeking to heal the soul without reference to the ecological system of which we are an integral part is a form of self-destructive blindness. Ecopsychologists are drawing upon the ecological sciences to reexamine the human psyche as an integral part of the web of nature.*
>
> (Brown, 1995, p. xvi)

Ecopsychology raised fundamental questions about the inner organization of human beings and how it is represented in psychological constructs. As Hillman (1995) claims,

> *the paradigm shift in psychology places it at a crossroads. It may go along the well-worn track, declaring subjectivity consists essentially only in human nature, thereby making its cut close to the skin and regarding as secondary what lies outside its bell jar. No doubt this path has its virtues, for it allows a special culture to bloom in a bubble, a culture today called egocentric, self-referential, and narcissistic.*
>
> (p. xxii)

## Environmental and Ecopsychology Perspective on Personality Formation

Ecotherapy needs an ecologically grounded personality theory. The philosophical and psychological category of nature establishes the core of ecopsychology and ecotherapy theory and its particular methods including eco-arts therapies theory. According to this theory our ideas of personality and its formation, health and pathology, curative and pathogenic factors of diseases, therapeutic relations, and even goals of therapy can be constructed. Whereas in most conventional therapies the category of nature is simply ignored, or considered to be secondary with regard to one's relation to the human world, primary caregivers (parental figures) and other people with whom significant relations can be established throughout the life span, one's relations with the more-than-human world, nature as a form of life and even a Subject, assumes the same significance in ecotherapy.

According to environmentally or ecologically grounded personality theory one's relationship with nature assumes a special role, being considered as a vital factor of personality formation having the same significance as one's relations with people. Emotional bonds with nature and attachment of human beings to nature, together with their bonds with people, serve as a vital factor of healthy personality formation beginning with the early developmental stage and ending with the final stage of the human life span.

Barrows (1995) points out that Piaget, Stern, Fordham and others whose theories inform our work now may serve as a bridge to a more ecologically based understanding of child development.

> *The place where transitional phenomena occur, then (to use Winnicott as a sort of bridge to a new formulation), might be understood, in this new paradigm of the self, to be the permeable membrane that suggests or delineates but does not divide us from the medium in which we exist. It is in this realm that distinctions between subjective and objective begin to blur and intersubjectivity is possible.*
>
> (pp. 106–107)

According to an ecopsychology perspective, personality development takes place within a wider matrix of being and relationships that enables the formation of Eco-Identity. The notion of an Eco-Identity can be preeminent for the fields of ecopsychology and ecotherapy and challenges most "conventional" personality theories. It can be defined as the interiorized dynamical structure of relationship with nature that embraces both human and more-than-human worlds and serves as one of the significant foundations for self-perception and self-concept. This is a kind of self-perception and self-understanding that is linked to one's mutually sustaining relationship with nature and implies one's responsibility and care for nature. Ethical and aesthetic perception of the natural environment and some practical action aimed at its preservation and cultivation serve as important factors of one's own health and well-being (Kopytin, 2016).

Eco-Identity is considered to be opposed to a "consumer false self" (Kanner and Gomes, 1995), "an ideal that is taken to heart as part of a person's identity. . . . The consumer false self is false because it arises from a merciless distortion of authentic human needs and desires" (p. 83). Kanner and Gomes believe that "the currently lost capacity to live in balance with nature will need to be rediscovered and revitalized and that therapists must help clients to identify, awaken, and nourish long-dormant needs, abilities, and inclinations buried and denigrated by the false self" (Kanner and Gomes, 1995, p. 88).

### *Nature as the Third Part in Therapeutic Relations*

Ecotherapy is sometimes believed to be "radical" in regard to most modern therapies due to its different perception of conditions, goals and therapeutic relationship involved. Ecotherapy as most other therapies is based on *relational theories* of therapeutic action, with their focus "on the larger relational system established by the client and the therapists, within which psychological phenomena crystallize and in which experience is continually and mutually shaped in a dialogue of the client and the therapist" (Bridges, 1999, p. 292). However, while the main parties in this relational system in most therapies are client and therapist, nature assumes the role of the third party in ecotherapy and the fourth party in expressive/creative arts therapies in which the arts are considered to be the third part. Within this relational system the crucial role is given to affective attachment both to the therapist and nature in the process of therapeutic change. As Berger (2009b) puts it, nature therapy as a particular form of ecotherapeutic practice

> *explores the ways in which nature and relationship with nature can add to the mainstream psychological/therapeutic framework, extending not only its physical space of performance, as it moves from a static and closed environment into the dynamic and open natural environment, but relating to it in a way that expands the "person to person" discourse, by opening it up to the non-human and larger-than-self.*
>
> (p. 57)

Similarly to the ecofeminist approach, nature is perceived in ecotherapy as a subject of a kind and requires environmental ethics that include emotional and subjective elements built on a relationship of care between humans and non-humans and the particular environments in which they are located (Palmer, 2003, p. 19). Ecotherapy invites clients to get involved in the relationship with nature as a significant factor of therapeutic action. Clinebell (1996) postulated that ecotherapy is characterized by the three-way relationship of person, therapist and nature, in which nature is considered to be a kind of a co-therapist or educator.

Understanding nature as the third party in therapeutic relationships implies specific psychological, moral and existential attitudes toward nature. As Berger (2008) puts it,

> *generally speaking, there are two main moral, perhaps ethical attitudes towards nature. The first, an instrumental standpoint, values nature only in relation to its usefulness in terms of its human interests. The second, an intrinsic standpoint, values nature for itself and for its own right with no dependence on outside factors or its contribution to people.*
>
> (pp. 63–64)

Perceiving nature as Subject with which some affective bond can be established is also possible as a result of intensified human-nature relationships typical within ecotherapy. Our perennial experience of interaction with the natural environment as a source of life, protection and nurture, enables this effect. Corbett and Milton (2011) even emphasize that therapeutically, the natural world could bring another dimension into the transferential relationship. Further exploration would be required to develop this, for example drawing on the work of various attachment, personality and object relations theorists (Bowlby, 1969; Erikson, 1950; Sullivan, 1940). If we recognize that nature cared for human beings for millions of years and perhaps still does, so our affective bond and attachment to the natural environment is possible, although its quality can vary depending on the developmental circumstances of the particular individual.

It should be recognized, however, that ecotherapy and eco-arts therapies as one of its forms, like any other therapy requires appropriately structured and accompanied therapeutic process. The presence of the therapist throughout a whole course of eco-arts therapeutic work provides the client with the sense of safety, containment, order and comprehensibility and helps her/him to shape and crystallize experience.

## *Environmental and Ecopsychology Perception of the Therapeutic Setting*

According to the traditional clinical (arts-psychotherapy) model of the arts therapy setting, it is both "an environment conducive to creativity" (Malchiodi, 2007, p. 80) and a container for powerful and unregulated experiences (Killick, 2000), "the space in which the relationship between therapist and client develops" (Case and Dalley, 1992, p. 19). The need for a client to reach a certain state of mind necessary to provide symbol formation in the atmosphere of the arts therapy setting is emphasized. Symbol formation as a means of effective therapeutic communication and the main focus for the analytical discourse is given importance in clinical arts psychotherapy. It is believed that "Visual imagery—the quintessential stuff of symbolism—is the raw material of art therapy" (Wilson, 2001, p. 40), which then can materialize through art making. Because the symbol is defined as a representational object that can be evoked in the absence of an immediate stimulus, the therapeutic environment is arranged to evoke symbol formation based on the client's immersion in her/his inner realm rather than in the outer reality and to help the client to begin using images as a reflection of her/his inner world based on the concept of "drawing from within" (Malchiodi, 2007, p. 56).

In art psychotherapy, a clients' relations to the outer environment is sometimes discussed to offer them additional opportunities for connecting to their inner worlds. As Case and Dalley (1992) explained,

> *The outer environment in which the institution is set will also directly and indirectly impinge upon and influence the sessions as clients make use of the content of the rooms and whatever is offered by the external environment (for instance, offering clients views of the outside world can evoke memories, feelings and fantasies).*
>
> (p. 32)

However, as we stated in our previous publication (Kopytin, 2016), "it is unusual for most arts therapists, especially those following a psychodynamic orientation, to consider environmental factors implied in socio-cultural and natural surroundings as having much significance in the therapeutic process (action). The emphasis is made on interpersonal therapeutic interaction and psychological exploration of the arts product as a reflection of the client's symptoms and her/his inner dynamics connected to therapeutic relations with minimum or no attention given to immediate environmental stimuli. A client's connection to the wider environment and crossing the therapeutic boundaries was usually considered to be less significant and even counterproductive" (p. 7). That is why some arts therapists like Moon (2010) questioned whether they had become "stuck" (p. 5) within a "client-creates-art-object focus" (p. xvii).

Environmental psychology and ecopsychology, together with socially sensitive approaches in expressive arts therapies and in contemporary therapies in general, expanded our understanding of the therapeutic environment. Modern meanings of the term "therapeutic environment" often embrace not only factors necessary for facilitating therapy, but healthcare facilities and "therapeutic team" as well as community. The therapeutic environment is designed and applied not only to support and facilitate state-of-the-art medicine and technology, patient safety and quality patient care, but to also embrace the patients' family and caregivers in a psychosocially supportive therapeutic space. It is believed that the characteristics of the physical, social and psychological environment in which a patient receives care affects patient outcomes, patient satisfaction and safety, staff efficiency and satisfaction as well as organizational outcomes. Environmental psychology and ecopsychology seem to be congruent with the modern ideas of the therapeutic environment, but give even more importance to natural environmental factors.

Because both ecopsychology and ecotherapy recognize synergy between human health and well-being and the health and ecological integrity of the natural environment, eco-therapeutic practices usually take place within natural environments or in other ways somehow related to nature. Although some ecotherapy practices, at least during certain parts of the session, can take place indoors, in the arts therapies settings special significance is given to participants' involvement in certain activities outdoors. Outdoor spaces used throughout these activities can vary considerably.

The wide continuum of environments used in nature-based or eco-arts therapies can embrace spaces with prevailing natural objects and characterized by greater biodiversity on the one hand, and those with mostly built objects on the other hand. The answer to the question "How much nature is needed in order to practice eco-arts therapies?" would be a wide variety of environments in which nature is present in one or another form. It could be the garden in a mental hospital or a public school, or more distant wilderness areas, "as long as the setting is maintained as a central reference to the process and its conduction" (Berger, 2009b, p. 240).

The Green Studio model was introduced (Kopytin, 2016) to define a special place where eco-arts therapeutic sessions can take place. The Green Studio/Eco-Studio can be characterized as a therapeutic indoor or outdoor space with certain abundance of natural living forms and materials, possibly some natural landscape, a part of the natural environment that can be chosen, maintained and personalized by the client or community. Sometimes it cannot be as permanent as the traditional therapeutic setting and is characterized by a unique equilibrium of static and dynamic qualities. Its dynamic qualities are dependent on greater transparency of its boundaries and natural processes involved.

As we defined it (Kopytin, 2016, p. 20), the Green Studio can be created as an accessible green area, a part of the institution (hospital, rehabilitation center, shelter, residential home, etc.), or aligned to a private practitioner's office. It can also be a kind of a "portable studio" (Kalmanowitz and Lloyd, 2005, 2011) arranged in the municipal (park, garden, beach, etc.) or in the "wild" environment. But even in this case a sense of order, permanence and comprehensibility for the client is possible as a result of her/his relationship with the therapist and various activities that give her/him a possibility to personalize a natural space.

A combination of different factors, including the twofold relationship of the client with the therapist and nature in which she/he becomes an active side who arranges, creates, inhabits and "nourishes" her/his space, "facilitates an affect driven experience of meaning in matter and a love of place that holds us" (Fenner, 2012, p. 17).

The Green Studio can be perceived as the place of attachment that is "made special," a vivid manifestation of the behavior of art (Dissanayake, 2002). It can also represent the function of *poiesis* that transcends traditional perception of the role of art as a mere means of self-expression and implies the capacity to respond to the world in which we find ourselves (Levine, 2011). Therefore it is possible and even necessary to perceive the Green Studio as providing a two-pronged system to achieve both individual health (at the micro level) and public and environmental health outcomes (at the macro level). For people seeking personal recovery also, through their creative care of green spaces, their Green Studio "may achieve unanticipated social capital and natural capital outcomes and thereby meet current multi-disciplinary policy targets" (Burls, 2007, p. 24).

## *Environmental and Ecopsychology Concept of the Creative Function*

In recent years, new ideas of the arts and the creative function of the psyche that are more congruent with the ecological movement emerged as a result of some innovative ideas in the field of expressive arts therapies. Some of them strive to integrate world traditions with their wider understanding of creativity into the scientific platform of arts therapies. One of examples could be the concept of *poiesis* (Levine, 1992, 2011). As Levine (1992) puts it,

> *Within the framework of expressive arts, we could say that* poiesis *implies the capacity to respond to the world in which we find ourselves. We suffer, both individually and collectively, when we find ourselves unable to respond, when this capacity for poietic action is restricted and we experience ourselves as being in a helpless situation. . . . The work of the change agent in the field of expressive arts, then, is to restore the capacity for poiesis that the individual or community has lost, and to help them expand the range of play within which they can act.*
>
> (p. 27)

He emphasizes that *poiesis* happens only in the world with others:

> *We have made this world together; this means that we can make it differently. The particular power of the expressive arts in the field of social change is to help us find our ability to make a new world together. Only by doing so can we leave to future generations a world which they will find worthy of response.*
>
> (Levine, 1992, p. 29)

Another prominent theorist of expressive arts therapy, Shaun McNiff (2011, 2015) developed his idea of creativity that is sympathetic to the environmental and ecological platform in a number of publications—in particular in his recent book *Imagination in Action: Secrets for Unleashing Creative Expression* (McNiff, 2015). He understands creativity as a defining quality of the human spirit, a force of nature, the mainstream of imagination accessible to all.

> *Yet it is not free to run in schools and societies still repressed by restrictive ideas about the nature of creative intelligence, how it can be cultivated and taught, who can do it and who cannot, and how it changes the world. The shackles to be cast off are largely fashioned by misperceptions that creativity and art are the domain of a talented few rather than the truly universal pulse advancing life everywhere.*
>
> (p. 10)

McNiff (2015) indicates that

> *art has been viewed as representing and interpreting nature but not enough attention has been given to how the process of creation in all its forms acts like nature. Making art is closely related to how things grow and move in the physical world.*
>
> (pp. 10–11)

As Levine, McNiff also emphasizes the value of collective creative expressions as an incremental building process of responsive acts. "We can do so much more in creating what I call 'slipstreams of expression,' where group and environmental forces carry us much further that we will go alone" (McNiff, 2015, p. 12).

His empirical observations of artistic expression as a force of nature are discussed in relation to classical Chinese thought. Correspondence to nature is fundamental to the Taoist and Confucian traditions, both grounded in the idea that *qi/ch'i* (vital energy/life force) is the energetic basis of creative transformation. The principle of *te*, applied to spontaneous and authentic expression, according to this tradition is explored in relation to practical approaches to helping people everywhere access their unique and natural creative powers.

The ethological understanding of the human "behavior of art" (Dissanayake, 2002), together with modern arts therapeutic ideas of creativity (Levine, 1992, 2011; McNiff, 2011, 2015), help us to recognize the arts as supporting the interaction of human beings with the more-than-human world, and reach ecotherapy goals such as provide healing and well-being as an inner state of consonance that exists in a healthy environment and is based on a harmonious connection with that ecology.

Our notion of Eco-Identity assumes a greater significance as related to the human ability to do arts as meaningful environmental action and even as a form of co-creation, in which human beings can participate, together with other living forms that establish a wider "community of subjects." Doing arts in and with nature, together with many other activities typical for ecotherapy, such as gardening, animal encounters, simply spending more time in ecologically healthy settings, or more actively working on maintaining and restoring eco-health, can be regarded as a type of environmental action that is characteristic of a person with an established Eco-Identity, with a strong self-regulating function related to coping skills and adaptivity.

Creative environmental function, as one of the core functions of Eco-Identity, is expressed through one's initiatives to care for and respect the environment and see local green spaces as a source of health and well-being for oneself and others who belong to both human and more-than-human worlds. Eco-Identity often makes one sociopolitically active, able to engage further in eco-health promotion and become an agent of change in educative, public health and environmental spheres.

Eco-Identity is linked to Creative (Artistic) Identity and rooted in one's love of life and biodiversity called *biophilia* (Kellert and Wilson, 1993; Wilson, 1984). It means a developed sense of beauty experienced through human encounters with nature, and compassionate attitude to life and nature both within and around. Eco-Identity enables the person to become involved in *the art of biophilia* (Kopytin, 2016), which can be recognized as form of creative activity in and with natural environments (green spaces). Creative acts related to the art of biophilia can be considered as based on a strong motivation to support and serve nature and life.

## References

Barrows, A. (1995). The ecopsychology of child development. In T. Roszak, M. E. Gomes, and A. D. Kanner (Eds.), *Ecopsychology: Restoring the earth, healing the mind* (pp. 101–110). San Francisco: Sierra Club Books.

Berger, R. (2008). Building a home in nature. *Journal of Humanistic Psychology, 48*(2), 264–279.

Berger, R. (2009a). Being in nature: An innovative framework for incorporating nature therapy with older adults. *Journal of Holistic Nursing, 27*(1), 45–51.

Berger, R. (2009b). *Nature therapy—Developing a framework for practice.* A PhD School of Health and Social Sciences, University of Abertay, Dundee.

Bowlby, J. (1969). *Attachment and loss: Attachment. (Vol. 1).* London: Hogarth.

Bridges, N. A. (1999). Psychodynamic perspective on therapeutic boundaries. *Journal of Psychotherapy Practice and Research, 8*(4), 292–300.

Brown, A. (2014). *Art and ecology now.* London: Thames & Hudson.

Brown, L. (1995). Ecopsychology and environmental revolution: An environmental foreword. In T. Roszak, M. E. Gomes, and A. D. Kanner (Eds.), *Ecopsychology: Restoring the earth, healing the mind* (pp. xiii–xvi). San Francisco: Sierra Club Books.

Burls, A. (2007). People and green spaces: Promoting public health and mental well-being through eco-therapy. *Journal of Public Mental Health, 6*(3), 24–39.

Burns, G. W. (1998). *Nature-guided therapy: Brief integrative strategies for health and well-being*. Philadelphia, PA: Brunner/Mazel.

Case, C., and Dalley, T. (1992). *The handbook of art therapy.* New York: Routledge.

Chalquist, C. (2007). *The environmental crisis is a crisis of consciousness: Bringing the psychological dimension into the discussion*. Speech delivered at 'Voices for Change,' organized by students at Sonoma State University, November 2007.

Clinebell, H. (1996). *Ecotherapy: Healing ourselves, healing the earth: A guide to ecologically grounded personality theory, spirituality, therapy and education*. Minneapolis, MN: Fortress.

Corbett, L., and Milton, M. (2011). Ecopsychology: A perspective on trauma. *European Journal of Ecopsychology, 2*, 28–47.

De Young, R. (2013). Environmental psychology overview. In S. R. Klein and A. H. Huffman (Eds.), *Green organizations: Driving change with IO psychology* (pp. 17–33). New York: Routledge.

Dissanayake, E. (2002). *What is art for?* Seattle and London: University of Washington Press.

Erikson, E. (1950). *Childhood and society*. New York: Norton.

Fenner, P. (2012). What do we see? Extending understanding of visual experience in the art therapy encounter. *Art Therapy: Journal of the American Art Therapy Association, 29*(1), 11–18.

Gibson, J. J. (1986). *The ecological approach to visual perception*. Hillsdale, NJ: Lawrence Erlbaum Associates.

Gregory, L. A., Fried, Y., and Slowik, L. H. (2013). 'My space': A moderated mediation model of the effect of architectural and experienced privacy and workspace personalization on emotional exhaustion at work. *Journal of Environmental Psychology, 36*, 144–152.

Grese, R. E., Kaplan, R., Ryan, R. L., and Buxton, J. (2000). Psychological benefits of volunteering in stewardship programs. In P. H. Gobster and R. B. Hill (Eds.), *Restoring nature: Perspectives from the social sciences and humanities* (pp. 265–280). Washington, DC: Island Press.

Halpern, D., and Bates, C., with Beales, G. and Heathfield, A. (2004). *Personal responsibility and changing behavior: The state of knowledge and its implications for public policy*. London: Cabinet Office.

Heimets, M. (1994). The phenomenon of personalization of the environment. *Journal of Russian & East European Psychology, 32*(3), 24–32.

Hillman, J. (1995). A psyche the size of the Earth: A psychological foreword. In T. Roszak, M. E. Gomes, and A. D. Kanner (Eds.), *Ecopsychology: Restoring the earth, healing the mind* (pp. xvii–xxiii). San Francisco: Sierra Club Books.

Kalmanowitz, D., and Lloyd, B. (2005). Inside the portable studio: Art therapy in the former Yugoslavia 1994–2002. In D. Kalmanowitz and B. Lloyd (Eds.), *Art therapy and political violence: With art without illusion* (pp. 106–125). New York: Routledge.

Kalmanowitz, D., and Lloyd, B. (2011). Inside-out outside-in: Found objects and portable studio. In E. G. Levine and S. K. Levine (Eds.), *Art in action. Expressive arts therapy and social change* (pp. 104–127). London and Philadelphia: Jessica Kingsley.

Kanner, A. D., and Gomes, M. E. (1995). The all-consuming self. In T. Roszak, M. E. Gomes, and A. D. Kanner (Eds.), *Ecopsychology: Restoring the earth, healing the mind* (pp. 77–91). San Francisco: Sierra Club Books.

Kaplan, S. (1995). The restorative benefits of nature: Toward an integrative framework. *Journal of Environmental Psychology, 15*, 169–182.

Kellert, S. R. (1993). Introduction. In S. R. Kellert and E. O. Wilson (Eds.), *The biophilia hypothesis* (pp. 18–25). Washington, DC: Shearwater Books/Island Press.

Kellert, S. R., and Wilson, E. O. (Eds.). (1993). *The biophilia hypothesis*. Washington, DC: Island Press.

Killick, K. (2000). The art room as container in analytic art psychotherapy with patients in psychotic states. In A. Gilroy and G. McNeilly (Eds.), *The changing shape of art therapy* (pp. 99–114). London and Philadelphia: Jessica Kingsley.

Kopytin, A. (2004). Photography and art therapy: An easy partnership. *Inscape: The Journal of the British Association of Art Therapists, 9*(2), 49–58.

Kopytin, A. (2016). Green Studio: Eco-perspective on the therapeutic setting in art therapy. In A. Kopytin and M. Rugh (Eds.), *Green Studio: Nature and the arts in therapy* (pp. 3–26). New York: Nova Science.

Kuhn, T. (1962). *The structure of scientific revolutions*. Chicago: University of Chicago Press.

Levine, S. K. (1992). *Poiesis: The language of psychology and the speech of the soul*. Toronto: Palmerston Press/Jessica Kingsley.

Levine, S. K. (2011). Art opens to the world: Expressive arts and social action. In E. G. Levine and S. K. Levine (Eds.), *Art in action: Expressive arts therapy and social change* (pp. 21–30). London and Philadelphia: Jessica Kingsley.

Linden, S., and Grut, J. (2002). *The healing fields: Working with psychotherapy and nature to rebuild shattered lives*. Published in Association with the Medical Foundation for the Care of Victims of Torture. London: Frances Lincoln.

London, P. (2004). *Drawing closer to nature: Making art in dialogue with the natural world*. Boston and London: Shambhala.

Louv, R. (2005). *Last child in the woods: Saving our children from nature-deficit disorder*. Chapel Hill, NC: Algonquin Books of Chapel Hill.

Malchiodi, C. A. (2007). *The art therapy sourcebook* (2nd ed.). New York: McGraw-Hill.

McNiff, S. (2011). From the studio to the world. In E. G. Levine and S. K. Levine (Eds.), *Art in action. Expressive arts therapy and social change* (pp. 78–92). London and Philadelphia: Jessica Kingsley.

McNiff, S. (2015). *Imagination in action: Secrets for unleashing creative expression*. Boston and London: Shambhala.

Moon, C. H. (2010). *Materials and media in art therapy: Critical understandings of diverse artistic vocabularies*. New York: Routledge.

Palmer, C. (2003). An overview of environmental ethics. In A. Light and H. Roston (Eds.), *Environmental ethics: An anthology*. Oxford: Blackwell.

Peterson, C. (2013). Mindfulness-based art therapy: Applications for healing with cancer. In L. Rappaport (Ed.), *Mindfulness and the arts therapies: Theory and practice* (pp. 64–80). London: Jessica Kingsley.

Shepard, P. (1995). Nature and madness. In T. Roszak, M. E. Gomes, and A. D. Kanner (Eds.), *Ecopsychology: Restoring the earth, healing the mind* (pp. 21–40). San Francisco: Sierra Club Books.

Sontag, S. (1990). *On photography*. New York: Farrar, Straus and Giroux.

Sullivan, H. S. (1940). *Conceptions of modern psychiatry*. New York: Norton.

Tishkov, L. www.privatemoon.ru

Ulman, E. (1961). Art therapy: Problems of definition. *Bulletin of Art Therapy, 1961, 1*(2): 10–20.

Ulman, E. (1971). The power of art in therapy. In I. Jakab (Ed.), *Psychiatry and art*, Vol. 3. (pp. 93–102). New York: S. Karger.

Van Gogh, V. The letters. www.vangoghletters.org

Wilson, E. O. (1984). *Biophilia*. Cambridge, MA: Harvard University Press.

Wilson, E. (1993). Biophilia and the conservation ethic. In S. R. Kellert and E. O. Wilson (Eds.), *The biophilia hypothesis* (pp. 31–40). Washington, DC: Shearwater Books/Island Press.

Wilson, L. (2001). Symbolism and art therapy. In J. Rubin (Ed.), *Approaches to art therapy: Theory and technique* (2nd ed., pp. 40–53). New York: Brunner-Routledge.

# 3

# NATURE THERAPY—HIGHLIGHTING STEPS FOR PROFESSIONAL DEVELOPMENT

*Ronen Berger*

## Introduction

This chapter presents three facets of the rapidly expanding field of environmental expressive therapies, nature therapy in particular. The chapter starts by presenting the basic nature therapy theory and concepts—specifically *touching nature, the triangular relationship (therapist-client-nature), choosing the right space and back to ritual*—and continues with an example that illustrates its implementation in practice. The second section of the chapter relates to nature therapy's development within the context of establishing environmental expressive therapies: the creation of a wide range of therapeutic programs and their official recognition, the development of academic training programs, the organization of conferences and the formation of a professional community. This chapter concludes with issues and questions dealing with the further development of this approach as a young field of expertise, as well as its academic and professional development and recognition.

## Nature Therapy—A Theoretical and Applied Framework

Nature therapy is a method that can be included in the spectrum of environmental expressive therapies that takes place in nature, and perceives nature as a partner in constructing a therapeutic setting and process (Berger, 2009, 2016a, 2016b; Berger and Lahad, 2013; Berger and McLeod, 2006; Berger and Tiry, 2012). This integrative method was conceptualized and developed by the author of this article as part of his PhD (Berger, 2009) and in subsequent work, and has been further developed by graduates of the nature therapy training and colleagues. The method integrates elements from creative and postmodern approaches such as ecopsychology (Roszak, Gomes, Kanner, 1995; Kimder, 2002; Kuhn, 2001; Totton, 2003) and ecotherapy, play therapy, drama therapy, Gestalt and the narrative approach, along with elements from traditional rituals and shamanism. Nature therapy is like other postmodern approaches that have developed societal theories to explain the rise in psychological distress such as depression, anxiety and trauma (Cushman, 1990; Gergen, 1991; Jordan and Hinds, 2016; Kopytin and Rugh, 2016; McLeod, 1997; West, 2000).

Nature therapy views the process from a psycho-eco-social perspective. It is based on the assumption that people's estrangement from nature is linked to a broad spectrum of psychosocial disorders and manifestations such as loss of self-esteem and meaning, depression, anxiety, loneliness and alienation (Berger, 2009, 2016a; Berger and Lahad, 2013). Thus, its intervention approaches and methods are grounded in an environmental-social framework that aims to strengthen mind–body and interpersonal relationships, along with self-inclusion and normalization skills.

Nature therapy views the relationship with nature as the main axis in a process that involves the use of creative methods to explore the relationship with nature in a metaphorical and symbolic way. It is thus akin to the work of other arts therapists who have developed methods implemented in nature (Chown, 2014; Jordan and Hinds, 2016; Kellen-Taylor, 1998; Kopytin and Rugh, 2016; Whitaker, 2010). A distinction should be made, however, between these arts-based approaches and adventure therapy or wilderness therapy that implement a more task-oriented perspective (Berger, 2009; Garst, Scheider, and Baker, 2001; Kaly and Heesacker, 2003).

## Touching Nature

The core of nature therapy, consistent with the fundamental assumptions of ecopsychology and deep ecology, is the claim that by reconnecting with nature people can be infused with healing forces that can lead to recovery (Roszak, 2001; Totton, 2003). *Touching nature* is a basic term suggesting that direct contact with nature can deepen a person's connection with his/her own nature. It can connect clients to a feeling of inner power and authenticity by enabling them to develop and express important personal qualities. It can help people strengthen the mind–body connection, reach higher levels of consciousness, and widen their spiritual connections and guidance (Berger, 2016; Berger and Tiry, 2012). This process is especially important given the intensity and rapid pace of modern life that may push one away from his/her center (Berger, 2009).

## The Triangular Relationship: Therapist-Client-Nature

The *triangular therapist-client-nature relationship* is a central concept in nature therapy, which seeks to broaden the classical therapeutic relationship between therapist and client by introducing nature as a third factor. The concept of a triangular relationship prompts the therapist to relate to nature as an active partner in the process. It impacts the design of the therapeutic setting as well as the therapeutic process itself. In this way, it differs from the perception of the artistic product as a third medium in art therapy, because in nature therapy, nature plays an active role and has a dynamic and a life of its own.

This concept of a triangular relationship helps the therapist decide what role to take within the therapeutic relationship. Therapists can take a central, dominant role in the interaction with the client, such that nature is a backdrop and a supplier of materials, an approach that can also be regarded as therapy *in* nature. Alternatively, the therapist can take a secondary position as a mediator between the client and nature by being a witness to a process occurring directly with nature, an approach that can be regarded as therapy *with* nature. In general, when the client or group is involved in investigating processes connected with relationships and interpersonal communication such as questions of trust and control, the therapist can focus on interpersonal interactions and relate to nature as a setting or as a supplier of material.

On the other hand, when the client is concerned with broader issues of identity and meaning, the therapist can invite the client to interact directly with nature, its cyclicality and its perennial sequences, and remains a witness whose function is to intensify the individual's encounter with nature. Clearly, in many cases, as the dynamics and the issues being examined evolve, the role of the therapist can also change. Changes in position and attitude, which can occur several times during the same session, also enable the client to move along the axis between the interpersonal and the transpersonal, and thus extend the framework and perspectives on the issues at hand (Berger, 2008, 2016; Berger and Tiry, 2012).

## Choosing the Right Space

The concept of *choosing the right space* highlights the importance of the issue of space in nature therapy in general and the choice of the specific space and time to work in particular (Berger and Lahad, 2013). The assumption that underlies this concept is that different natural locations, habitats and environments have different impacts upon different processes and different people. A beach, a desert or a forest will have different meanings for different clients and in different phases of therapy. An open environment like the beach can be experienced as a space that symbolizes freedom and relaxation for one person while causing anxiety and stress for another. The choice of the season and the time of day can also have an influence, and therefore should be taken into consideration in the choice of the time of the session. At sunrise and sunset, the Israeli beach is a wonderful place to work in the summer because the temperature and setting are pleasant and the symbolism of the environment can connect a person with feeling and thoughts about the cycles of life, thus providing perspective, acceptance and hope (or sadness, loneliness and depression). However, the same beach at noon, with its high temperatures and direct sunlight, can be too intrusive for emotional work and therefore might be unsuitable for the therapeutic process. The concept of *choosing the right space* helps the therapist take these issues into consideration when selecting a suitable time and environment to work for the specific client and for the therapeutic goal.

## Back to Ritual

One of the unique features of nature therapy is its fundamental connection to the concept of ritual and its use in therapy. This applies both to collective ritualistic ideas, such as the connection between people and nature, mind-spirit-body within the community, as well as to the integration of performance and arts into the therapeutic process (Berger, 2014, 2015). It also relates to the concept of the sacred space, the idea of a rite of passage, and the three phases constitute rituals (Berger, 2014; Marcow-Speiser, 1998; Van Gennup, 1960). By acknowledging people's basic need for rituals, for instance by helping them deal with uncertainty, loss, sickness and transitions in life, and the role modern therapy plays in the creation of secular rituals (Berger, 2014, Jennings, 2012; Marcow-Speiser, 1998).

Nature therapy incorporates and utilizes elements in nature to create rituals. It generally does not use existing rituals borrowed from various cultures, but creates them according to the culture of the group and connections to the here and now. It utilizes the dynamics and culture of the group, links them to collective and universal phenomena present in nature (such as the changing of the seasons, the transitions between high and low tide, sunrise and sunset, birth and death) and uses natural elements (water, wind, fire, earth) to create rituals that are meaningful to the client and group. This approach allows clients to connect their personal to their cosmic stories by giving them a feeling of acceptance, normality and oneness. It can also help people assimilate painful stories, explore their significance in general, and when dealing with loss, trauma and stress in particular. The use of rituals can also help individuals to connect mind and body, establish a sense of connectedness and oneness within themselves, with others and with things larger than the self.

## Methods and Intervention Techniques

Nature Therapy implements several unique methods and intervention techniques that can be used with different clients and settings. Two of these methods are presented here.

### *Arts Within Nature*

Arts within nature refer to selected concepts and techniques from creative arts therapies such as drama therapy (Jennings, 1995, 1998, 2012; Jones 1996; Pendzik, 1994, 2006), dance-movement therapy (Chaiklin, & Wengrower, 2009), art therapy (Rubin, 1984; Whitaker, 2010) and music therapy as integrated into nature therapy. These concepts and techniques encourage the client to creatively explore the natural environment (Berger & Lahad, 2013, Berger & Tiry, 2012). This symbolic way of creative work in the environment is associated with arts-based therapy concepts such as fantastic and dramatic realities (Lahad, 2002; Jennings, 1995, 1998, 2012; Jones 1996; Pendzik, 1994, 2006), distancing (Landy, 1983, 1996) and the concept of ritual (Al-Krena, 1999) that is at the core of nature therapy practices (Berger, 2015). In this approach, metaphors and physical-sensory experiences with nature are believed to help the individual experience the world through additional perspectives, undergo recovery processes, and create a preferred, alternative reality.

Unlike drama therapy and other creative arts therapies, which are usually located indoors, creative arts activities within nature relate to nature as a provider of symbols and materials or as a backdrop for dramatic happenings. It also views nature as an active partner in designing the stage, the story, and the process relating to its intrinsic value and the influence of its independent dynamics. Special attention is given to environmental phenomena and processes that can be included in therapeutic references in order to support therapeutic changes. Therefore, the story is extracted from nature and the environment can merge with the recounting of a personal challenge and can be used as a healing metaphor or the basis for a spontaneous ritual. For example, burying a porcupine can help a child to cope with a father dying of cancer (Berger, 2007) and immersion in water can evoke processes of birth and renewal (Berger and McLeod, 2006).

By linking the personal with the universal and eternal, an individual can normalize difficult experiences, put them in a wider context, and explore new, beneficial meaning I them (Berger, 2009; Berger and McLeod, 2006). Linking individual and natural or universal coping mechanisms as well as personal or psychological time with cosmic or eternal time has great therapeutic value. It connects the individual to a sense of the eternal and affords a sense of belonging and context. This is significant in therapeutic work in general, but even more so in therapy that focuses on coping with uncertainty and loss (Berger, 2016a; Berger & Lahad, 2013).

### *Building a Home in Nature*

Building a home in nature draws on people's basic need to find or create a space where they feel safe and protected from uncertainty, unfamiliarity and from the dangers of the world outside. Building a camp or a home is a well-known spontaneous activity amongst children who tend to create such spaces in their homes, neighborhoods or at school. This activity takes on even greater importance in a natural setting that is not privately owned and contains many uncertain elements. Delineating a physical site not only provides safety in terms of the powers of nature and general uncertainty, but also defines the place of the individual with reference to others and to the environment.

Working with this model includes a preparatory stage of choosing the location, followed by building the home, and planning its ongoing maintenance. The basic assumption of the model is that this active, concrete yet symbolic process facilitates observation and work on basic intra-personal and inter-personal issues, as well as on the relationship between the individual and the environment.

The story of a child whose home in nature is located in the center of the group village will differ from the story of a child whose home is on the outskirts of town, or from someone who did not build a home, or a child whose home is invisible in terms of location and shape. The boundaries of the home will hint at the individual's inner boundaries and between this person and the environment. A home lacking boundaries will tell a different tale than a home with boundaries made of prickly bushes, or a home surrounded by a brick wall. This method of observation considers the building process, the image, shape, location and size of the home as metaphorical clues about the participant's real home. Aside from the diagnostic perspective inherent to the home in nature model (Berger, 2009), it allows the individual and the group to view the home and subsequently receive feedback from the others in the group. In this case, the facilitator's intervention can induce a certain type of construction that promotes specific socialization and communication processes.

Another significant aspect of the model stems from the fact that the constructed space is larger than the individual or the group. It allows entry, offers containment, and can even host other participants, unlike other therapeutic techniques in which small models of homes are built and observed from the outside. In this model, the individual can enter the constructed home, feel the containment it provides, and even look outside from within.

Building a home from natural materials teaches the participants that they can create the reality of their lives in the immediate present from pre-existing materials, thus instilling hope and a sense of control over life and its renewed creation. Ordinary visits to the home, session after session, allow the individual to encounter basic issues of control, in light of independent changes in nature that change and redesign the home. Ongoing maintenance and confrontation with the changes caused by nature develop flexibility and creativity, as well as acceptance of imperfection and loss of control. The physical-creative-concrete construction of a home circumvents cognitive defense mechanisms, enables the observation of additional facets of the participants' life stories and helps expand coping resources.

## From Theory to Practice—An Example

It was the concluding encounter of a group participating in a training program for nature therapy. The meeting took place on the beach, in the light of the full moon, between sunset and sunrise, from the afternoon hours until the following morning. After creative work in the sand, during which each participant created or sculpted a map or path marking the development she/he had experienced during the learning process, we sat around a campfire to share. David, a man in his late twenties, shared his complex feelings with the members of the group and thanked them for their support in his process of leaving his parents' home and moving to his new home with his partner.

The group members listened and told him how they viewed his developing maturity and the progress toward separation that he had made in the group. They also shared the sadness they were feeling at their own separation from the group and their fear of life after the end of training. When the sun came up a number of hours later, they would be asked to begin a personal journey, to imagine every step in the sand as a step in their lives, from the past to the present, and then to the future. Some of the participants walked away from the fire and some sat not far from it, looking at the sea. An hour later, after the sun had risen, they were asked to choose a place on the beach and to create a shape symbolizing their present status and feelings about leaving the training and their new independent way.

Using his whole body, David dug two funnel-shaped channels in the space between the sand and the water. The narrow part of the funnel pointed to the east, to the sunrise, and the wider part was oriented toward the sea. After the group members had walked through each of their peers' personal spaces and listened to the stories, David invited the group to gather around his creation.

> *First of all, when I moved and rolled around and played with the sand, I had no idea what I was doing and what I would create. Now, standing here with you and looking down on it from above, it seems to me that I have created a birth canal.*

I invited David to participate in a spontaneous ritual that we would invent for him then and there. David agreed, took off his shirt and sat down at the entry to his funnel, while the other group members created a tight-fitting human channel in both directions, toward the sunrise and toward the sea, continuing the channel dug into the sand. A few minutes later, shouting, pushing and crawling, David made his way from the narrow channel to the open beach. Seconds later, while still lying, panting, on the sand, a great wave washed over him from behind. "I'm alive," he shouted. "I have been reborn." The participants gathered around him and wrapped him in blankets. There were prayers mixed with tears and laughter, stories about birth and death; participants spontaneously broke into hymns, melodies and songs as the sea covered the drawings we had made in the sand, washed over them and cleared them away. The night took its leave and made way for a new day. . . .

The example illustrates how the theory and concepts of nature therapy can support the therapist's choices in practice. It began with the concept of *choosing the right space*, which helps the therapist make the connection between the aim and issue to be dealt with in the session and the choice of place and time of the workshop. In this case, the aim of the workshop was to help participants in processes of closeness and separation, help them leave each other and the training program as well as to connect to a feeling of continuity and faith. The beach on a night with a full moon is a setting that contains and tells a story of change and cycle: the movement between day and night, high tide and low tide related to the group's story and process. It is also an open place when one can see the horizon. The sand is a dynamic medium and can tell a parallel story about the dynamics of life and its uncertainties. It is easy to make figures in the sand, but at the same time it has its own dynamics. One can build a castle in the sand and a wave can easily wash it away. In this sense, the sand symbolizes the cyclic movement between creation and destruction, life and death. This example shows how that the concept of *choosing the right space* can be used in action, by looking for a natural location and time that can support the specific journey.

The concept of *back to ritual* and the creation of rituals were also presented. The example showed not only how the whole workshop was designed in a ritualistic way, but also how spontaneous and unique rituals were created. It illustrates the symbolic orientation of nature therapy and its emphasis on the physical connection with nature. The presence of group work and group support was highlighted, as well as the implementation of the concepts *of touching nature and the triangular relationship: therapist-client-nature.* The unique therapeutic influence of nature when the wave washed over David was illustrated, as well as the position of the therapist within the triangular relationship. There were times when the therapist took a background position by letting the participants work mainly with nature and the creation process. This contrasted with other times such as the sharing around the fire when nature became the background for the conversation the therapist was leading. The example highlighted the "dance" of the creative process and the spiritual facet fostered by nature therapy that takes place in the facilitation between the therapist-client-group and nature.

## The Professional Development of Nature Therapy and Other Environmental, Nature-Assisted Expressive Therapies

The professional development of nature therapy and other nature-assisted environmental expressive therapies involves the creation of a wide range of recognized therapeutic and training programs, and the development of a professional community. This process has taken place parallel to the field's academic development, which included in particular PhD study (Berger, 2002–2008), research, publications and the conferences.

A. *The development of wide-ranging therapeutic programs.* I conducted the first nature therapy work in Israel during my work as a drama therapist in schools for children with learning disabilities in the north in 2001–2003. I took children who did not feel comfortable doing therapy indoors into nature and conducted the sessions there (Berger and McLeod, 2006). My dissertation constituted the basis for the development of nature therapy as a theoretical framework for practice.

Based on the success of this pioneering work in schools, in 2004 I developed the first wide-ranging nature therapy program called *Encounter in Nature*, an official program under the auspices of the Department of Special Education of the Israel Ministry of Education. It included a 30-hour training program for arts therapists working in schools followed by weekly supervision. The therapists worked with a variety of children in different schools for children with learning disabilities including institutions that specialize in working with children with psychiatric problems, pervasive development disorder (PDD), behavioral problems and late development (Berger, 2006, 2008).

In 2006, following the second Lebanon War, I developed the Safe Place program together with Doron and Berger-Glick and under the supervision of Prof. Lahad to help traumatized children (Berger and Lahad, 2010, 2013). This program was also recognized by the Ministry of Education and later by the Ministry of Social Affairs that expanded the program to families. The success of these programs, the ensuing conference presentations and research publications opened the door to the recognition of other, smaller programs such as Eytan Yogev's Yealim program, which works with youth at risk under the Ministry of Education; Shulamit Horowitz's program dealing with kindergartens under the Ministry of Education; Maya Goldberg's program working with people with late development under the JDC foundation; and Ronit Shwartz's program that works with the elderly under auspices of the EMDA Association.

B. *The development of training programs.* As nature therapy is not yet formally recognized as an acknowledged form of therapy in Israel, the training programs are designed and delivered as nature therapy group counseling training. The diploma is awarded for in-group counseling and not therapy.

However, now that the program has been expanded to two full years, which includes a year-long practicum, professionals who enroll as therapists can complete their practicum in clinical settings and work with individuals and then be awarded a nature therapist diploma.

Nature therapy is a postmodern discipline that integrates several approaches. For this reason the training syllabus includes courses that provide participants with the psychodynamic, group-oriented, art-based, spiritual and ecopsychological background they need for the facilitation of groups in nature therapy. It does not include courses dealing with clinical issues such as trauma, psychiatry or the therapist-client relationship. The program has two main courses: a course about group processes with a psychodynamic and artistic orientation, and a nature therapy course. The courses take place in 8-hour days throughout the academic year. In addition, two long workshops are held: a 3-day workshop in the desert focusing on the ritualistic aspects of nature therapy, and a whole-night workshop on the beach focusing on the process of closeness and separation. These workshops also show the impact and meaning of untrammeled nature upon processes (as opposed to "man-made" nature near the campus). It also highlights issues concerning working for long periods (as opposed to 2-hour weekly sessions).

Participants are accepted for postgraduate training on the basis of a BA degree or higher and previous experience in educational or therapeutic work. The courses are held on campuses near natural areas that enabled the nature therapy classes to take place in nature. The coursework combines theory and experiential work with a focus on personal and group process as a basis for conceptualization and learning.

The first nature therapy training program in Israel took place in 2004 at Tel-Hai College, as a 1-year program lasting 180 hours. When it was realized that the learning process needed more time, in 2006 the program was extended to 224 hours by adding a second year for a practicum. The practicum includes facilitation of groups in different organizations and with different clients, followed by weekly 4-hour group supervision on campuses.

In 2009, a larger training program was developed and was inaugurated at Tel Aviv University. It consisted of a 2-year, 414-hour training course. It extended the two main existing courses in group process and nature therapy while adding courses in Gestalt and those dealing with issues such as creativity, spirituality and ethics in group counseling. This program was run until 2015, when I began teaching an MA drama therapy program and retired from running the nature therapy programs.

Since then, graduates of the program have opened a few smaller courses that focus on issues they developed. Tal Paner runs a course on the spiritual aspects of nature therapy, Eytan Yogev runs a course on the use of nature therapy with youth at risk, Ronit Schwartz runs a course on the use of nature therapy with the elderly through a mind-body perspective, and Maya Goldberg runs a course about the use of nature therapy with late developers. These courses do not award a diploma.

Another development that has taken place since 2012 is the integration of nature therapy courses within drama therapy and art therapy MA programs: the College of Arts and Social and Tel-Hai Academic College.

C. *Development of professional community.* Alongside the development of therapeutic and training programs and publications on nature therapy, several conferences were held. The first took place at Tel-Hai College in 2004 in collaboration with the Ministry of Education. After that, annual conferences took place until 2015, in the institutions that hosted the trainings programs—Tel-Hai College and Tel Aviv University. In addition, an experiential 2-day conference took place in nature in 2013. Each conference focused on a different issue with presenters from within the nature therapy community and outside it. The conferences created a place for the members of the community to meet and exchange and to kindle new collaborations. In addition, presentations, workshops and keynote lectures have been given in different conferences that have drawn attention to the contribution of nature therapy to different processes and with different clients.

It is worth noting that although nature therapy is a therapeutic approach with clinical applications, it is not yet officially recognized as a clinical profession in Israel. This is because full clinical training in nature therapy probably requires a 3-year MA program that would also be more expensive and demanding. Furthermore, the original program was designed as training in group counseling and not therapy. In addition, these courses are considered postgraduate programs and not MA programs that do not have academic accreditation. This creates a disparity between students' experience of training led by experienced therapists with deep personal and group processes and the development of their own skills, and the absence of recognition of the diploma they were awarded. This also affected career opportunities because it was unclear how nature therapy differed from group facilitation, group counseling or therapy. I believe that the development of full MA clinical training programs is essential for the further development of the field.

## Summary

This chapter presented nature therapy as a method within a growing professional field of environmental expressive therapies and outlined its theory, training programs and professional development. It presented the basic concepts of *touching nature, the triangular relationship: therapist-client-nature* and *choosing the right space* as well as the concept of *back to ritual*. The chapter highlighted the issues concerning the development and establishment of environmental expressive therapies as a specialized professional field such as the wide range of recognized therapeutic programs, training programs, conferences and the growing efforts of an expanding professional community of clinicians who practice environmental, nature-assisted expressive therapies.

## References


Al-Krena, A. W. (1999). An overview of rituals in western therapies and interventions: Argument of their use in cross-cultural therapy. *International Journal for the Advancement of Counseling, 21*(1), 3–17.

Berger, R. (2006). Using contact with nature, creativity and rituals as a therapeutic medium with children with learning difficulties: A case study. *Emotional & Behavioural Difficulties, 11*(2), 135–147.

Berger, R. (2008). Going on a journey: A case study of nature therapy with children with learning difficulties. *Emotional & Behavioural Difficulties, 13*(4), 315–326.

Berger, R. (2009). *Nature therapy—Developing a framework for practice.* A PhD School of Health and Social Sciences, University of Abertay, Dundee.

Berger, R. (2014). Nature therapy—integrating nature in therapy. In R. Berger (Ed), *Arts—The Heart of Therapy* (pp. 441–443). Kiryat Byalik: Ach Publication. (Hebrew).

Berger, R. (2015). Back to ritual. In V. Buchanan (Ed.), *Art therapy: Programs, uses and benefits* (pp. 71–84). New York: Nova Science.

Berger, R. (2016a). Nature therapy: A framework that incorporates nature, the arts and ritual in therapy. In A. Kopytin and M. Rugh (Eds.), *Green Studio: Nature and the arts in therapy* (pp. 27–46). New York: Nova Science.

Berger, R. (2016b). Renewed by nature: Nature therapy as a framework to help people deal with crises, trauma and loss. In M. Jordan and J. Hinds (Eds.), *Ecotherapy: Theory, research and practice* (pp. 177–186). Basingstoke: Palgrave Macmillan.

Berger, R., and Lahad, M. (2010). Safe place. Ways in which nature, play and creativity can help children cope with stress and crisis: Establishing the kindergarten as a safe haven where children can develop resiliency. *Early Child Development and Care, 180*(7), 889–900.

Berger, R., and Lahad, M. (2013). *The healing forest in post-crisis work with children.* London: Jessica Kingsley.

Berger, R., and McLeod, J. (2006). Incorporating nature into therapy: A framework for practice. *Journal of Systemic Therapies, 25*(2), 80–94.

Berger, R., and Tiry, M. (2012).The enchanting forest and the healing sand: Nature therapy for people coping with psychiatric difficulties. *Arts in Psychotherapy, 39*(5), 412–416.

Chaiklin, S., & Wengrower, H. (2009). *Dance/movement therapy. Life is dance.* New York: Routledge.

Chown, A. (2014). *Play therapy in the outdoors.* London: Jessica Kingsley.

Cushman, P. (1990). Why is the self empty: Towards a historically situated psychology. *American Psychologist, 45*, 599–611.

Exler-Levi, T. (2007). The ethical perception of animal assisted therapy. *Animal and Society, 33*, 28–37.

Garst, B., Scheider, I., and Baker, D. (2001). Outdoor adventure program participation impacts on adolescent self-perception. *Journal of Experiential Education, 24*(1), 41–50.

Gennup, A. van (1960). *The rites of passage*. Chicago: University of Chicago Press.
Gergen, K. J. (1991). *The shattered self: dilemmas of identity in modern life*. New York: Basic Books.
Jennings, S. (1995). *Theatre, ritual and transformation*. London: Routledge.
Jennings, S. (1998). *Introduction to drama therapy*. London: Jessica Kingsley.
Jennings, S. (2012). Theater of resilience: Ritual and attachment with marginalized groups—We are all born dramatized and ritualized. In C. Schrader (Ed.), *Ritual theatre—The power of dramatic ritual in personal development, groups and clinical practice* (pp. 200–216). London: Jessica Kingsley.
Jones, P. (1996). *Drama as therapy, theater as living*. London: Routledge.
Jordan, M., and Hinds, J. (2016). *Ecotherapy: Theory, research and practice*. Basingstoke: Palgrave Macmillan.
Kaly, P. W., and Hessacker, M. (2003). Effects of a ship-based adventure program on adolescent self-esteem and ego-identity development. *Journal of Experiential Education*, *26*(2), 97–105.
Kellen-Taylor, M. (1998). Imagination and the world: A call for ecological expressive therapies. *Arts in Psychotherapy*, *25*(5), 303–311.
Kinder, D. W. (2002). *Nature and psyche-radical environmentalism and the politics of subjectivity*. Albany: University of New York.
Kopytin, A., and Rugh, M. (Eds.). (2016). *Green Studio: Nature and the arts in therapy*. New York: Nova Science.
Kuhn, J. L. (2001). Toward an ecological humanistic psychology. *Journal of Humanistic Psychology*, 41, 9–24.
Lahad, M. (2002). *Creative supervision*. London: Jessica Kingsley Publishers.
Landy, R. (1983). The use of distancing in drama therapy. *The Arts in Psychotherapy*, *10*(3), 175–185.
Landy. R. (1996). *Essays in drama therapy*. London: Jessica Kingsley Publishers.
Marcow-Speiser, V. (1998). Ritual in expressive therapy. In J. Rubin (Ed.), *Therapeutic presence* (pp. 204–218). London: Jessica Kingsley.
McLeod, J. (1997). *Narrative and psychotherapy*. London: Sage.
McLeod, J. (2003). *An introduction to counselling*. Buckingham: Open University.
Pendzik, S. (1994). The theatre stage and the sacred space. *The Arts in Psychotherapy*, *21*, 25–29.
Pendzik, S. (2006). On dramatic reality and its therapeutic function in drama therapy. *The Arts in Psychotherapy*, *33*, 271–280.
Roszak, T. (2001). *The voice of the earth*. Grand Rapids: Phanes Press.
Roszak, T., Gomes, M. E., Kanner, A. D. (1995). *Ecopsychology: Restoring the mind, healing the earth*. San Francisco, CA: Sierra Club Books.
Rubin, A. J. (1984). *The art of art therapy*. New York: Brumel Mazel.
Totton, N. (2003). The ecological self: introducing eco-psychology. *Counseling and Psychotherapy Journal*, *14*, 14–17.
West, W. (2000). *Psychotherapy and spirituality: Crossing the line between therapy and religion*. London: Sage.
Whitaker, P. (2010). Groundswell—The nature and landscape of art therapy. In C. H. Moon (Ed.), *Materials and media in art therapy: Critical understandings of diverse artistic vocabularies* (pp. 32–39). New York: Routledge.

# PART II

# Nature-Assisted Expressive Therapies Practice

# 4

# DRAWING NATURE

*Jean Davis*

## Introduction

Perhaps you are a creative arts therapist or another type of therapist looking to expand the paradigm of your practice. Maybe you are undergoing psychotherapy or are considering entering treatment. Maybe you are not attracted to therapy and you are focused on personal development and societal improvement. In any case, this is a call to all of humanity—especially those who have considered engaging in the process of evolution and improvement, personally, collectively and environmentally.

The simple drawing activity I will describe may help to facilitate your efforts by seaming the divide between the internal and external constructs of humanity and nature. It is okay if you are ambivalent about this matter. Contending with resistance, or the unconscious action to protect ourselves from awareness of that which we fear will overwhelm us, is an important part of the process!

I invite you to ponder human potential when going outdoors to draw nature. My personal journey alongside clinical vignettes will hopefully provide you a springboard into your own journey and one filled with creative investigation and environmental stewardship.

## Why Draw From Nature?

In this section I am addressing the concept of gathering from and being inspired by nature. Honing in on the practice of drawing nature with art materials will follow this section. Children easily move in their bodies and make physical contact with the environment. As adults, we frequently become much less connected. When was the last time you saw an adult climb a tree? Open their mouths to catch falling snow? Jump in rain puddles while skipping down the street? Roll in the sand at the beach? There are a lot of emotions lodged in our senses and, as many ecopsychologists believe, and as I believe myself, we have cut ourselves off from the natural environment and hence, in crucial ways, our essential selves.

The practice of ecopsychology is based upon the belief that the separations between humanity and nature underlie the environmental dilemmas we face and, in a direct link, many of the emotional disorders from which we suffer. When we are attuned to our natural environment, we are more internally aligned—and our physical and emotional well-being is enhanced.

Largely defined, we could posit nature is everything, but in its most narrow of definition, it is that which comes directly from the earth and has not been transformed through human manipulation. The definition upon which I settle is between these extremes. I believe that human manipulation is natural, although not always in line with or in support of other natural elements and processes. The invention and use of plastic, for example, creates an opposition to plant-based products and does not move in rhythm with composing and recycling.

Due to its relatively low cost, ease of manufacture, versatility and imperviousness to water, plastic was created and used in abundance, but became and continues to increasingly become a problem in other ways including, very significantly, their resistance to natural processes of degradation and contribution to modern waste. As I see it, nature is making mistakes or participating in forces out of sync with nature and then making adjustments or corrections, over and over again. The goal is not perfection, but about an ongoing awareness and willingness to address oversights. I support Theodore Roszak's claim that natural occurrences are happening all the time, wherever we are in a skyscraper apartment in an urban environment or on the top of Mount Olympus (Roszak, Gomes and Kanner, 1995).

I've included a sampling of research that demonstrates the efficacy of experience in nature on our emotional, physical and psychological well-being. Nature is an inexpensive and effective tool for dampening the impact of illness and dulling the intrusion of everyday stress (Alter, 2013). Contact with green spaces is like going back home, and fills us with the same sense of safety and belonging. We crave nature in the same way that a child needs a mother, and derive the same feeling of comfort from it (Taylor, 2012). Miyazaki has taken more than 600 research subjects into the woods since 2004. He and his colleague Juyoung Lee, also of Chiba University, have found that leisurely forest walks, compared with urban walks, yield a 12.4 percent decrease in the stress hormone cortisol, a 7 percent decrease in sympathetic nerve activity, a 1.4 percent decrease in blood pressure and a 5.8 percent decrease in heart rate. On subjective tests, study participants also report better moods and lower anxiety (Williams, 2012).

Studies by the Kaplan and Kaplan (1989) show that after short walks in greenery, or even spells of looking at nature images in a lab, subjects' directed-attention capabilities at least partly recover—people perform significantly better on cognitive tests and report feeling happier. Other studies suggest that nature helps maintain and restore positive psychological mood states (Kaplan, 1995; Shibata and Suzuki, 2001, 2004; Van den Berg, Hartig, and Staats, 2007).

A recent pilot study by psychologists Paul and Ruth Ann Atchley of the University of Kansas and David Strayer of the University of Utah (Atchley, Atchley, and Strayer, 2012) found that after 3 days of hiking and camping in the wilderness, participants in an Outward Bound course improved their scores on tests of creativity by 50 percent. Even when we don't enjoy spending time in nature, like during lousy winter conditions, we benefit from it just the same. At least that's what Toronto's Berman found when research subjects took walks in an arboretum on a blustery winter day. The walkers didn't really enjoy themselves, but they still performed much better on tests measuring short-term memory and attention (Berman, Jonides, and Kaplan, 2008).

## Why Draw Nature?

Art therapy brings art making to the therapeutic relationship as a way to facilitate the work. A wide variety of populations, including those who experience illness, trauma, and other serious challenges, regularly benefit from the experience. But the central question in this exploration is: why draw nature as opposed to the many different ways in which individuals could utilize art materials?

My thesis is that drawing nature offers a clear guideline, structure and discipline. Starting with a blank sheet of paper can be very intimidating, so a directive of picking an object or scene to draw outdoors can give a much appreciated structure and focus to an art-making task. Not only does the structure lay the groundwork for control; it also allows the artist to make choices about what to incorporate and what to eliminate in order to continue the theme of control. The ability to have some form of control while drawing is particularly important when drawing nature because it helps the artist recognize the importance of being with the moment and moving with ongoing changes while still being able to freeze and capture a moment. While the reality of time and space are present, the choices one makes artistically can transcend time and place.

Drawing nature increases observational skills. What we observe outside ourselves is not in our control, but something we witness. As Eastern philosophies, spiritual belief systems and certain psychological approaches have taught us, we are often stuck in our heads and less in our experience. As Fritz Perls, father of Gestalt therapy, said repeatedly, "Lose your mind and come to your senses." When one draws from observation, one is forced to truly see, and experience the continual change that is nature—whether it's a rising sun, blowing grasses or shadows that grow longer and darker. Observing and moving with change allows us to practice getting more comfortable with change and, thereby, practicing being fully awake! Nature is alive and creates aliveness in all that it touches, just as the late afternoon sun casts an orange light on a cement sidewalk or the dry winter air creates clarity to the skyline of New York City. These observations not only keep us in touch with nature, but they force us to be *with* nature as we observe and then depict what we observe, over and over again.

So how is this practice actually performed? Drawing nature simply means taking art materials of choice outdoors and drawing from the natural environment. As ecopsychologist Michael Cohen has expressed, finding one's attraction to nature is imperative to the process of making a connection with nature (Cohen, 2007). There is a lot in nature that is unappealing and even downright scary—making it difficult to summon the desire to try to connect. Therefore, one's choice in materials also needs to come from a participant's attraction to the materials utilized so the experience is supported and palatable. As one glides the oil pastels across the page and feels the calm of the ocean's tide while incorporating it, a good feeling is likely to arise and the wish to continue surfaces as well.

I believe it is imperative that the drawing occurs outdoors—whether it be an urban, suburban or rural environment. Our senses are heightened outdoors because we feel the temperature and air quality, hear the noises around us more clearly, and often have more depth in the visual realm. When we think of our senses, we typically think about the five senses we were taught in school—sight, smell, hearing, taste, touch. Michael Cohen outlines 53 nature senses (Cohen, 2007)! The object or the scene that one chooses to draw is often metaphoric or indicative of something about the participant. Illustrating this point might be a man who continues to draw man-made structures such as buildings and cars, tending to the details and underplaying the wild grasses lurking underneath and moving dark clouds that envelop the landscape. The safety of these structures offers the man a form that is comfortable and static and is a way to stay away from the unknown. He is in the natural landscape, but finding safety within it. In addition to the content, the process by which one draws nature also begs exploration. Imagine a nervous teenager, drawn to colored pencils, forming scratchy, non-committed lines and quickly seeking an eraser to undo that which isn't intended. He is fidgety and unsure of direction at the pivotal time of adolescence. But he is staying with it—trying different ways, undoing them, trying again.

In my own practice of regularly drawing nature as well as working with clients to do so, I seek to extrapolate themes and set the stage for more formal research.

## Clinical and Personal Observations—Clinical Examples (Manny, Charles, Jamie)

Twelve-year-old Manny struggles with issues of attention and psychosis. Once living in a homeless shelter, he now resides in a small one-bedroom apartment with his mother and many siblings. His artwork is filled with grim images of monsters, decapitated figures, blood and satanic rituals. Manny reports feeling more at ease with the thought of death as opposed to when he was younger and frightened by such imaginings, but he remains preoccupied with the subject. Like others in the combined school and day treatment program he attends, Manny is supported by a team of clinical and educational professionals and he receives adjunctive individual and group art therapy services.

In approaching his desire to be more creative and the team's goal to help him decrease psychotic symptoms, individual art therapy is taken outdoors with the directive of drawing nature. Although Manny is always agreeable, his distractibility, both verbally and non-verbally, is often in contrast to his congeniality. However, once he is able to focus on a scene or object of his choice in the natural setting, his artwork changes. It's observably less graphic and much more spontaneous in gesture and seems to indicate more flexibility in his ability to improvise. His eyes are focused outward and his conversations shift from a focus on death and technology to the difficulty of artistically capturing leaves dancing in the wind and insects he notices and the reminder of what he's learned about them in science. These moments seem to allow Manny a more dimensional experience as opposed to the repetitive, less relatable conversations that often ensued.

Fifteen-year-old Charles attends the same facility as Manny and is diagnosed with autistic spectrum disorder and anxiety. He has a soft, pleasant demeanor and an interest in art therapy, but he struggles with making contact with others and expressing himself. Frequently, Charles attempts making fingerless gloves or oddly shaped clothing, but his products do not satisfy him. My sense was he was reaching too far inward and needed to be encouraged to try a more external and reality-based approach. He was receptive to the notion of drawing nature (just outside the facility), and within a few short sessions he created a drawing of a tree that was aesthetically pleasing as well as strong, bold, grounded and connected. Over several weeks of going outside to draw, Charles was mostly silent during the experiences. However, when he spoke, he expressed that he was enjoying the process and I noted a distinct calmness in his voice. He also verbalized satisfaction with his art products, unlike his more frequent frustrating art-making experiences indoors.

Jamie is a 55-year-old female referred to my private practice for myriad reasons. Over the course of her life, among the many difficulties with which she has struggled are depression, childhood sexual abuse and substance abuse. Jamie is well aware that she dissociates and, in consideration of this,

I ask her to perform homework assignments that entail drawing outdoors and then bringing these drawings back to session for review. This was an exercise she engaged with for several weeks, but one session in particular stands out. Prior to going outdoors to draw, Jamie was highly anxious and so she was encouraged to draw what she saw out of the window while still remaining in the comforts of her apartment. The pencil-drawn image in her journal depicts a view from her living-room window and the scene, directly outside, within a park. Her portrayal of the transition between inside and outside is stunted, avoided and bizarre. The line indicating the edge of the window morphs into the tree well beyond it. I bring this to her attention and she acknowledges that going outside, both literally and in this drawing, is extremely frightening. However, in simply honing in on this issue through the drawing, she sees that she keeps herself in, literally and emotionally. With my encouragement, Jamie soon goes outdoors to draw from nature. Her images are stunning and they remind her of parts of her childhood that are no longer cut off and, by her standards, aren't traumatic, but rather warm, joyous, colorful and celebratory.

These examples offer an indication of the short-term effects of drawing nature. Like any kind of workout, I believe that the repetition of this activity over time would result in a deeper, sustained favorable effect.

## Personal Examples of Drawing Nature in the Initial Phase

Over a period of about one year, I engaged in a personal investigation into drawing nature—going outdoors, daily drawing what my eye found. The amount of time spent on the activity was unprescribed, but I rarely spent more than 5 or 10 minutes on each occasion. My intention was to observe my emotional and physical experience before and after drawing. Images were drawn with a range of materials, depending on my preference in the moment—colored pencils, charcoal, a regular pencil and later, paints and/or oil pastels. I started in the fall and my initial drawings were of a turning leaf or tree. Autumn is my favorite season so it wasn't difficult to find a moment in my day to go out before heading out to work or taking a break in the late afternoon to partake in this activity. In addition to drawing nature, I documented in writing my physical and emotional feelings both before and after the exercise—and consistently, I felt better after drawing nature—in nature.

The words or phrases that I jotted down prior to drawing were clenched jaw, racing heart, restless, distracted, tired, stiff, tense, sad, nervous/anxious, awareness of feelings in stomach, awareness of temperature, and a variety of experiences focusing on my heart. Overriding these feelings were a kind of buzz, static movement and contained energy. I envisioned catching a fly and putting it into a jar and watching it move about, bouncing up against the walls repeatedly. The fly can see out and is able to envision the freedom, but isn't allowed access. The breathable air dissipates. This image creates anxiety, sadness, panic and depression in me. I realize that the ways in which I enclose myself fuel a false impression of control and, ultimately, keep me contained and, eventually, emotionally dead.

Many of the words/phrases that I wrote after drawing were more tuned in, more open, more comfortable in stomach and throat, calm, relaxed, rested, settled, more in my center, more focused, feeling good emotionally and physically in body and breath, quiet within, senses opening up more (awareness of sounds, smells, stimulated by colors, repeated sensations on skin), repeatedly more optimistic thoughts, more connected to art and myself, peaceful and slower inside. Clearly the experience afterward is more favorable and offers me a sense of self that is expansive, but not overwhelming. The pace is slowed, my senses are heightened, and there's nothing to do other than simply being. Even as I write this, I can feel the cool air blowing past my legs and the thoughts of entrapment floating away. I am aware less of words, more of sensation.

**Figure 4.1a** Nature drawn by Jean Davis during the initial phase of investigation

**Figure 4.1b** Nature drawn by Jean Davis during the initial phase of investigation

**Figure 4.2** Nature drawn by Jean Davis prior to period of resistance

## And Then the Outset of Winter—and Resistance

In the early phase of the project, the task of drawing nature and recording my physical and emotional responses, before and after the task, felt simple and proved worth the little investment. But then winter turned its icy face in my direction. This meant bundling myself before venturing outdoors. My before-and-after notes indicated a fair amount of preoccupation with my extremities feeling cold and/or numb. Although my drawings were somewhat interesting in their starkness, the lack of color and life and my physical discomfort left me feeling a bit empty. That's when the resistance to engage in this activity began. Every day I thought about going out to draw—and somehow I couldn't. The list of excuses I made for myself was comprehensive. It was too cold, there was too much to do, the daylight to draw had passed and was too dim, the materials weren't satisfying.

By the time spring busted out with the early signs of what would become crocuses, daffodils and cherry blossoms, my inner experience had not changed along with it. So I waited, and waited. Finally as the end of spring sunk in, I wrote some words about my feelings with regard to the task I had set forth to accomplish. My hopes were that this would shift something. I found this quote from my journal:

> *Ugh. I try to just think about going out to do this exercise and my unwillingness is unbelievably thick and catatonic. Thoughts are: It's too cold, takes too much planning and effort. Like a child, "I don't want to." I'd rather do anything else. Going outside is too vulnerable, too exposing, I put myself at risk of being in touch with something I don't want to know or already know too much. It's too close, too intimate. Is this resistance? Or is it hibernation? And today was nice. . . . I could almost push through resistance to the other side. But I didn't. I just thought about it. That's something. Maybe not. I love making art. I'm grateful for that.*

Like my own, personal resistance with regard to drawing nature, I've seen similarities manifest with people I work with, students and clients alike.

**Figure 4.3a** Nature drawn by Jean Davis during the final phase of investigation

**Figure 4.3b** Nature drawn by Jean Davis during the final phase of investigation

**Figure 4.3c** Nature drawn by Jean Davis during the final phase of investigation

## Clinical Examples of Resistance

In my private practice, I have clients that fluctuate between wanting to engage in art-making alongside nature and resisting it. This is also true at a major university, Pratt Institute, where I have been a faculty member for many years. I have seen graduate art therapy students become not only interested in, but some who have become enthralled in environmental art therapy. At the same time, classes that have brought about opportunities to go outside or work with found/natural objects have sometimes brought about negative feelings and statements that indicate opposition. "I'm too tired, it's too cold, picking things off the ground disgusts me."

A poignant example of resistance comes from an recent experience in my clinical work. In the same facility as Manny and Charles, I took four kids in their early adolescence—Jason, Carl, Dana and Simon—outside for our weekly art therapy group. "Try drawing what you ACTUALLY SEE," I said. I explained how this is a very difficult task because most people are accustomed to only drawing the way they *think* a tree looks as opposed to what it actually looks like when we are intently use our eyes. Carl said, "But I have an idea about what I can draw from Minecraft"! I was tempted to simply let him draw the details of this video game because he's not always interested in art-making. However, I adhered to the plan and said, "Just give it five minutes and then you can draw what you would like, okay?" He reluctantly agreed.

Dana sat right down at the picnic table and began drawing the apple tree with tremendous attention. Simon went and gathered some sticks, assuring me that he would follow my instructions as soon as he completed making a screen and video game within. Jason, dancing around on tiptoes with tremendous anxiety said, "I hate being outdoors, can we please go inside?" I tried everything to help Jason calm from an exploration of bees and their high unlikelihood of stinging him, red ants from biting him, sun from burning his skin, and the addressed concerns went on with very little change in his emotional state.

Finally, I suggested that I take a chair from inside, place it on the cement pathway, and allow him to have something synthetic to hold onto as he painstakingly took in the natural environment. "What time is it? Is it time to go in yet? I don't like it out here!" Jason said, but this time with less insistence. "We have 15 minutes," I said. "Now, I will hold your pad of paper while you draw whatever you see and would like to put on your paper. Pick anything!"

Jason began drawing the same tree that Dana was so patiently and persistently drawing. Carl had quickly drawn the same tree and was playing in the dirt with sticks alongside Simon who had, in fact, transitioned from stick collecting to drawing the sticks that he had tenderly organized into an interesting and strange structure on the ground. What happened next was a surprise and, at the same time, very much understandable. These teens, each struggling with varying psychiatric diagnoses including issues of attention, were now focused and engaged with the environment and their drawing. Then, in what felt like a miracle, Jason said, “How much more time do we have?” When I told him we had about five more minutes, he protested, “But I like it here! I don’t want art therapy to be over!”

## Meaning and Power of Resistance

Research reveals that children spend less and less time outdoors because our environment isn’t safe enough: nature-based recreation has declined 35 percent in the United States in the past four decades (Cordell, 2008). We build barricades both literally and emotionally to ward off intruders considered dangerous individually, within our local society and, increasingly, globally. This effort creates what Jordan would describe as a split between self and nature as a protection against vulnerability. He posits that taking the risk to love and become attached means that which is loved can be lost, harmed or can even betray us (Jordan, 2009).

The clinical definition of resistance is the automatic and unconscious retreat from emotional pain. This act protects us, but also leads to internal fragmentation. But if it does not rigidify and is directly acknowledged and addressed, it is as healing as openness. Often the feelings in the resistance itself are the heart of the work (Porter, 1995).

When I finally acknowledged this resistance as my own and not something imposed on me (like the weather), something shifted. I recognized my need for control and fear of the unknown. There was nothing else to do but push myself—with love and a continual reminder of the appeal for the task. I brought my drawing materials to the beach, a setting that brings me much respite and enjoyment. I watched the dark waves lighten into swampy green-lit sleeves as they stretched onto the dry, yet hardened sand. I painted and scratched with watercolor and oil sticks, sometimes overdoing it to the point of shaving slivers of paper off its surface. But I took pleasure in the process and was relatively satisfied with the result, and thereby encouraged to repeat the experience. The next afternoon, I watched the sun go down over the bay and the colors changes drastically and continuously over a period of only about 45 minutes. It was difficult to keep up, but the challenge kept me present and alive. I came back to myself and my environment—if only for these moments.

## Nearing the End and Beginning a New Chapter

It is my belief that drawing nature is a highly active form of meditation that offers significant health-improving and life-affirming opportunities. At the same time, some form of resistance needs to be identified and acknowledged, embraced and then addressed.

Anything worthwhile requires earnest effort, whether it be focused on personal growth or our collective work to bring more authenticity, empathy and enlightenment to this planet, to this mystery. As we slow down from our the frenzy of our culture, we may well recognize the larger but more hidden messages indicating what's happening to us individually and as a species on intellectual, emotional, psychological, physiological and spiritual dimensions. I believe that facing these metaphysical matters directly will enable us to encounter a new realm of possibilities.

## Acknowledgments

The author would like to recognize the editorial contributions of Danny Rosenthal.

## References

Alter, A. (2013, March 29). How nature resets our minds and bodies. *Atlantic*. Retrieved from www.theatlantic.com/health/archive/2013/03/how-nature-resets-our-minds-and-bodies/274455/

Atchley, P., Atchley, A., and Strayer, D. (2012). Creativity in the wild: Improving creative reasoning through immersion in natural settings. *PLoS ONE*. http://journals.plos.org/plosone/article?id=10.1371/journal.pone.0051474

Berg, van den A. E., Hartig, T., and Staats, H. (2007). Preference for nature in urbanized societies: Stress, restoration, and the pursuit of sustainability. *Journal of Social Issues*, *63*(1), 79–96.

Berman, M., Jonides, J., and Kaplan, S. (2008, December). The cognitive benefits of interacting with nature. *Psychological Science*, *19*(12), 1207–1212.

Cohen, M. (2007). *Reconnecting with nature: Finding wellness through restoring your bond with the earth* (3rd ed.). Lakeville, MN: Ecopress.

Cordell, K. (2008). The latest trends in nature based outdoor recreation: Proceedings of the national academy of sciences. *Forest History Today*. Retrieved from www.foresthistory.org/publications/FHT/FHTSpring2008/Cordell.pdf

Jordan, M. (2009). Nature and self-ambivalent attachment? *Ecopsychology*, *1*(1), 26–31.

Kaplan, R., and Kaplan, S. (1989). *The experience of nature: A psychological perspective*. Cambridge: Cambridge University Press.

Kaplan, S. (1995). The restorative benefits of nature: Toward an integrative framework. *Journal of Environmental Psychology*, *15*(3), 169–182.

Porter, K. (1995). Resistance. In H. Bernard and R. Mackenzie (Eds.), *Basics of group psychotherapy* (pp. 103–107). New York: Guilford Press.

Roszak, T., Gomes, M. E., and Kanner, A. D. (1995). *Ecopsychology: Restoring the earth, healing the mind*. San Francisco: Sierra Club Books.

Shibata, S., and Suzuki, N. (2001). Effects of indoor foliage plans on subjects' recovery from mental fatigue. *North American Journal of Psychology*, *3*(3), 385–396.

Shibata, S., and Suzuki, N. (2004). Effects of an indoor plan on creative task performance and mood. *Scandinavian Journal of Psychology*, *45*(5), 373–381.

Taylor, S. (2012, April 28). The power of nature: Ecotherapy and awakening. *Psychology Today.* Retrieved from www.psychologytoday.com/blog/out-the-darkness/201204/the-power-nature-ecotherapy-and-awakening

Williams, F. (2012, November 28). Take two hours of pine forest and call me in the morning. *Outside.* Retrieved from www.outsideonline.com/1870381/take-two-hours-pine-forest-and-call-me-morning

# 5

# INNER AND OUTER LANDSCAPES

## Bringing Environment Into the Therapeutic Relationship Through Expressive Writing

*Mary Reynolds Thompson and Kate Thompson*

### Introduction

In this chapter we explore three widening circles of self and existence, from ecological and existential perspectives, and demonstrate specific writing techniques for each part of the model. We move from the smaller self, isolated and disconnected from the larger world, to a more expansive sense of self, embedded in a web of connections of both the human and non-human variety, and finally to a place where meaning and values are constructed.

The authors, one an eco-coach and facilitator of poetry therapy, the other an existential and journal therapist, show how writing about landscapes—real, imagined, and literary—helps break down barriers between interior and exterior worlds that are then seen to shape and impact one another in a reciprocal relationship.

Mary: As a facilitator of poetry therapy I work with groups and individuals exploring nature's metaphors and archetypes as aspects of the wilder self. My clients are looking to find ways out of lives that often feel too domesticated or tame. They long to feel more alive.

Kate: As an existential therapist, I see my clients as embodied beings. I am curious about the places they inhabit and have inhabited, their sense of place, their sense of their being in the world. I see in many of them a desire to connect with and experience nature—sometimes a part of our work is how to restore this in their lives and through that a restoration of well-being for the self.

Together we have been leading workshops on the relationship between outer and inner landscapes for over five years at the time of writing. We've held these workshops in different settings and under different titles: *A Sense of Place; Inner and Outer Environments*; and *Literature, Landscape and Imagination*. The workshops explore a variety of perspectives, but they share a common focus: that we are shaped by the places we inhabit, literally, psychologically, and spiritually, just as we shape the places around us. As Robert Macfarlane puts it:

> *I have long been fascinated by how people understand themselves using landscape, by the topographies of the self we carry within us and by the maps we make with which to navigate these interior terrains. . . . For some time now it has seemed to me that the two questions we should ask of any strong landscape are these: firstly, what do I know when I'm in this place that I can know nowhere else? And then, vainly, what does this place know of me that I cannot know of myself?*
>
> (Macfarlane, 2012, pp. 26–27)

Despite our different training, backgrounds, and professional activity, in developing and facilitating these workshops we discovered much in common. The similarities in our approaches became ever clearer as we developed a series of writing prompts that allow our clients to examine a deeper and evolving sense of self through their relationship to environment. The ecological self, introduced by the founder of the deep ecology movement, Arne Naess (1995), comprising those beings, both human and non-human, with which a person identifies (feels for, or sees themselves in), is analogous to the existential therapist's view of the self as ever changing and being formed by the relationships to people, place, and experience in time. Both the existential therapist and the eco-coach notice that clients experience a sense of enlargement of being as a result of exploring an ever widening web of relationships.

Merleau-Ponty's work speaks to both approaches, particularly in his phenomenological emphasis on describing the lived experience in the world, being "connatural" with the world. "The world is not what I think but what I live through" (Evernden, 1993, p. 43). For Merleau-Ponty our connection to and interrelatedness with the world is essential and primary (van Deurzen-Smith, 1997) to our being human. He also sees language, which here we interpret as written and read, rather than spoken, as the way in which we make sense of and create meaning out of these experiences.

The writing prompts we offer elicit memories of direct experiences that are often at odds with what clients have been told, or think, is acceptable or true. This disparity between unexamined beliefs and what is actually encountered, emerges most vividly in the feedback writes (Thompson, 2011) that are a central part of this process. For the existential therapist, this provides an opportunity to become both the writer and the reader of her own experience, the author of her own story. For the ecotherapist, it is also fertile ground for exploring how our direct experiences of the real world inform the real self (Snyder, 1990).

Finally, the power of writing is core to both approaches, and can be experienced in almost any setting. Eco-therapy, counseling in nature, and wilderness therapy (Jordan, 2015) are developing practices in which the therapeutic encounter takes place outside, however in this chapter we are particularly looking at how, through writing, we bring environment into the therapeutic relationship, as distinct from taking the therapeutic relationship out into the environment. This is not to say that all our work takes place within the built environment, but we are curious about how the recollection of and imaginative inhabiting of landscapes offers a therapeutic opportunity in our work with others.

## An Ecological Approach

"Ecopsychology proceeds from the assumption that at its deepest level the psyche remains sympathetically bonded to the Earth that mothered us into existence" (Roszak, 1995, p. 5). Ecopsychology (Roszak, 1992) calls for us to heal the human-nature split believed to be the root cause of our environmental crisis and an array of social and psychological ills. If humans view themselves as integral to the earth, it asserts, then ecological destruction will be seen as self-destruction. Moreover, nature is the matrix through which we experience our most natural and alive selves. Bill Plotkin similarly states in *Wild Mind* that the core insight of the developing field of ecopsychology is that we are separated from the greater earth community, especially its untamed qualities and powers (Plotkin, 2013, p. 7). Eco-alienation therefore can be seen as an estrangement from our own nature as much as an estrangement from the natural world (Watts, 1958).

The ecological approach, with its emphasis on interrelatedness, is both aligned with indigenous wisdom and supported by new science. The age of scientific atomism, when each thing was perceived as a thing unto itself, disconnected and disparate, is giving way to an understanding of the universe as an interconnected and complex web of relationships. In this new vision, humans are part of "a single, if multiform, energy event" (Berry, 1988, p. 24). This radical shift in perspective—that we are related to everything that has ever existed (Plotkin, 2013)—offers us new insights into what it means to be wholly human. We broaden and deepen our sense of self when we feel for, and see ourselves in, the world about us (Naess, 1995). As we move through the ecological model, exploring a widening and deepening sense of self through three circles of being (the egoic, the ecological, and the cosmological) we examine how our experience of who we are and how we make meaning in the world changes as we learn how to dismantle the notion that what is "in here" is somehow separate from what is "out there."

## An Existential Approach

Existential therapy is concerned with how people live and what it means to them to be alive and to be fully human. Existential therapists seek to understand their client's worldview, in order to make sense of the way in which the client navigates existence and identify areas that cause distress, dissatisfaction or dis-ease. An existential approach assumes that the self is continually changing, that it is not fixed but rather evolves in response to the circumstances of life. The task of the existential therapist is to help clients face up to their predicaments in life, understand how they live, and help them to explore how they might enlarge their lives. In order to understand how someone navigates the world and creates their existence it is helpful to have a broad map or scheme of human relating in the world; having a model of the self or an approach to individual experience can provide a framework for understanding and guide the therapeutic journey.

Ludwig Binswanger (1888–1966) was the first physician to combine psychotherapy and existential/phenomenological theory in a clinical model. He believed that thinking about a patient as a being-in-the world, as situated in and part of the world, gave a structure for human existence that was more useful, when working with patients, than simply considering their behavior. He identified several worlds (*Welts*) in which people exist:

*Eigenwelt*, the subjective experience of the world and the relationship with self;
*Umwelt*, the relationship between self and environment;
*Mitwelt*, the interactions between people, relationships with others, and how that affects our being in the world.

He also implied the existence of the *Uberwelt*, the spiritual dimension, further developed by Van Deurzen (1951–) in her model of four dimensions of the self:

*Psychological dimension*, or being with the self;
*Physical dimension*, or being with the world;
*Social dimension*, or being with others;
*Spiritual dimension*, or the dimension of meaning, values and spirituality.

> *Each of these levels of operating is as important as any of the others. There are connections and overlaps between them and it is merely a matter of clarification to try and distinguish these different forms of world relating in the first place. Each level has its own paradox and tension, its particular human objectives and aspirations, its preferred mode of operating and medium, its evils and ideals.*
>
> (van Deurzen-Smith, 1997, p. 100)

**Table 5.1** Aligning the models

| Reynolds Thompson | Van Deurzen Dimensions of the Self | Binswanger Worlds |
|---|---|---|
| The Egoic Self: The smaller me/more isolated/more self-referential, tribal. | Psychological dimension: Being with self, the creation of selfhood and a personal world. Thinking. | Eigenwelt: Private world of the psyche. |
| The Ecological Self: The Self in relationship to the rest of the earth community and part of an integral web of life. | Social/physical dimension: Being with others/being with nature, interacting with the world using our senses. Feeling. | Mitwelt/Umwelt: Physical world/public world. |
| The Cosmological Self: The Self embedded within a 13.8-billion-year evolutionary story that is both scientifically understood, but also a cosmology (a worldview of interconnection). | Spiritual dimension: Values and meaning, a world of ideas, beliefs and intuition, a sense of purpose. | Uberwelt: Ideal or spiritual world. |

## Expressive Writing

The medium that we here explore in the therapeutic encounter is expressive writing. Expressive writing, particularly prose writing, is an often overlooked part of the family of expressive arts therapies. The ability to give voice to, and make meaning out of, our connection to the world about us through personal writing, becomes the key to bearing witness to a larger sense of self, bringing greater insight and understanding to the way that self behaves.

To write about the outside world is to return us to the inner world. Place is both literal and psychological and metaphorical. As Hillman asserts, the "bad" place we are in may refer as much to the bleakness of our physical surroundings as it does to the depression in which we sink (Hillman, 1995). We are always embedded in place, we exist in a given place and time, we are thrown into this world and its physical reality, and then it is up to us to make sense of it. When we write about place we come into contact with different aspects of our experience and deepen the relationship with the self and psyche. Magritte says of his painting *La Condition Humaine*, where a painting is placed in front of the view it depicts:

> *This is how we see the world, . . . We see it as being outside ourselves even though it is only a representation of what we experience on the inside.*
> (Schama, 1995, p. 12)

In writing our stories of place and our relationship to it, we begin to make tangible the reality that self does not end at the edges of our own skin; as Hillman argues it has been defined (or confined) by psychology (Hillman, 1995). The self is in constant relationship to a web of connections, seen and unseen. Thus, we don't just imprint the world through what we do; the world also imprints us. Whenever morale is low, interests tend to narrow; one way to break down self-preoccupation is by stimulating thoughts and imagination (Hynes and Hynes-Berry, 1994). Through writing about our lives, we seed and begin to cultivate a deepening relationship with the world. In essence, we are moving from the narcissistic self described by Woodman and Dickson (1996) as alienated from the earth and our own feelings, to one where we are firmly anchored in both our outer and inner landscapes.

As we move through the three circles, the writing that emerges often becomes a more embodied, or somatic, presence with roots and tendrils that dig deep into the earth. When we write from a place of connection, we draw to us a web of natural symbols, sounds and onomatopoeia, the symbols and the rhythms of the other/more-than-human world. Gary Snyder beautifully expresses this sense of language as animate: "Language is not a carving, it's a curl of breath, a breeze in the *pines*" (Snyder, 1990, p. 74).

Writing offers an additional key to healing, both for the individual in therapy and in healing the rift between our inner and outer worlds. Through the act of writing, eco-therapy clients may be seen to be co-creators with the universal spirit of creativity that flows through all of life, just as existential therapists are co-creators with their clients in exploring a life. Telling or writing stories about the places we love, the forest we played in as a child, stories of animals and rocks and backyards, also reminds us that we are not trapped in a Hobbesian view of life that is short, brutish, and hard, but exist as part of a vibrant, interconnected world: "Where beauty is perceived, an integration of self takes place" (Hynes and Hynes-Berry, 1994, p. 27).

Expressive writing allows people to tell their stories in their own words, to see themselves afresh through the words on the page. In this way people can begin to escape from the dominant story of their lives, perhaps one that is "told to" rather than "told by." Writing in therapy, rather than simply engaging in talking therapy, is a way of re-authoring experience: "It can be argued that writing provides one mechanism through which persons can be more active in determining the arrangement of information and experience and in producing different accounts of events and *experience*" (White and Epston, 1990, p. 37).

The neurologist Oliver Sacks reminds us that memory is not a static entity but a dynamic process in which material is "transformed, disassembled and re-categorised with every act of recollection" (Sacks, 2012, p. 154). Author and plant ecologist Robin Wall Kimmerer quotes Gary Nabhan as saying, "we can't meaningfully proceed with healing, with restoration, without 're-story-ation.' In other words, our relationship with land cannot heal until we hear its stories. But who will tell them?" (Kimmerer, 2013, p. 9).

We use expressive writing as a re-story-action, or re-storying (White and Epston, 1990), process. As Sartre reminds us, we cannot change the facticity of the past, we can only change how we think about and understand it from the position of the present (Sartre, 1992). Writing autobiography in place allows us the opportunity to re-story our present by learning from the biographical memories embedded in the landscapes of the past.

Part of our work as therapists and healers, therefore, is to get curious about people and the landscapes and places (organic and inorganic) they inhabit. Questions we ask include:

- Where do people spend most of their time: in an office, out of doors, with animals, with technology?
- Where do people feel most alive? Most connected?
- Where do they experience a sense of the sacred (meaning)?
- Are there landscapes and places that hold a deep resonance?
- Are some of the landscapes inhabited not with bodily presence but through the imagination, from reading books?
- Can we actually discover more of our own being in literary landscapes?

So perhaps, after all, what is really important is to pose our fundamental question not as:

*Who am I?*

But rather:

*Where am I?*

## Landscapes in Literature

Landscapes in literature provide another opportunity to bring about a therapeutic interaction (Hynes and Hynes-Berry, 1994). In our work, the outer environment is the primary text, explored for its richness of images, metaphors, and archetypes. However, literary landscapes also provide a foundation for examining the relationship of self and world. Literature here is used to stimulate memory and inspire a feeling response toward landscape. In bibliotherapy, sessions in which literature is used to bring about a therapeutic interaction (Hynes and Hynes-Berry, 1994), the facilitator usually chooses the text. But we invite people into their own choices, helping them to remember books with landscapes that spoke to them at different periods in their lives. In exploring their choices, participants are often surprised into fresh insights about their current situations. Beginning with writing about literary landscapes, rather than personal ones, has the advantage of allowing clients to enter a realm where they, through their creativity and imagination, have autonomy. Literary landscapes have a similar ability to mirror aspects of the self as does the natural world.

Kate: The Lake District landscape in Arthur Ransome's *Swallows and Amazons* books deeply affected me as a young reader. And, before I could read, in the Beatrix Potter books that were read to me. It gave me a richer sense of the possibilities within landscapes which were familiar but overseen by adults. This landscape recurred in my later reading, in poets from Wordsworth to Norman Nicholson. My deep connection with the Lake District, first through books and then as I experienced it for myself was a formative experience in developing my own independence of mind and spirit and my enduring connection to the natural wild.

Mary: Looking back, *The Secret Garden* by Frances Hodgson Burnett, a story of children bringing a garden back to life and in the process healing both physically and psychologically, was my first insight into the relationship between healing the earth and healing the self. Later, the wild moors of Emily Brontë's *Wuthering Heights* mirrored my own tumultuous and sometimes brooding adolescent self. My love affair with wild landscapes continues until this day. I feel freer, more alive, and more myself in wide open spaces.

## Creating a Safe Place

Writing can be an overwhelming experience. As writing therapists, we know how important it is to guide and support our clients carefully through the processes we use.

In her work on Journal Therapy, Kathleen Adams says: "Under several sets of circumstances, freewriting is simply *not* the best choice" (Adams, 2013, p. 44). She goes on to mention writers with a history of trauma, left-brain writers, writers with cognitive impairments. She urges the introduction of filters of structure, pacing, and containment to create a safe writing practice. Her model, the Journal Ladder (Adams, 1998), is a set of writing exercises which progress from the most structured on the lower rungs of the ladder to freewriting at the top, which when followed creates a safe, structured, and containing writing environment. These are the principles which inform the exercises we present in this chapter.

## Two Central Techniques

### *The Warm-Up Write*

This tends to be a short and fairly contained write, similar to a gymnast stretching, that allows clients to warm-up their writing selves. It may also be viewed as a threshold exercise that marks entry into the therapeutic space and that helps build a safe container for the work that follows.

### *The Feedback Write*

The therapeutic potential of expressive writing is deepened when we add a feedback write after each initial piece of writing. This allows the writer to move from the descriptive to the reflective mood "when he causes the commitment of immediate spontaneity to advance, for himself and others to the reflective" (Sartre, 1988, p. 77). The feedback write is a way of recognizing, deepening, and integrating the insights of the initial write. It takes the form of a reflection in writing, just a few observations or thoughts on the process or content. This simple device allows people to come into contact with themselves in a new way—first by reading and witnessing their own words, then by writing about the experience (Thompson, 2011).

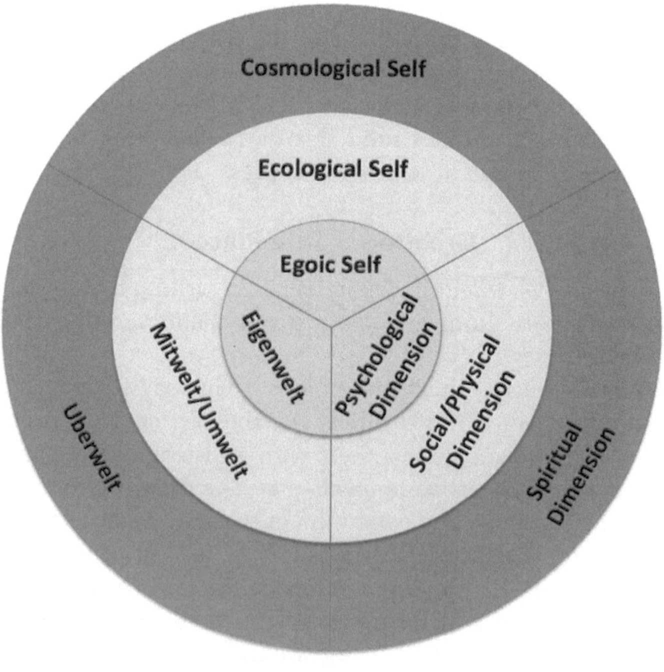


**Figure 5.1** Concentric circles of the self and dimensions of existence

In the next section we present the three circles of the self and dimensions of existence, illustrating each with writing exercises appropriate to the stage. The ability to negotiate the different circles is what makes a fully realized, healthy human being.

## Circle One: Egoic Self/Eigenwelt/Being With the Self/Private World of Psyche

In this stage of the model, the client often needs to speak of a private world of grief, sense of frustration or sadness, confusion, or despair. Here we use expressive writing techniques that are the equivalent of opening a window in a stuffy room: they let in some air, but they don't overwhelm the client with sensory overloads. What provides this safety is structure, pacing, and containment (Adams, 1993), matching the exercise to the stage of the client and the work they are doing.

### *The Ecological Approach*

It is important to recognize that the client's state of mind may be influenced by factors sometimes overlooked in other approaches. A client's feelings of emptiness and alienation, for example, might be compounded by a dominant worldview that perceives humans as separate from the natural world. The devastating, and devastated, state of the environment could also add to their despair. Theodore Roszak writes: "As nature around us unfolds to reveal level upon level of structural complexity, we are coming to see that we inhabit a densely connected ecological universe, where nothing is 'nothing but' a simple, disconnected, or isolated thing" (Roszak, 1995, p. 8). Thus, the loss experienced by clients may also include a loss of connection to nature in general, or to a special place. They may feel a sense of underlying anxiety because the places in which they are "most at home" are under threat—or have already been paved over, deforested, or irrevocably altered. Solastalgia is a neologism that describes the pain or sickness a person feels when the home they inhabit is under assault. It is the lived experience of dislocation, while still in place (Albrecht, 2005). Experiencing solastalgia further undermines a person's sense of security and identity.

In 1926, just four years before his death, D. H. Lawrence visited his childhood home in Nottinghamshire where he played as a boy. After describing all the ways in which the countryside had been built over and despoiled, he writes, "It's all a concrete arrangement now, like a sewer" (McDonald, 1961, p. 822). This sense of loss is echoed in the experience of a client who wrote of his grief when, upon returning to his childhood home, he discovered that the new owners had cut down the large tree that had once spread its wide branches over a grand swath of the garden. The tree had sheltered him as a young boy, both physically and psychologically, and now he grieved its passing. Such losses, while painful, can help us to move beyond our egoic states and open to feelings of attachment to place.

### *The Existential Approach*

The innermost circle is Binswanger's *Eigenwelt* (private world), and Emmy van Deurzen's psychological dimension of existence. This is the private world of intimate relationships where the primary relationship is with the self. This is the relationship that often needs to be developed, to find a more intimate way of relating, first with the self, then with others. When this is a healthy part of the self, when people are able to be stable in the Eigenwelt, it gives them a secure base from which to navigate the other areas of the self and world. Where people suffer from mental dis-ease, psychological disturbance, or are given diagnoses such as "borderline personality," they may be immured in the personal dimension because the physical or social dimensions feel unsafe and too hard to navigate. Finding balance between the psychological self and the other dimensions of existence, between withdrawal and engagement in the world is one of the fundamental challenges of being human.

### *Circle One Exercises*

#### *Warm Up*

Write for 3–5 minutes on the following questions in any way you choose:

*Who am I?*
*Where am I?*
*What do I want?*

Feedback write: *read through what you've written and write a couple of sentences, beginning: "Reading this I notice . . ."*

#### *My Journey Here*

This is a 7-minute writing sprint. "Here" corresponds to the time and space that you find yourself reading these words. Allow your words to flow freely and keep your pen moving or the keys tapping.

Begin with: "My journey here . . ."

Feedback write: *read through what you've written and write a couple of sentences, beginning: "Reading this I understand . . ."*

#### *Steppingstones Part One*

Steppingstones originated with Ira Progoff (Progoff, 1975). It is a technique that allows people to connect the threads of their lives in thematic ways. It is presented here in three parts, providing a thread through the three circles of self. Landscape Steppingstones (Thompson, 2011) looks at the internal psychogeography of an individual, seeking the places imbued with emotional significance or personal landmarks in the landscapes of our lives. Steppingstones is therefore an act of biogeography (Macfarlane, 2012).

1. Think back over the course of your life. Allow your attention to rest on the different places that you have known and begin to list them (with simply a word or a phrase) as they come to you. Don't pause to ask "Why?" or "What?"
2. Stop when you have about eight.
3. Number them in chronological order.
4. Read the list aloud in chronological order. Progoff says that the point of reading aloud is to receive your own words back to you in a different form, not have them heard by an audience.

Feedback write: "*When I read this I notice . . .*"

### *A Framed Literary Landscape*

Sometimes landscapes in books can become as real and affective as actual inhabited landscapes. "Books, like landscapes, leave their marks in us" (Macfarlane, 2015, p. 12). As Sartre and Macfarlane remind us, we are all readers before we are writers (Macfarlane, 2015; Sartre, 1988).

In this exercise structure, pacing and containment are provided by the idea of a framed picture, capturing a moment in time, as a photographer frames a shot through the camera lens or an artist places a creation in a frame. The use of a literary rather than an actual landscape allows people to be less immersed in the lived experience of their own lives with all its potential for anxiety.

1. Think of a book that made an impression on you at some time in your life, where the landscape has entered your imagination and memory because it was almost a character in its own right.

Allow the landscape to come into focus as though you are looking through a camera, or at a picture in a frame.

2. Describe what you see within that frame, as though you were looking at a picture hanging on your wall.
3. Using the present tense, notice the colors, imagine the sounds, smells, see the relationships between the objects that make up the landscape.

Feedback write: "*When I read this I feel . . .*"

> *The Arable's farm—"everywhere you look is life." The lilacs are blooming scenting in the air with a fragrance that has never been duplicated in a laboratory. The apple blossoms are promising apples in a few short months. There are sheep bleating—shearing time is on the horizon and pigs, geese and all manner of insects are commenting and consulting on affairs in the barn. It is a myth that the country is a quiet place. Machines run a distant second regardless of their horsepower claims. It is the smell of life in the fullness of the cycle—calves, foals, manure, pig slop, fresh cut hay and all manner of things that are pushing, shooting and insisting on bursting forth. Punctuated by a riot of color—every shade of green, and as the tomatoes ripen along with corn, peppers, squash and berries there is a rainbow of reds, oranges, yellows, blues and purples. Tucked into the corner of the barn—the largest building on the farm is a gossamer web. The product of the resident spider, Charlotte. She spins words into her web—"Some Pig," referring to Wilbur, the runt of the litter who was saved and nurtured by Fern, the Arable's daughter.* Charlotte's Web *is part cheer, part commentary and an ode to a deep abiding friendship. Everywhere you look is testimony to interdependence, the web of life and a fierce desire to protect, champion and document what is truly important.*

Feedback write: "*When I read this I feel the immense power of story to transport. I read* Charlotte's Web *almost 60 years ago and it remains one of my favorite stories to this day. I also understood in a new way why I am so drawn to farms and why my excursion last weekend to a farm market that was set up on a working farm was such a restorative experience. When I hear the phrase, 'teeming with life,' it's not the cities that I grew up in that I think of—it's the farms that I've known. And I got that in a different way with this write."—Deborah*

## Circle Two: The Ecological Self/Mitwelt/Umwelt—the Physical-Social Dimension

In this circle, expressive writing becomes the bridge that connects our inner and outer worlds. Clients are encouraged to begin to free associate, write with the immediacy of the first person, present tense, imagine a reader outside of the self and begin to explore the reflections that nature offers us in making meaning of understanding our own lives and relationships (Fox, 1997). The writing exercises in this section have less structure, more freedom than in Circle One.

### *The Ecological Approach*

In this second circle of being, what we have been taught about the world (that we are separate from nature) is often found to be at odds with how we experience the world (as part of nature). This juxtaposition can cause clients to question old assumptions.

*How does being part of nature alter my identity? To what and whom am I responsible now?*

The writing exercises here encourage a "call and response" between our inner and outer worlds. By paying attention to the landscapes we inhabit and how we respond to them internally, the boundaries between inner and outer nature begin to blur. We begin to see how we experience ourselves differently, depending on the environments (natural and built) that we inhabit. Here, the client is discovering a self described by psychologist and pastoral therapist James B. Ashbrook as the whole mind that "comes out of nature and does not function apart from nature" (Clinebell, 1996, p. 42). So much of language, according to ecopsychologist Larry Robinson, "tends to de-animate the world, reducing it (and us) to a collection of objects being acted upon by other objects" (Buzzell and Chalquist, 2009, p. 25).

Through writing about our relationship to place, we are coming to view the universe as "a communion of subjects, not a collection of objects" (Berry, 1999, p. 82). Arne Naess describes how we downplay our relationship to place in order to conform to some intellectual standard that is more comfortable with two separate entities—self and place—joined by an *external* rather than an *internal* relationship. "We may try to make the sentence, 'This place is part of myself' intellectually more understandable by reformulations—for example, 'My relation to this place is part of myself' " (Naess, 1995, p. 231). However, in the ecological model, the first statement, "This place is part of myself," stands without need of apology or correction.

## The Existential Approach

In this circle we have elided the Mitwelt/Umwelt, the physical and social dimensions, because both represent the self in relationship to the world, the physical world (the Umwelt—the biological world and the environment) and the social world (the Mitwelt—the world of relationships to people). Every individual is situated in a world of relationships to place and people. Understanding our clients' relationships to their natural world is an important step in understanding their being in the world (*Dasein*) and therefore the way in which they navigate and construct their world. "Of the four dimensions the natural world is the most fundamental. Clearly human existence is always anchored in a physical presence in an actual material world" (van Deurzen-Smith, 1997).

Each client has his or her own unique, subjective experience of the world, and by helping them to explore this we are helping them to explore in writing the inner self. Any two people would have a different experience of the same place, just as each child in the same family experiences "different" parents.

In terms of the natural world, differences may be based on perspective, on preferences (one person loves the heat, another finds it overwhelming; one is drawn to the woodland scenery, another finds it dark and claustrophobic). In family therapy, asking members of the same family to describe the place they went for many holidays together can elucidate strong emotions, painful history, or wounds, or recover a shared pleasure—all responses give useful material for exploration.

Although the notion of "a beautiful view" may be to some extent a cultural construct, located in a particular set of socio-historical circumstances, the individual's idea of such a view is governed by his or her own experiences.

## *Exercises for Circle Two*

### *Warm-Up Write: Clustering the Places We Inhabit*

Clustering is also called Mind Mapping or Webbing (Adams, 1990, p. 87). Not everybody finds clustering easy or natural, but breaking through this resistance can result in fresh insights because this technique encourages free association.

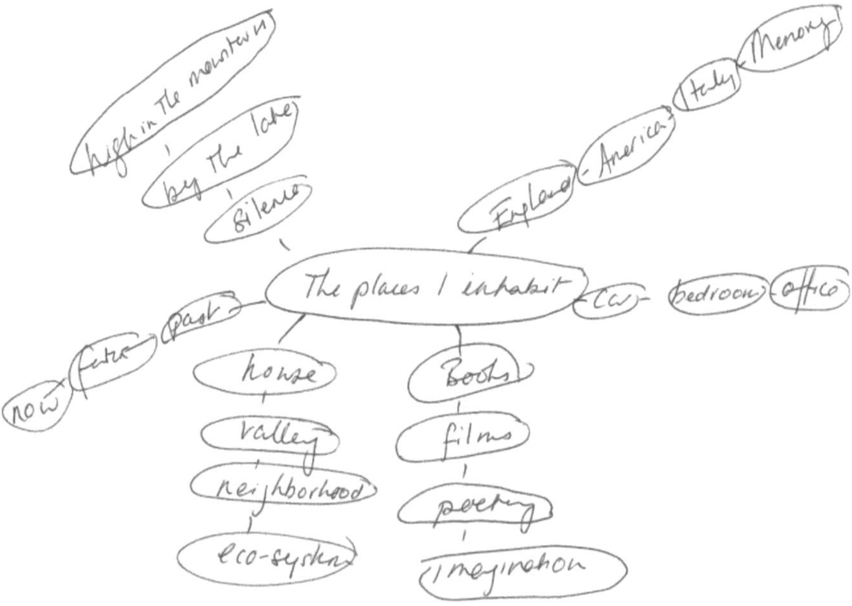


**Figure 5.2** Model of cluster

Adapted from an exercise in *Writing the Natural Way* by Gabriele Lusser Rico

1. Write the phrase *The Places I Inhabit* in the center of your page and draw a circle round it.
2. Start to free associate, writing down any words or phrases that spring to mind, spinning them out and circling each one.
3. Stop clustering when you feel a strong urge to write, which is often after one or two minutes. It may appear as a feeling of, "This is what I want to write."

Feedback write: *Write no more than a paragraph or two about the ideas generated by your cluster.*

### *Steppingstones Part Two*

In Circle One, Steppingstones Part One ended with a list of places from life, numbered in chronological order.

Look at that list again, notice which place calls for your attention now.

Close your eyes, allow that place come into focus, notice where you are in it, what's happening, re-enter the memories.

When you are ready begin to write.

Write in the first person; use the present tense.

Feedback write: "*When I read this I realize . . .*"

### *Writing About a Natural Object: The Character Sketch*

A character sketch is a written portrait. It describes not only outward appearance, but imagined or sensed characteristics and attributes (Adams, 2013). Choose a natural object that you can physically get close to. It can be anything from a towering tree to a small pebble.

Begin by describing everything you notice about the object, using all your senses. Write for ten minutes.

Feedback write: "*This [name the object] reflects my. . . . This [name of object] makes me feel . . .*"

### *Unsent Letter to Place*

Framing a piece of writing in an unsent letter is a common therapeutic technique in many modalities, perhaps because letter writing is a familiar process. Letters can be written to people (living or dead), parts of the self or objects outside the self, such as a landscape. Framing the writing as a letter with an intended reader is both freeing and focusing.

Choose a place that has been important to you—it could be where you are now, a place from the past, a literary landscape or a place you would like to visit.

Write a letter to that place.

Say who you are and why you are writing, what you know of that place.

Feedback write: "*This place represents . . .*"

*Dear Poland,*

*I long to visit you and I don't know what I'm looking for or where to search within your borders to find it. Perhaps I hope you'll be a mirror to some previously unknown part of me. Perhaps I hope you'll fill the hole or provide some information/insight into the family and ancestry I've never known. I know that I want to walk your land, take you in with my senses, have my ears filled with your language that will make no sense to me, savor some tastes that were maybe familiar to my ancestors. You are as mysterious and unapproachable to me as my extended family but you seem easier. I just have to show up, not so much to interact or impress or understand. I want to soak something into my skin. I picture your cities as rather magnificent but faded, crumbling. I picture your skies as overcast and your air as damp. I imagine something strong, heroic about you—through WWII perhaps, where you were so victimized but fought back. Oh, maybe that is what we have in common. You rose again from ashes just as I did. I guess I want to see how you turned out! Or do I want to show you how I turned out?*

Feedback write: "*This place represents my family and heritage and seems very foreign and incomprehensible, yet has called to me over many years now. That was a fresh insight/twist at the end, seeing both Poland and myself as survivors of history—wanting to see how she turned out and wanting to show off my own strength and renewal!*"*—Carolyn*

## Circle Three: The Cosmological Self/Uberwelt—Ideal or Spiritual World

In this circle the writing shifts again as the writer takes on different perspectives. This is the meaning-making circle where something transcendent can happen. The prompts here invite people to become observers of their own lives, to take a reflective stance through the device of the omniscient narrator or, even more mystically, to speak in a voice from the environment, becoming part of it. The place from which we are writing may be seen to be located both in the outer and inner environments, and as such belongs to both worlds. The outer circle allows empathy and imagination to be fully explored in writing. We are inhabiting, psychologically and imaginatively, the places and beings around us, giving utterance to both ourselves and the other than human world.

### *The Cosmological Self*

The ecological self is bonded to the earth and to particular locales or ecosystems within it; the relationship to environment is based on life experience, the places we have lived, visited, or read about and is framed by a particular geological era and physical location, Earth. The cosmological self, however, expands to include the all; that is, everything that has ever existed throughout time and space. There can be no bigger context or physical environment from which to view our lives. Science now reveals an awe-inspiring reality. Rather than existing in a mechanical, reductionist universe, we are part of a seamlessly interconnected universe. The self cannot be separated from the rest of creation (Pfeiffer, 2012). In some sense we were present at the origin of the cosmos. If ecotherapy's purpose is to rekindle a sense of belonging to the natural world (Chalquist, 2009) then the new universe story provides a context for the deepest kind of belonging (Swimme and Berry, 1992). We were there at the very beginning of the story. Swimme and Tucker help us to appreciate the wonder of this when they suggest that the essence of this new understanding is that the stars are our ancestors (Swimme and Tucker, 2011). We only have to imagine looking up at the stars in the night sky and experiencing them as kin to feel how this shift in perspective infuses our lives with meaning and sacredness. This awareness of being inextricably linked to the whole of creation, this overwhelming sense of oneness and unity, describes the feelings we most often associate with religious or mystical experiences. In Circle Three of the self, we come to know ourselves as interpenetrated by and flowing into the world and universe. As we begin to realize how deeply embedded we are in this living cosmology, we might feel: "Deep in the heart each of us knows that the mystery of the self is as great as that of the universe—perhaps it is the same mystery" (Shepherd, 1978, p. 210).

### *The Existential Approach*

Circle Three is the Uberwelt, the spiritual dimension, the circle where meaning is made. It is the circle of values and beliefs or "the meta-world where all the rest of our experience is put into context" (van Deurzen-Smith, 1997, p. 123). When existential therapists work in this dimension, they are helping clients to explore the system of meaning and values by which they live and how they make sense of the world. This circle explicitly considers beliefs and how those beliefs are derived. The task in this dimension in existential therapy is to find out why you live, what you really live for, and what you want to live for.

"The inner world of each client is immense, perhaps larger than will ever be consciously known to yourself or others. This vast unknown territory is the landscape through which we accompany our clients on their psychotherapeutic journeys" (Heery and Bugental, 2005, p. 254).

### *Circle Three: Writing Exercises*

#### *Warm-Up*

What language from nature do you want to learn to speak? Tree? Wind? River? A certain color? Let your imagination lead the way. Write for five minutes on the following:

> *I want to learn how to speak the language of . . . (blank)*
> Feedback write: *When I read this I experience . . .*

This exercise is inspired by a passage in Terry Tempest Williams' *Red: Passion and Patience in the Desert.*

### *Steppingstones Part Three*

1. Now return to the place you wrote about in Steppingstones Part Two.

This time, as you let it come into focus, look at it from a distance, draw back from it, take a wider lens view.

2. See yourself in the landscape, notice how old you are, what you are doing.
3. When you are ready begin to write in the third person, present tense.

Begin:

*She/He is. . . .*
Feedback write: *When I read this I understand . . .*

### *Unsent Letter From Place to You*

In Circle Two you wrote a letter to a place in your life.

This time let the place write back to you. What does it have to say to you?

Feedback write: *My connection to this place is . . .*

### *Landscape of the Soul*

Certain types of landscapes (mountains, seascapes, valleys) draw us to them. The stronger the attraction, the more powerful our response to them. In the presence of such places, it is as if we don't only inhabit the landscape, it also inhabits us.

Choose a type of landscape that calls to you.

Write for 10 minutes: *The (name of landscape) in me knows . . .*

Feedback write: *Reading this I realize . . .*

*The ocean in me knows the waves of emotion that lie within me. It understands how that power can be overwhelming. It also helps to wash the slate clean when needed. Again, an element of calm and structure . . . and the wild and destructive.*

Feedback write: *"Reading this I realize . . . I am feeling the parts of me that are out of control. My sense is I want the calm and structure and am getting the wild and destructive, but learning to find high ground."—Karen*

## The Combined Model

From a starting point of two apparently separate approaches, it can now be seen how different dimensions can be mapped onto each other, not completely nor exclusively but rather as a set of overlapping scales. Correlations between the ecological model of the self and the existential model become more apparent as we move through the different circles; it may be expected that other modalities and approaches will find common ground here. When we link different models of the self we find ourselves in new territory where we can think about the different inner and outer environments that constitute the human experience.

Expressive writing provides a further bridge between these different approaches, revitalizing the exploration of self and world, or self-in-the-world (Dasein), and thus engendering fresh possibilities. In writing our own stories of place we are constructing our individual experience, discovering a widening and deepening sense of self, emerging from our own understanding and imagination. Thus a key goal of ecotherapy, to heal the human-nature split, can also be realized within more established and mainstream therapies, through the use of expressive writing. By gaining control (authorship) over the kinds of stories we tell about ourselves and the world, we begin to envision and create the kind of world we want to inhabit.

Building on the work of Jerome Brunner, White and Epston (1990) wrote:

> *We would like to rest our case for a therapy that incorporates narrative and written means. We have found these means to be of great service in the introduction of new perspective and to a* range of possible worlds, *to the privileging of vital aspects of lived experience in the* recreation *of unfolding states, in enlisting person in the reauthoring of their lives and relationships.*
>
> (White and Epston, 1990, p. 217)

In light of these words, we would suggest that any environmental therapy that seeks to support a mutually flourishing connection between people and the planet would benefit from using expressive writing techniques to "re-story" and "re-author" the relationship we have with the world about us. By writing about the places we inhabit we come to see that "landscape has long offered us keen ways of figuring ourselves to ourselves, strong means of shaping memories and giving form to thought" (Macfarlane, 2012, p. 193). As therapists of any persuasion we can use this as a reason for bringing nature into the therapeutic relationship and letting our clients tell their stories in new ways.

## References

Adams, K. (1990). *Journal to the self: Twenty-two paths to personal growth.* New York: Warner Books.

Adams, K. (1993). *The way of the journal: A journal therapy workbook for healing* (2nd ed., p. xi). Madison, Lutherville: Sidran Press.

Adams, K. (1998). *The way of the journal: A journal therapy workbook for healing.* Madison, Lutherville: Sidran Press.
Adams, K. (2013). The journal ladder. In K. Adams (Ed.), *Expressive writing: Foundations of practice* (pp. 43–51). New York: Rowman & Littlefield.
Albrecht, G. (2005). Solastalgia: A new concept in health and identity. *PAN: Philosophy Activism Nature, 3*, 41–55.
Berry, T. (1988). *The dream of the earth.* San Francisco, Sierra Club Books.
Berry, T. (1999). *The great work: Our way back into the future.* New York: Random House.
Chalquist, C. (2009). Ecotherapy research and a psychology of homecoming. In L. Buzzell and C. Chalquist (Eds.), *Ecotherapy: Healing with nature in mind* (pp. 69–82). San Francisco: Sierra Club Books.
Clinebell, H. (1996). *Ecotherapy: Healing ourselves healing the earth.* Minneapolis, MN: Fortress Press.
Deurzen-Smith, van E. (1997). *Everyday mysteries.* London: Routledge.
Evernden, N. (1993). *The natural alien: humankind and environment* (2nd ed.) (p. 43). Toronto: University of Toronto Press.
Fox, J. (1997). *Poetic medicine: The healing art of poem-making* (pp. 191–222). New York: Tarcher/Putman.
Heery, M., and Bugental, J.F.T. (2005). Meaning and transformation. In E. van Deurzen and C Arnold-Baker (Eds.), *Existential perspectives on human issues.* London: Palgrave Macmillan.
Hillman, J. (1995). A psyche the size of the earth. In T. Roszak, M. E. Gomes, and A. D. Kanner (Eds.), *Ecopsychology: Restoring the earth, healing the mind* (pp. xvii–xxiii). San Francisco: Sierra Club Books.
Hynes McCarty, A. and Hynes-Berry, M. (1994). *Biblio/poetry therapy: The interactive process: A handbook.* St. Cloud: North Star Press.
Jordan, M. (2015). *Nature and therapy, understanding counselling and psychotherapy in outdoor spaces.* London. Routledge.
Kimmerer, R. (2013). *Braiding sweetgrass: Indigenous wisdom, scientific knowledge and the teachings of plants.* Minnesota: Milkweed Editions.
Macfarlane, R. (2012). *The old ways, a journey on foot.* London: Hamish Hamilton.
Macfarlane, R. (2015). *Landmarks* (p. 12). London: Hamish Hamilton.
McDonald, E. D. (Ed.). (1936). *Phoenix: The posthumous papers of D. H. Lawrence* (p. 822). London: William Heinemann.
Naess, A. (1995). Self-realization: An ecological approach to being in the world. In G. Sessions (Ed.), *Deep ecology for the 21st century: Readings on the philosophy and practice of the new environmentalism* (pp. 225–239). Boston: Shambhala.
Pfeiffer, B. (2012). *Wild earth, wild soul: A manual for an ecstatic culture.* Alresford, Hants: Moon Books.
Plotkin, B. (2013). *Wild mind: A field guide to the human psyche.* Novato, CA: New World Library.
Progoff, I. (1975). *At a journal workshop.* New York: Dialogue House.
Rico, G. L. (1983). *Writing the natural way.* Boston: J. P. Tarcher.
Rilke, R. M. (2005). Widening circles. In *Book of hours* (A. Barrows, trans.). New York: Penguin Books.

Robinson, L. (2009). Psychotherapy as if the world mattered. In L. Buzzell and C. Chalquist (Eds.), *Ecotherapy: Healing with nature in mind* (pp. 22–29). San Francisco: Sierra Club Books.

Roszak, T. (1992). *The voice of the earth: An exploration of ecopsychology.* Grand Rapids, MI: Phanes Press.

Roszak, T. (1995). Where psyche meets gaia. In T. Roszak, M. E. Gomes, and A. D. Kanner (Eds.), *Ecopsychology: Restoring the earth, healing the mind* (pp. 1–17). San Francisco: Sierra Club Books.

Sacks, O. (2012). *Hallucinations.* New York: Random House.

Sartre, J.-P. (1988). *'What is literature?' and other essays.* Boston: Harvard University Press.

Sartre, J.-P. (1992). *Being and nothingness* (H. E. Barnes, trans.). New York: Washington Square Press.

Schama. S. (1995). *Landscape and memory.* New York: Alfred A. Knopf.

Shepherd, P. (1978). *Thinking animals: Animals and the development of the human intelligence.* Athens: University of Georgia Press.

Snyder, G. (1990). *The practice of the wild.* San Francisco: North Point Press.

Swimme, B., and Berry, T. (1992). *The universe story: From the primordial flaring forth to the Ecozoic Era: A celebration of the unfolding cosmos.* New York: Harper Collins.

Swimme, B., and Tucker, M. E. (2011). *Journey of the universe.* New Haven: Yale University Press.

Thompson, K. (2011). *Therapeutic journal writing: A guide for professionals* (pp. 103–111). London: Jessica Kingsley.

Watts, A. (1958). *Nature, man and woman* (pp. 2–3). New York: Pantheon Books.

White, M., and Epston, D. (1990). *Narrative means to therapeutic ends.* New York: W. W. Norton.

Williams, T. T. (2002). *Red: Passion and patience in the desert.* New York: Vintage Books.

Woodman, M., and Dickson, E. (1996). *Dancing in the flames: The dark goddess in the transformation of consciousness.* Boston: Shambhala.

# 6

# THE ART OF UTILIZING THE METAPHORICAL ELEMENTS OF NATURE AS "CO-THERAPIST" IN ECOPSYCHOLOGY PLAY THERAPY

*Janet A. Courtney*

> *The best remedy for those who are afraid, lonely or unhappy is to go outside, somewhere where they can be quiet, alone with the heavens, nature and God. Because only then does one feel that all is as it should be and that God wishes to see people happy, amidst the simple beauty of nature.*
>
> Anne Frank, *The Diary of a Young Girl*

## Introduction

After reading about the devastating 2014 tragedy on Mount Everest, where several mountain workers lost their lives, I learned something profound that has caused me much contemplation. A young Sherpa, Nima Chhiring, set out early in the morning from base camp with a load of 65 pounds when a premonition caused him to suddenly abort his work duties. Brown (2014) explained:

> *In Nepal premonitions of danger are sometimes experienced as a buzzing, a high-pitched sound, a phenomenon called kan runu, or crying ear. Nima Chhiring, who had been to the summit of Everest three times, had heard his ear cry before and knew better than to ignore it. He was racked with indecision: Continue dutifully on to Camp I with his load, or deposit the gas canister as far as he'd carried it and go down immediately? [He decided to descend.] Other Sherpas asked him what he was doing. I said, "My ear is crying and we will hear something bad has happened, I am going down and you should go down too."*
>
> (p. 61)

Word quickly spread about Nima Chhiring's "crying ear" and some turned about, but sadly within minutes, an avalanche occurred and killed 16 mountain workers and injured 8 others. After reading this, I could not get this young man and the notion of a "crying ear" out of my mind. I was intrigued that he was able to be so acutely attuned with nature and that his body was able to send him a signal of warning. And, not only did he experience the internal message—he acted upon it; because he had an inner *knowing*—he *knew* that something bad was going to happen. As well, this was not some isolated phenomenon for Nima Chhiring; he came from a culture where this type of occurrence was common enough to have a label.

This stirred within me a great longing and a feeling of something missing or lost, and hours of deep contemplation with many questions: Did my pioneer ancestors, who lived close to the land, have a sense of intuitive connection to nature—something that has been lost through the generations? And, if so, what was that knowledge? What internal messages have I missed or not paid attention to, perhaps failing to read my internal signs related to nature—both positive or dangerous? Did my younger, little girl self, understand that sense of connection? Something I have forgotten? Are there ways that I can rekindle that sense of interconnectedness? It created a sense of craving deep within my being—a longing to reconnect with nature at an intimate level.

Connecting to this intense yearning experience helped me to fully appreciate what Wilson (1993) formulated as the *biophilia hypothesis*, which postulated a pervasive attraction—an "emotional affiliation" (p. 31)—that draws people to nature. Kellert (1993) defined it as a "human dependence on nature that extends far beyond the simple issues of material and physical sustenance to encompass as well the human craving for aesthetic, intellectual, cognitive, and even spiritual meaning and satisfaction" (p. 20). Likewise, I could also relate to the *Ecological Self*, originally coined by the Norwegian philosopher, Arne Naess, in the 1970s, and elaborated by Macy and Gahbler (2010) to denote the "radical interrelatedness of all life forms . . . Deep ecology broadens one's sense of identity and responsibility, freeing us to experience what Naess calls the ecological self" (p. 67). And spiritually these words by Zen master Thich Nhat Hanh rang true:

> *You carry Mother Earth within you. She is not outside of you. Mother Earth is not just your environment. In that insight of inter-being, it is possible to have real communication with the Earth, which is the highest form of prayer.*

I felt an affinity to all of these perceptions and have related this deeper level of connection to the natural world directly into my therapy work with children and families.

## Societal Concern for Children

In today's society, for a variety of reasons from technological distractions to schools cutting back on recess, children are missing essential nature exploration. Many of today's children experience nature, not by direct contact but by classroom representations, internet exposure, video games and now "Instagram." Land restrictions, fear of litigation, and safety concerns have all made their contribution to this ever increasing disconnect between children and the natural world. As well, Conn (1995) noted, "The most obvious effect of the industrial age is that much of what we touch in our everyday lives is far removed from its roots in the Earth" (p. 160).

Some professionals are exploring the possibility that many of the behavioral disorders observed in children might well be, in part, a consequence of this disconnect (Louv, 2008, 2012; Platt, 2012; Rivkin, 2014; Swank and Shin, 2015). A phenomenon coined by Richard Louv (2008) called Nature Deficit Disorder speaks to the detrimental effects that can occur when children have decreased access to the world of nature.

Many therapists who work with children in a playroom setting have, for the most part, neglected to include nature objects such as plants, flowers, shells, and stones, and the wonderful and meaningful metaphors that they inspire, substituting instead a room of plastic objects (Courtney, 2008). On the upside, practitioners who work with children are now embracing nature through creative interventions and research, and are discovering its mental health benefits for children (and adults) for a multitude of diagnoses and problem areas (Annerstedt and Währborg, 2011; Courtney and Mills, 2016; Cutillo et al., 2015; Faber Taylor and Kuo, 2009; Mills, 2015; Mills and Crowley, 2014; Montgomery and Courtney, 2015; Rivkin, 2014; Swank and Shin, 2015).

Now wonder about this: what happens when youngsters are given a chance to unplug from technology and their overscheduled lives and spend time in nature? Recently a monastic from a Buddhist monastery shared his experiences following a five-day mindfulness retreat with a group of adolescents (paraphrased here with permission):

> *On the first day of arrival, some of the monastics, calling themselves the "Technology Liberators" collected . . . (imagine this) . . . 100 cell phones so the teenagers could then be "technology liberated." [Prior to the retreat, the teens knew that this was a condition for attendance.] The outcome? Through the time out in nature, including camping out in tents, stone-circle sharing groups, and "Mindful" trail hikes, among other nature-based activities, it was observed that the teenagers started to connect and share more with their peers—making new friendships and discovering more about themselves. One girl shared that because she was no longer distracted by her phone that she had the opportunity to then be with her thoughts and stated, "I like my thoughts, I'm kind of funny." And,*

**Figure 6.1** Kids need opportunities to spend extended time in nature. The author's son, Austin, age 16, hiking the Appalachian Trail, North Carolina—in a kilt!

Photo by Doug McPherson and Boy Scout Troop 132, Palm Beach Gardens, Florida

*another teen enjoyed being with others of "like-mind" and shared, "It's like you took all of the best people from 100 different schools and put them all together." At the end of the retreat the feedback of their experience was this: Many related that the retreat was "too short" and that they wished it had been "longer."*

[After hearing this story, I smiled . . . Ah, hope springs eternal! Refer to the Deer Park Monastery website: Deerparkmonastery.org.]

## The Importance of Childhood Play and Nature

As a child I took delight roaming the woods surrounding my home in the Northeastern United States. It was my playground—my protected world of make-believe. Sometimes I played alone and other times with friends. But I was always outdoors first thing in the morning, and I would return home only when hungry and then be out the door again. Sometimes I imagined I was an Indian running fast through the woods barefoot, dodging rocks and trees along the way; and another day I played homemaker, sweeping with a tree branch a clearing I created encircled by fallen tree stumps—my pretend house. One time I crawled into a rock cave pretending I was a bear—exploring, risk-taking, daring. I swam for hours in cool mountain lake water—pretending I was a dolphin and mastering new physical skills such as learning the butterfly stroke. Other times I played flashlight tag with my friends excitedly running through the woods trying to get back to base without being found. I needed that play, that freedom. It taught me how to take risks, overcome fear, build courage, problem solve, practice life encounters, learn new skills, and rebalance myself emotionally. It is a part of me and makes up who I am today.

It is often stated that play is the *language* of the child and in therapy children's play allows them a safe psychological distance from their problems. The Association for Play Therapy (APT) defines play therapy as "the systematic use of a theoretical model to establish an interpersonal process wherein trained play therapists use the therapeutic powers of play to help clients prevent or resolve psychosocial difficulties and achieve optimal growth and development" (APT website: www.a4pt.org). Overall play—whether playing alone or with peers—helps children to develop the following Twelve "C's" of Competency (expanded from O'Connor, 2015):

- To inspire Curiosity
- To foster Courage
- To develop Caring
- To feel Capable
- To build healthy empathetic Connections
- To feel like they Count
- To grow in Confidence
- To promote Creativity
- To learn to be Careful
- To develop Concentration
- To kindle Compassion
- To grow a sense of Community.

**Figure 6.2** Carefully planning the waterfall journey. Taking risks. Building courage. Practicing leadership skills. This parallels later life formulating of accomplishments

Photo by Janet Courtney

**Figure 6.3** Successfully mastering the plan of action. Growing in confidence and sense of capability

Photo by Janet Courtney

Most practitioners who work with children make a dedicated effort to learn about life from the point of view of the child. They also try to understand and connect to their own child within and to remember what it is like to be a child, and to put themselves in the "child's shoes." Educator Marjorie Spock, sister of Dr. Benjamin Spock (the famous pediatrician of the 1940s), asserted that the reason for the communication gap between adults and children is that the consciousness of children is different from that of adults. Spock (1986) advised:

> *Adults no longer remember their own state of being during early childhood, and insight into a consciousness so different from their own; the education to which most of us were subjected has done little to sensitize us to the phenomena of other individuals' inmost experience. Moreover, we habitually conceive of children as sharing our own state of being.* (p. 58)

Because of this, practitioners may need to relearn how to play and to also connect and remember their own "child within." Of course, we have our adult ways of playing—good thing—but the childhood type of spontaneous playfulness is different, especially play in nature. This is also related to understanding about the parents we work with and the need for them to remember their playful time in nature. The following exercise can be used to help reconnect to a childhood time in nature. (Have someone read this to you to enhance your experience.)

### *Let's Take a Nature Journey Back in Time*

Find a comfortable place to sit away from distractions. Begin to get in touch with your breathing. Starting with the exhale, blow a long breath out through your mouth . . . and then breathe in . . . and then on the exhale imagine that you are blowing out of your body any tension or undesired feelings. While on the inhale, feel the nurturance of the oxygen entering your body and sense the calming and relaxing feeling that each breath brings you. In this relaxed state, allow yourself to search for a memory when you had a pleasant experience in nature as a child. Experiences can be varied. Maybe it's a time when you were by yourself, with your family, or playing with friends. Where in nature did you feel most relaxed, comfortable, and at home? Maybe you were at the ocean, by a lakeside, or a rushing stream. Or maybe you were in the mountains, a forest, or running on sand dunes in the desert. Recall also about the season—Is there snow on the ground? Are leaves falling off the trees? Are the flowers blooming in the spring? Or is everything fully awake in the summer? Recall the sounds surrounding you. What do you hear? What about the air? How does it smell? Try to reconnect to the aroma of that smell. Take a few moments now to use your imagination to reconnect with that childhood experience . . . And, when you are ready to "return back" from your journey, take some time to jot down a few of those sensations and memories.

> Note: A great read about the importance of play can be found in Stuart Brown's (2010) book, *Play: How It Shapes the Brain, Opens the Imagination, and Invigorates the Soul.* And for a comprehensive foundation of a varied selection of play therapy interventions, refer to Crenshaw and Stewart (2015).

## The Profound Experience of Touching Nature

The Greek philosopher Aristotle, who lived between 384–322 bce, in trying to figure out exactly what *organ* touch is related to (such as the organ of hearing is the ears) finally surmised that it must be the *heart* and that touch is so crucial to living that "its absence spells doom to man and all animals" (as summarized by Weber, 1991, p. 18). The anthropologist Ashley Montagu (1986) wrote, "Touch is the parent of our eyes, ears, nose, and mouth" (p. 1). It is how humans learn about the world, and touch can also lead to transformative experiences for children through many types of therapeutic interventions (Courtney and Nolan, 2017). Our skin receptors (the largest sensory organ of the body) are connected to our central nervous system and therefore send messages of kinesthetic experience to the brain. And our fingertips are extremely sensitive to feeling. According to Elbrecht (2013), "every square inch of skin [on our fingertips] has about 16,000 touch sensors that communicate with our brain" (p. 42)—more than any other part of the body.

Montgomery and Courtney (2015) advised that any time we connect to the natural world such as relishing the "feel of a gentle breeze on the skin, anticipating the taste and texture of apples as they are harvested, and enjoying the scent of a bouquet of lilacs," these primary experiences are "sensory impressions that belong to a pre-verbal, pre-narrative world—the biophilic component of human experience" (p. 20). When children see the objects of nature in the office, they want to reach out and touch them. It is not enough to look with the eye—they are connecting to an inner primordial urge to know their world through engaged contact. The varied sensory experiencing of the natural objects has a profound effect upon them. Stones, sand, clay, shells, flowers, and other nature items provide a rich variety of tactile sensation. For example, stones come in all different sizes, weights, and textures. Some stones are rough, smooth, bumpy, heavy, lightweight, and initially cool to the touch, but can warm up when held.

## The Power of Metaphor, Storytelling, and Direct Suggestion: Your Words Have the Potential to Transform

Metaphors can act as symbolic bridges of personal connection inspiring solutions that strengthen a child's own inner resources and resiliency. Storytelling with children can help to provide an emotional and psychological dissociation from their problems and can also help lower resistance. Lankton and Lankton (1989) advised that "therapeutic metaphors do not engender the kind of resistance to considering new ideas that direct suggestions often can. They are considered as gentle and permissive, not a confrontive or demanding way to consider change" (pp. 1–2). Additionally, Milton Erickson advanced that indirective positive messages embedded in a metaphoric story will activate inherent healing processes that can reach a child at a deeper level of consciousness (Lankton and Lankton, 1989; Mills, 2015; Mills and Crowley, 2014; Short, Erickson, and Erickson Klein, 2005). Marvasti (1997) wrote, "The justification for the utilization of metaphors relies upon the premise that metaphors will pass the conscious level and enter the unconscious of the child" (p. 288).

The following story is offered to provide a thought-provoking example of just how impactful the power of suggestion (albeit a manipulative one) can have on the receiver.

### *The Story of the Brown Monkey*

In a faraway land there lived a beguiling street swindling Sorcerer. He had a bag of gold coins that he would hold out and show to people as they walked past him. He would tell them that if they added their own coin to the bag they could then have all of the coins by simply reaching their hand into the bag and grabbing the coins. However, the seemingly simple exercise had a catch as the clever but crooked Sorcerer revealed more about the task. He would step closer to his innocent, intrigued onlooker as his voice changed to a softer and slower paced mesmerizing tone. And then, with a mischievous smile he uttered: "If you put a coin in this bag, you can then reach in and grab out all of the coins in the bag to keep, but only on one condition . . . as you do so you are not to *think about* the BROWN MONKEY. If you *think about* the BROWN MONKEY, then you cannot have the coins. And, he repeats the conniving imprint a third time—if you *think about* the BROWN MONKEY you cannot have the coins."

So, dear reader, what do you think might happen? Could they do it? Could they reach in and grab out the coins without thinking about the BROWN MONKEY? Could you do it?

The point of this story is to demonstrate just how impactful the power of our words and suggestions can have on a listener. Because once the suggestion was made (*not to think about the Brown Monkey*), it would be very difficult to completely remove the thought from one's mind. Many marketing and advertising executives know this and use subliminal messaging to their advantage to sell products. Of course ethically, in therapy, we *only* use our words with the highest of integrity and authenticity and only to impart the highest of good for the client. (This point and how it is used therapeutically with children will be elaborated further in the following sections and in the case study.)

## Utilizing the Metaphor of Nature as "Co-therapist" in the Playroom Setting

Ecopsychology theory and research is an essential underpinning for all therapeutic work that is nature based (Conn, 1995; Courtney and Mills, 2016; Metzner, 1995; Montgomery and Courtney, 2015; Pollan, 2002; Roszak, Gomes, and Kanner, 1995; Swan, 2000). As global culture becomes more disconnected from nature, many practitioners are searching for ways to optimize the beneficial aspects of nature into a client's life (Conn, 1995; Courtney and Mills, 2016; Kopytin and Rugh, 2016; Mills, 2015; Mills and Crowley, 2014; Montgomery and Courtney, 2015; Scull, 2009). Berger and Mcleod (2006) view nature as partner or "co-therapist" in the healing process and believe in "using the relationship with nature as the key reference point for therapy" (p. 81). Swank and Shin (2015) advocated that child practitioners can bring elements of nature into the therapy room—especially if there are reasons why a child may not be able to be outdoors (e.g., children with allergies, children diagnosed with obsessive-compulsive tendencies related to germs, or impulsive children that need the containment of an office for safety). With this in mind, the following questions arise:

- How can practitioners create a therapeutic space that incorporates nature?
- How can practitioners utilize nature therapeutically in the office/play therapy room space with children and families in sessions?
- How can practitioners bridge what happens in therapy sessions to ground and encourage nature-based healing experiences beyond the therapy hour?
- Are there ways that practitioners can help encourage within the child a sense of an ecological self or awaken a sense of interdependence in relationship to the grander natural world?

The following sections and case study focus on addressing these questions.

## Expanding the Nature Metaphor in the Play Therapy Space

I consider myself extremely fortunate that I was able to acquire an office that offered a natural connection to nature. It came in the form of a second-floor large office window that looked out into a wooded area with a huge oak tree abounding with life—butterflies, birds (hawks, blue jays, and cardinals that would often come to tap on the window to say "hello"), squirrels, lizards, and even a raccoon family! What fun!

Metaphors related to nature abound. Horticultural therapists Linden and Grut (2002) used the metaphor of the garden in working with victims of torture in London to address issues of loss, renewal, growth, and change. They advised that "Metaphor is at the heart of the work of the Natural Growth Project, and parallels are drawn between the cycle of the natural world, with its successes and failures" (Linden and Grut, 2002, p. 42). The multi-sensory experience of having a variety of natural objects in the playroom for children to visually explore, touch, listen to, and smell broadens the opportunity for storytelling. And, each child's problems must be assessed in order to utilize (and adapt) the best metaphor for that particular child. For example, if a child's presenting problem is impulsivity, not thinking things through before acting, and a lack of patience in life, I might hold an acorn in my hand for the child to see and say, for example, the following:

> *Ben, I want to show you this acorn I found while I was* slowly *hiking in the Blue Ridge mountains. I was so amazed when I came upon a large scattering of acorns on the trail—they were* sitting so still *with their sweet little caps on them. And, then I* slowed down *and* stopped myself for a minute *and* started to think *about what I know about acorns . . . [At this point I invited Ben to hold the acorn so that he could have a kinesthetic experience of nature.] I then pointed to the huge oak tree outside of my office window and asked him, do you know that within this little acorn is that whole tree? It's true. [Metaphor speaks to the inner potential of child.] But it takes a lot of time and sometimes this little acorn has to* wait and wait very peacefully, and calmly, and patiently for the right time *and season to sprout. It needs just the right amount of rain, and the right amount of sunshine, and the right nourishment from the soil [reinforcing nurturing and caring themes]. And, then one day—magic! it begins to sprout and grow. [Instilling a sense of wonder for the natural world.] But it must* rest quietly *and be* very, very patient *in order for that to happen. [Interspersed messages provided suggestions of the need to slow down and have patience and that all things come in due time.]*

The therapist-storyteller also works with voice variety and inflection and pace of telling the therapeutic stories. As well, when the interspersed positive messages are delivered (note words in roman type), the therapist might soften and quiet his or her voice and speak slower when imparting what they want the child to understand at a deeper level of consciousness. In fact, this is a key element to the art of therapeutic storytelling. Telling the story is one part of the task, but it is in the *delivery* of the story that makes all of the difference. Additionally, there is very little need to ever explain the intention of metaphoric storytelling. From an Ericksonian paradigm, the therapist trusts and knows that metaphorical suggestions speak to the child intrinsically. It is an indirect planting of healing seed-thoughts of comfort, solutions, change, and hope.

Additionally, a StoryCraft or an EarthCraft, as Joyce Mills (founder of StoryPlay) labeled them (Mills, 2015), can be created with the child utilizing acorns (for example) in an art-craft project. StoryCrafts can ground and expand on the therapeutic metaphor and can encourage "the activation and utilization of the creative imagination to explore, innovate, and discover new pathways of healing, thinking, and being" (Mills, 2015, p. 180). It also gives the child a transitional object for home that is chock-full of metaphorical meanings.

**Figure 6.4** Acorns have long been used to represent metaphorical parallels to human potential

© Depositphotos.com/Umocha111, printed with permission

Courtney and Mills (2016) gave another example of the utilization of nature:

> *Handing a shell to a child diagnosed with ADHD and asking her or him to* listen carefully *to the sound of the ocean can immediately assist in calming and focusing the child. A story can be expanded by telling*

> *the child, "A baby sea animal once lived in this shell. This was its home, and any time he was feeling scared, worried, or upset, all the baby sea animal had to do was to crawl back into the shell where he felt all* safe, calm, *and* relaxed inside."
>
> (p. 16)

In the preceding example nature is viewed as a co-therapist that can support children to resolve emotional problems. Courtney and Mills (2016) wrote that in the playroom, "elements of nature as a *Natural World Library* whereby, the seasons, plants, animals, shells, the ocean, rocks/gems/minerals, and weather are the *metaphorical miniatures* containing valuable life lessons for achieving transformational healing" (p. 19).

**Potential metaphorical functions of nature:**

- Provides an experience to have contact with the earth in the therapy room;
- Helps to build a therapeutic alliance;
- Builds therapeutic safety and protection;
- Increases self-esteem;
- Reframes problems and self-perceptions;
- Plants seed-thoughts;
- Acts as a transitional object between the office and home;
- Exemplifies points of therapy;
- Comforts through touch and holding of nature objects;
- Sparks children's own inner resources;
- Decreases resistance;
- Suggests ways to solve problems (skill building);
- Offers a springboard to address emotions;
- Lessens fears and anxiety;
- Encourages respect for cultural heritage;
- Stimulates the imagination and magical thought in the healing process.

## Nature and Culture

Nature can also be culturally and geographically specific, and children in therapy can sometimes feel an instant connection to the varied nature objects in my play therapy room. For example, I have a sandtray of pink-hued sand from Bermuda. A child, age 12, an immigrant from a Caribbean island, rejected the three other types of sandtray options available and wanted to only work in the "island" sand as it helped her to feel a connection to her roots and identity. I also have a large collection of semi-gemstones scattered through my playroom—mostly raw and uncut or unprocessed stones (such as garnet still embedded in its parent stone) representing locations and countries from all over the world.

Mills and Crowley (2014) advised that in all indigenous healing philosophies and stories there is a deep-seated belief in the healing power of nature. They wrote:

> *The natural world is our relative, our teacher, and our healer, and that everything is sacred. In these wisdom teachings, the earth, sky, moon, sun, and stars are not viewed through a scientific lens . . . Instead, they are experienced as our* Mother Earth, Father Sky, Grandmother Moon, Grandfather Sun, *and the* Star Nation—*as* relatives *guiding, protecting, and teaching us many lessons along life's physical and spiritual paths.*
>
> (p. 3)

*Note: although I have worked with children to utilize the therapeutic aspects of nature outdoors, the following case study is provided to demonstrate some of the ways I have incorporated nature within the office playroom setting.* All identifying information for the case study has been changed to protect confidentiality.

## Case Study: "Penguin Man" Speaks

Joey, age 9, was referred for counseling by his school counselor due to low performance in school and an inability to concentrate and focus. He had recently been diagnosed with attention deficit disorder with hyperactivity by his pediatrician, who placed him on medication. However, this did not seem to impact any changes in his school performance. During the first appointment with his father, it became clear that his problems were far more complicated. Joey's parents divorced when he was five and the father had custody of Joey. The father advised that he was recently out of drug rehabilitation and that Joey's mother also suffered with drug addiction but had not sought treatment. The biological mother was living out of state and Joey had only sporadic and unpredictable telephone contact with her.

### *Treatment Plan*

1. Provide individual therapy to include nature-based metaphorical interventions, art therapy, and Gestalt play therapy sessions;
2. Address feelings of abandonment regarding separation from mother;
3. Provide Joey with tools to self-regulate to focus, calm, and manage difficult feelings;
4. Support Joey to develop an ecological-self of connection to nature;
5. Hold joint family sessions between father and Joey to build a more secure attachment relationship;
6. Help the father reconnect to his own childhood experiences in nature;
7. Encourage and support experiences and time in nature between Joey and his father.

### *Course of Treatment and Child's Perception*

Joey was seen for play therapy sessions over a two-year period. From his perspective, he felt that his father was unfairly hard on him and felt deep emotional pain regarding the absence of his mother. He shared that he was often picked on and made fun of by his peers, effecting his feelings of self-worth. He was also having difficulty coping with the stress of school academic pressure.

## SESSION EXCERPT: BEGINNING PHASE OF THERAPY

### *Stepping Stones: Building Upon Inner Resources Through Artistic Metaphor*

During one of the initial individual play therapy sessions with Joey, I wanted to draw upon his inner resilience and strengths to help build his confidence and feelings of self-worth. One way that I approached this task was by using an *Artistic Metaphor* (Mills and Crowley, 2014) activity of stepping stones. (I have a collection of flat sandstones that I collect on the beach that kids can choose from.) The following is a listing of the steps of how I completed this activity.

**Step 1**: I asked Joey what he wanted and hoped for himself and his life. He stated that he wanted to be "happy." I then had him select a stone for him to "draw a symbol" that represented "happy." This stone was then placed as the final stepping stone desired "goal." (Even with young children it's always important to know what they hope to gain from their time in therapy, not just what their parents want.)

**Step 2**: Next I asked him to pick out some other stones to draw on and to think of things in his life that helped him to feel "happy." I told him that he could draw an image (symbol) on each stone that represented these things.

**Step 3**: I then had him share each stone and highlighted and reinforced the positive images and messages that made him feel happy. He drew a dog (he stated his dog helped him to feel better); a fish (he remembered a time when he fished with his grandfather); vanilla ice cream (his favorite kind); an abbreviated name of his favorite teacher; and a polar bear (his favorite animal). (We discussed each one of these stones in detail to further expand on his own story related to each stone image.)

**Step 4**: Joey then took the stones home with him. This acted as a transitional bridge for the therapy session that was filled with positive affirmations related to his resilience. I also suggested to Joey, "I bet over the next week you will be able to think of a lot more things that you do in your life that help you to *feel happy*. And, next week when you come back you can tell me some of those ideas. I will be curious to learn."

**Figure 6.5** Stones can be utilized as transitional objects from the playroom to the child's outside world. Positive messages and stories that draw upon the child's inner strengths and resources are attached to the stones and act as a tangible metaphorical bridge to reinforce the therapy work. Image used with permission

## SESSION EXCERPT: MIDDLE PHASE OF THERAPY

### *Father and Son Nature-Based "Homework"*

Much of the parent-child therapy centered around growing the attachment relationship between Joey and his father. One intervention was to support the father to find ways that he could spend more positive and joyful time with Joey as the father was often focused on Joey's problem behavior—with complaints such as: "Joey does not listen," "He won't stop playing his video games," "Joey won't do his homework when asked," or "Joey won't clean his room or pick up after himself." The father's constant frustration with these issues created a tremendous amount of stress in the relationship for both the father and Joey. It was further assessed that there was virtually no time spent outdoors or together time in playful connection.

Building upon the strengths of the father, I learned that he had been involved in the Boy Scouts in his youth, spending much time outdoors hiking and camping. I then had him share with me some of his memories of those scouting experiences so he could be reconnected with those early memories about how beneficial those outdoor experiences were for himself. He smiled and spoke with enthusiasm when he shared some of his adventures, such as when he learned how to "fish" and jumping off a rope-swing into a freezing river.

Knowing that nature in and of itself can have a profound healing effect on the human brain and perception (Williams, 2016), my next step was to encourage the father to create similar types of nature-based experiences for his son. I also educated him about the emerging research that indicated positive effects of nature on children diagnosed with ADHD (see Special Note #1). Joey and his father decided to plan a weekend camping trip that I helped to facilitate the planning of during a therapy session. This shifted the conversation that was commonly full of a list of things that Joey had done wrong to an engaging discussion about the trip including where they could go to camp, what to bring, what to cook out, and what activities they would like to do. They scheduled for a month in advance so that they would have time to gather all they needed.

Prior to the camping trip I also gave two more tasks: To the father, I asked him to "catch Joey doing or being good" in order to focus more on what Joey did that he approved of instead of all the negative comments toward Joey. I also asked him to "tell Joey some stories" about some happy experiences that he had when he was a kid out in nature. For Joey, I asked him to take some pictures of nature and things he did outdoors with his Dad that he would like to share with me when he returned. I also hoped this would help to encourage within him an appreciation, respect, and connection to nature. (See Kopytin, 2016, for some creative ways to utilize nature photographs therapeutically.)

> Special Note #1: Research has shown the positive effects of nature on school in class behavior and with children diagnosed with ADHD (see e.g., Barros, Silver, and Stein, 2009; Faber Taylor, and Kuo, 2009; refer also to the *Children and Nature Network* website for a comprehensive list of articles on this subject, http://www.childrenandnature.org/?search=main&s=adhd).

### *Post-camping Trip Session*

It is a well-known truism that children often act out when they are not feeling connected to their parents. Therefore, creating opportunities for parents and children to have experiences of joy—especially in nature—helps to heal the disconnect. It is known that increased connection between a parent and child will directly impact increased cooperation on the part of the child. This is what happened after the camping trip between Joey and his father. There was an increased sense of lightness in their relationship and the father reported that there was less resistance by Joey to listen and follow through with home tasks.

One way that I helped to "ground" the experience into the therapy was to have Joey share with me the pictures he took on the campout and to then "tell me a story from start to finish about the picture." He had indeed taken a lot of photos via his phone and first showed me a picture of a box turtle. This was the story he shared:

> *Well, we were driving down the road to the campsite and then we saw a big box turtle sitting in the middle of the road. We were worried that the turtle would get run over so my Dad stopped the car and we got out and I helped my Dad get the turtle to the side so no one would run over it. It was so cool!*

He shared this story with much pride and respect for his father. I used the story to highlight his caring attitude toward the wildlife. I also took the opportunity to create a therapeutic metaphor, as Joey often felt a tremendous amount of anxiety and worry.

> *You know turtles are really amazing because they always carry their homes with them on their backs. And, whenever they get scared, frightened or worried, all they have to do in pull their heads inside their shell and they are all* safe *and* protected *inside.*

The words "safe" and "protected" were emphasized as positive suggestions to build upon his inner strengths and resilience, thus deepening the sense of safety and trust for Joey for himself, as well as within the therapeutic environment. I also used the opportunity to tell him Aesop's fable of the "Tortoise and the Hare"—emphasizing how the turtle won the race through his *slow and steady effort*—that the turtle *took his time and paced himself* to reach his goals. Again, the therapeutic positive suggestions were to help address some of his impulsivity.

## SESSION EXCERPT: LATER PHASE OF THERAPY

### *Therapy Turning Point: A Gestalt Encounter Through the Medium of Clay*

Joey bounced into the playroom carrying an empty water bottle and dashed to the children's table and asked if I could get out the clay (see Special Note #2). He seemed to have something in mind, and an indication that he had reached a point of inner self-direction in therapy. He used the wire to cut out from the clay block and silently set to work. I sat in attuned stillness as he intently molded the clay in his hands onto the bottle. Souter-Anderson (2010) described the process of creating in clay in the "presence of another" an "alchemical process," which is a fluid unfolding discovery of "what goes on between the client, the therapist, and the clay and what the emerging theme might be" (p. 64).

> Special Note #2: Clay is a developmental stage of stone and sand, and will vary in texture, color, and mineral content depending on its source. They (clay, rocks, sand) have a life cycle that starts with a beginning, a middle, an end, and then a beginning again. The same minerals get recycled over time again and again. Nothing ever dies, it just gets transformed. And, because we need those minerals for essential life-sustaining nourishment—these nature items that we bring into the therapy room are *alive*!

Most children enjoy working in clay, and it is a powerful therapeutic medium that can act as a bridge between a child's inner unconscious world into the outer world. Souter-Anderson (2010) advised that physical contact with the medium of clay is a "sensate experience . . . that appears to stir feelings and make contact with emotions, whilst simultaneously engaging with the world of imagination, thus incorporating a metaphorical contact" (p. 51). I have used clay successfully with children diagnosed with ADHD, anxiety disorders, and problems of encopresis.

### *A Gestalt Encounter With "Penguin Man"*

Within several minutes he finally looked up from his creation and seemingly very satisfied and proud of himself stated, "There!" allowing me to view his final product. The following is a Gestalt (see Special Note #3) encounter process recording of what emerged next.

Th: After a quiet listening pause, "Can you share with me what you have created?"

Joey: *Pointing*, "It's a penguin."

Th: "Hmmm . . . I see. Does the penguin have a name?"

Joey: *He considers for a moment*, "Penguin Man," he exclaimed.

Th: "Penguin Man . . . I am wondering if we could imagine if Penguin Man could speak. What do you think he would say to you?"

Joey: *He suddenly became very solemn and pensive as if contemplating very deeply*, "He would say . . . 'Your mother doesn't love you.' "

Th: *Heart sinking with deep compassion for Joey and suddenly understanding the extreme depth of sadness of separation and abandonment he felt for his mother. I also knew he was deep in process and wanted to see what emerged if I continued to facilitate the emerging inner conflict.* "Joey, how would you respond back to Penguin Man? What would you say back to him?"

Joey: *Considering the question and looking and speaking directly to Penguin Man,* "I would say, 'But she calls me on the phone and tells me that she loves me.' "

Th: "And, what does Penguin Man say back to that?"

Joey: "He would say, 'I think that you don't even have a mother.' " *At this point, Joey stopped the encounter and he suddenly began to cry and stated,* "Dr. Courtney, it's true, sometimes I feel like I don't even have a mother."

At this point, I reached out and held Joey's hand as a grounding anchor and so that he could feel my presence and my sense of care for him while he allowed himself to experience and feel the pain of loss and of missing his mother. This was something that he had never shared with me prior, and I

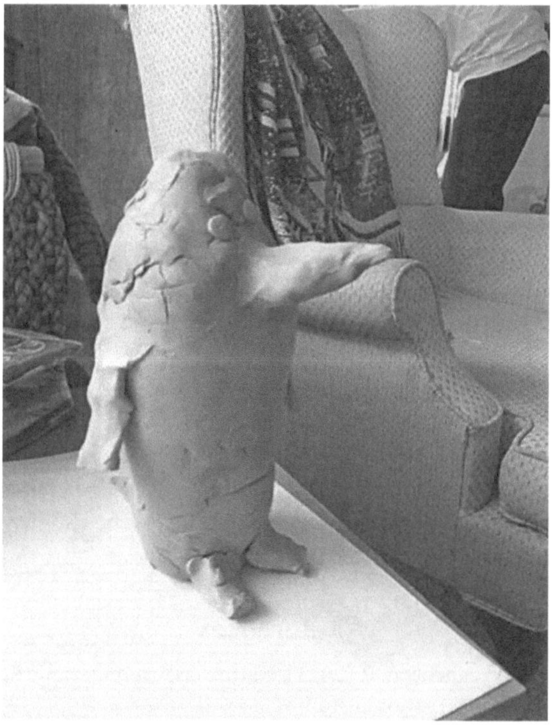

**Figure 6.6** Penguin Man speaks

Photo printed with permission

felt it was a turning point within the therapy. It also deepened his sense of trust and attachment to me, offering a corrective emotional experience.

> Special Note #3: Gestalt therapy was developed by Fritz Perls and is rooted in existential philosophy (Perls, 1969). Its main principles are to develop a deepening awareness of a continual focus of the "here and now" experiencing of the present moment. The preceding process recording is a variation of the Gestalt process of *dialoguing* stemming from what is commonly referred to as the "empty chair" technique (Congress, 2011). The preceding transaction focused on honoring the intrapersonal conflict of the emerging opposing "polarities" and allowing them an opportunity to rise to awareness. Thus the goal of the encounter was to not and try to "fix it" per se, but rather to allow the emerging process to have an opportunity to come to awareness, thus shedding light on Joey's innermost thoughts and feelings.

### *Case Summary Concluding Comments*

Some children grab hold of your heartstrings and do not let go—such was the case with Joey. Toward the end of therapy Joey's mother sought successful treatment for her addiction and Joey was able to regain a stable relationship with her that brought him much relief and joy. When our therapy time together came to a close, I gave Joey a naturally formed heartstone that I had found on the beach that could act as a tangible reminder of my love and care for him.

This case study exampled a few ways in which nature can be therapeutically incorporated and utilized metaphorically within therapy sessions. It also demonstrated how the therapist can support and encourage "homework" type nature-based activities between parents and children. Working with children and nature in the playroom focuses on the *alive* three-way relationship of healing between the therapist, the child, and the natural world. The task of finding creative ways to incorporate nature as "co-therapist" into sessions that can also inspire for the child an ecological sense of self can be rewarding for all, and potentially reach far beyond the therapy hour to touch our interconnected larger world humanity.

## References

Annerstedt, M., and Währborg, P. (2011). Nature-assisted therapy: Systematic review of controlled and observational studies. *Scandinavian Journal of Public Health*, *39*, 371–388.

Barros, R. M., Silver, E. J., and Stein, R.E.K. (2009). School recess and group classroom behavior. *Pediatrics*, *123*, 431–436.

Berger, R., and Mcleod, J. (2006). Incorporating nature into therapy: A framework for practice. *Journal of Systemic Therapies, 25*(2), 80–94.

Brown, C. (2014, November). Sorrow on the mountain. *National Geographic.*

Brown, S. (2010). *Play: How it shapes the brain, opens the imagination, and invigorates the soul.* New York: Penguin Group.

Congress, E. (2011). Gestalt theory and social work treatment. In F. Turner (Ed.), *Social work treatment: Interlocking theoretical approaches* (5th ed., pp. 255–270). New York: Oxford University Press.

Conn, S. A. (1995). When the earth hurts, who responds? In T. Roszak, M. E. Gomes, and A. D. Kanner (Eds.), *Ecopsychology: Restoring the earth, healing the mind* (pp. 156–171). San Francisco: Sierra Club Books.

Courtney, J. A. (2008, June). The perfect dollhouse. *Play Therapy, 3*(2), 6–7.

Courtney, J. A., and Mills, J. C. (2016). Utilizing the metaphor of nature as co-therapist in StoryPlay. *Play Therapy, 11*(1), 18–21.

Courtney, J. A., and Nolan, R. D. (2017, in press). *Touch in child counseling and play therapy: An ethical and clinical guide.* New York: Routledge.

Crenshaw, D. A., and Stewart, A. L. (Eds.). (2015). *Play therapy: A comprehensive guide to theory and practice.* New York: Guilford Press.

Cutillo, A., Rathore, N., Reynolds, N., Hilliard, L., Haines, H., Whelan, K., and Madan-Swain, A. (2015). A Literature review of nature-based therapy and its application in cancer care. *Journal of Therapeutic Horticulture, 25*(1), 4–15.

Elbrecht, C. (2013). *Trauma healing at the clay field: A sensorimotor art therapy approach.* London: Jessica Kingsley.

Faber Taylor, A. F., and Kuo, F. E. (2009). Children with attention deficits concentrate better after walk in the park. *Journal of Attention Disorders, 12*, 402–409.

Frank, A. (1993). *The diary of a young girl* (B. M. Mooyart, trans.). New York: Bantam.

Kellert, S. R. (1993). Introduction. In S. R. Kellert and E. O. Wilson (Eds.), *The biophilia hypothesis* (pp. 18–25). Washington, DC: Shearwater Books/Island Press.

Kopytin, A. (2016). Environmentally and eco-based photography: Ecotherapeutic application of photography as an expressive medium. In A. Kopytin and M. Rugh (Eds.), *'Green Studio': Nature and the arts in therapy* (pp. 155–178). New York: Nova Science.

Kopytin, A., and Rugh, M. (Eds.). (2016). *"Green Studio": Nature and the arts in therapy.* New York: Nova Science.

Lankton, C. H., and Lankton, S. R. (1989). *Tales of enchantment: Goal oriented metaphors for adults and children in therapy.* New York: Brunner/Mazel.

Linden, S., and Grut, J. (2002). *The healing fields: Working with psychotherapy and nature to rebuild shattered lives.* London: Frances Lincoln.

Louv, R. (2008). *Last child in the woods: Saving our children from nature-deficit disorder.* Chapel Hill, NC: Algonquin Books.

Louv, R. (2012). *The nature principle: Reconnecting with life in a virtual age.* Chapel Hill, NC: Algonquin Books.

Macy, J., and Gahbler, N. (2010). *Pass it on: Five stories that can change the world.* Berkeley, CA: Parallax Press.

Marvasti, J. A. (1997). Ericksonian play therapy. In K. O'Connor and L. M. Braverman (Eds.), *Play therapy: Theory and practice: A comparative presentation* (pp. 285–309). New York: Wiley & Sons.

Metzner, R. (1995). The psychopathology of the human-nature relationship. In T. Roszak, M. E. Gomes, and A. D. Kanner (Eds.), *Ecopsychology* (pp. 55–67). San Francisco: Sierra Club Books.

Mills, J. C. (2015). StoryPlay: A narrative play therapy approach. In D. A. Crenshaw and A. L. Stewart (Eds.), *Play therapy: A comprehensive guide to theory and practice* (pp. 171–185). New York: Guilford Press.

Mills, J. C., and Crowley, R. J. (2014). *Therapeutic metaphors for children and the child within* (2nd ed.). Philadelphia, PA: Brunner-Routledge.

Montagu, A. (1986). *Touching: The human significance of the skin* (3rd ed.). New York: Harper & Row.

Montgomery, C. S., and Courtney, J. A. (2015). The theoretical and therapeutic paradigm of botanical arranging. *Journal of Therapeutic Horticulture, 25*(1), 16–26.

O'Connor, N. (2015). *Family therapist suggests parents relearn to play.* Retrieved on February 17, 2017, from https://www.sciencedaily.com/releases/2015/04/150415102920.htm

Perls, F. (1969). *Gestalt therapy verbatim.* Moab, UT: Real Person Press.

Platt, L. (2012). Parks are dangerous and the sidewalk is closer: Children's use of neighborhood space in Milwaukee, Wisconsin. *Children, Youth and Environments, 22*(2), 194–213. doi:10.7721/chilyoutenvi.22.2.0194

Pollan, M. (2002). *The botany of desire.* New York, NY: Random House.

Rivkin, M. S. (2014). *The great outdoors: Advocating for natural spaces for young children.* Washington, DC: National Association for the Education of Young Children.

Roszak, T., Gomes, M. E., and Kanner, A. D. (Eds.). (1995). *Ecopsychology.* San Francisco: Sierra Club Books.

Scull, J. (2009). Tailoring nature therapy to the client. In L. Buzzell and C. Chalquist (Eds.), *Ecotherapy: Healing with nature in mind* (pp. 140–148). San Francisco: Sierra Club Books.

Short, D., Erickson, B. A., and Erickson Klein, R. (2005). *Hope & resiliency: Understanding the psychotherapeutic strategies of Milton H. Erickson, MD.* Bethel, CT: Crown House.

Souter-Anderson, L. (2010). *Touching clay, touching what?: The use of clay in therapy.* Dorset: Archive.

Spock, M. (1986). *Teaching as a lively art.* Great Barrington, MA: Anthroposophic Press.

Swan, J. A. (2000). *Nature as teacher and healer: How to reawaken your connection with nature.* Lincoln, NE: iUniverse.com, Inc.

Swank, J. M., and Shin, S. (2015). Nature-based child-centered play therapy: An innovative counseling approach. *International Journal of Play Therapy, 24*(3), 151–161.

Weber, R. (1991). A philosophical perspective on touch. In K. E. Barnard and T. B. Brazelton (Eds.), *Touch: The foundation of experience* (pp. 11–43). Madison, CT: International Universities Press.

Williams, F. (2016, January). This is your brain on nature. *National Geographic.*

Wilson, E. (1993). Biophilia and the conservation ethic. In S. R. Kellert and E. O. Wilson (Eds.), *The biophilia hypothesis* (pp. 31–40). Washington, DC: Shearwater Books/Island Press.

# 7

# THE ART OF MINDFUL WALKING IN EARTH-BASED ART THERAPY

*Beverley A'Court*

## Embodiment and Walking in Earth-Based Art Therapy

*This chapter describes continuing explorations into the role of mindful walking within 'Earth-based' or 'holistic eco art therapy'; mindful-movement-based, systemic and outdoor approaches divergent from traditional psychodynamic art therapy. Walking; from within studio constellations and installations, to ritual pathways and outdoor quests, can be part of a resource-based approach, illustrated here with examples from client sessions, supervision and trainings. The importance of the body as nature and 'first ground' is highlighted. Cultural traditions and archetypes referencing walking support this style of therapeutic work.*

In *Where Mathematics Comes From*, Lakoff and Nunez (2000, 2001) argue that 'the very structure of reason itself comes from the details of our embodiment' (McNerney, 2011, p. 1). All the defining parameters of perception and cognition, including psychotherapeutic concepts, are inseparable from our embodied existence. Industrialised societies have marginalised, and often exclude, this crucial factor from many scientific, medical and other analyses. Our anatomy and functioning are alive in our categories of thought. Writing 'about' a different, non-dual way of perceiving and its place in therapy is therefore challenging, and I refer readers to 'Speaking With a Boneless Tongue' (Jardine, 2002) for a prose style which may better replicate the experience of interdependence and co-arising in thought.

Art is made with the body and is at times a powerfully visceral, messy, physical process. It is now well recognised as valuable to consider the bodily aspects of the art therapy process further than has been customary in the psychoanalytic and psychodynamic tradition (Steinberg, 2010). During and

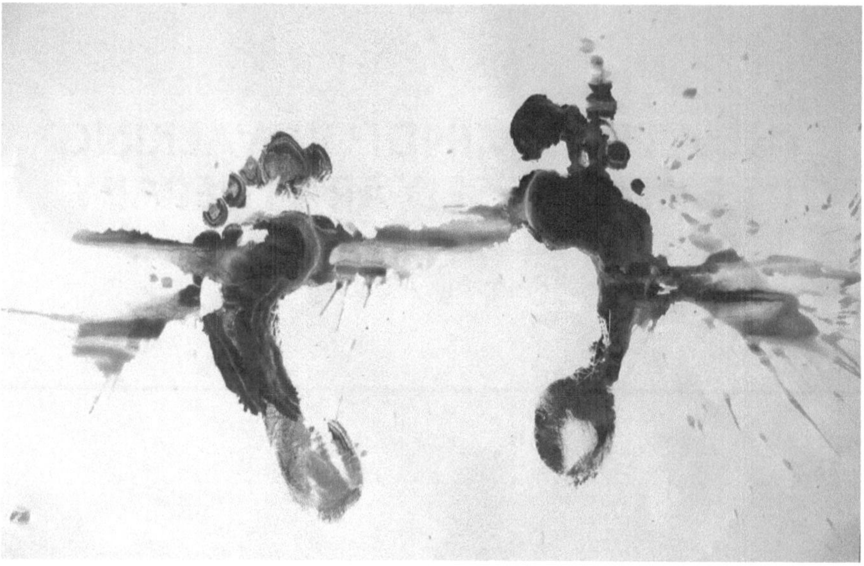

**Figure 7.1** Explorations in embodied art-making

Artist: Paul Batten. Photo: Paul Batten, printed with permission

following art-making, we can observe how clients interact with the art materials, how medium, moves, marks and meaning interpenetrate, and how they, and we as therapists, move and behave spatially in relationship within the field, including within the historical and socio-cultural traditions and conventions, bodily imperatives and contact taboos of which we are part.

In Earth-based art therapy, where we are concerned with helping people to recover from trauma or aim to restore well-being in ways that acknowledge the interdependence and value of all life, walking is a natural, step-by-step vehicle for titration techniques, providing gentle, progressive, incremental exposure to, increased tolerance and integration of, intense, traumatic experiences. We can combine spontaneous, expressive art-making with variations on ancient and modern mindfulness practices, bringing ourselves into close, compassionate witnessing observation of the 'ground' of our being, and its constantly shape-shifting nature; connecting in awareness,

- aspects of our walking body, its muscular-skeletal articulation, shapes, rhythms, accompanying somatic experiences and flow of thoughts and feelings.
- our conceptualised 'environment'; beings and phenomena in the 'field' of our art, movement and attention, the immediate natural and wider socio-cultural, world.

The quartet of art, mindful walking and nature, with the witnessing support of a therapist to enter gentler, open-body-minded observation of present reality, provides a potent field for therapy. It allows a 'sensory based attunement' (Malchiodi, 2016) of all parts that reveals and awakens insight and stimulates new perceptions and routes for action arising from the person's body-mind system, initially sensed as subtle somatic shifts, and spontaneous, poetic words.

> *Every step involves trust . . . and that moment when it's like you aren't anywhere, you could be floating, then you land back and the ground started to feel soft! not solid, receiving my foot. It moved me, I didn't know the ground could feel soft and gentle, and welcome me walking on it.*
>
> (Training workshop participant)

The relationship between walking, art-making, subjective mind-body state and responsive 'field' can be explored in the light of literary and other cultural traditions, current neuroscience and observations of occurrences in art-therapy practice.

## Introduction: Earth-Based Art Therapy

Walking occurs in art therapy, incidentally, in how the client arrives, enters, moves within and leaves the therapy studio, and more intentionally, in structured procedures which may be suggested for specific art therapeutic purposes. Posture and walking can be the first spontaneous, gestural responses to energy released or intensified by art-making and, when included in awareness, can reveal more for the client about their art, their body-mind and their situation. Gait, like spontaneous mark-making, is a distinctive 'signature' and our movement is 'the graphology of everything (we) are' (Alon, 1996, p. 34), and can be an indicator of deeper, systemic conditions (Holtzer, Wang, and Verghese, 2012). Mindful walking, with awareness of self and all that might be thought of as 'other' in the immediate surroundings, and the vibrant relationships between them, may not be instinctive but like an art, is a learned skill, fine-tuned by practice to become a psychological and therapeutic resource, in ways this chapter attempts to demonstrate.

During sessions, walking implies and involves space; the walk, the walker and the space walked constitute a unified field of phenomena in which characteristics of the place and its life forms have potential significance for the therapeutic journey. Walking can connect us physically, emotionally and spiritually to the vast field of our connections, enabling us to become conscious of even a tiny fractal of this in our body-mind:

> *Our bodies are a complex, arachnid world within . . . comprised of strands of glycogen that stretch and contract with every movement,*

> *every breath, with every heartbeat. We share the spider's sensitivity to the vibration and sound of its web.*
>
> (Bennett, 2011)*

An Earth-based psychology paradigm acknowledges a shared web and continuum of existence in communication with itself (Bohm, 1980; Mindell, 2007), whereby the natural life of the imaginative body emerges in interdependence, or co-dependent arising, with nature, and is the locus of, or portal to, 'spirit', understood as the subjective sense of connection and union with the infinite source of life, awareness and all manifestations. Body-mind-Earth resonances and interspecies interactions thereby become a spontaneous part of the dynamic field of therapy and potential catalysts for therapeutic insight (A'Court, in Kopytin and Rugh, 2016, pp. 47–77).

Earth-based art therapy draws inspiration from indigenous cultures which might be said not to have lost, or be seeking, connection with nature, but to embody and celebrate their place in the 'great mystery' of nature. From within Western European eco psychology, earth-based art therapy is about developing healing, creative modalities in which our relationship with the Earth is reinstated as primary; as a dynamic, active agent in therapy, a source of both support and challenge, akin to the speaking mirrors and singing forests of fairy tales, not merely a passive background. The linear progress of a walk evokes echoes of cultural narratives, of epic ancestral and fictional transformational journeys in relation to natural elements, beings and forces.

Evidence is accruing for the many roles played by nature in psychological well-being and the varied forms of nature-contact currently and potentially useful within eco therapy are reviewed in Kopytin and Rugh (2016, pp. xii–xviii). Simply walking barefoot outdoors on earth or grass, 'earthing' (Chevalier, Sinatra, Oschman, Sokal, and Sokal, 2012, Chevalier, Melvin, and Barsotti, 2015) has significant enhancing effects on blood viscosity, endocrine and nervous system function, heart rate, skin conductivity and sleep, and aids reduction in general tension and stress, inflammatory disorders, pain, fatigue, and hormonal and menstrual disturbances (Ober, Sinatra, and Zucker, 2014). How much more healing potential may there be when we linger for periods in nature, absorbed in mindful, physically and imaginatively engaged making? Much nature-based therapy incorporates forms of mindfulness practice in nature, combined with hands-on, physically vigorous, creative activities. Earth-based art therapy treats the act of making-in-relationship with the body and surrounding nature as a core influential element of the therapy, bringing together

- Sensory and somatic awareness and conscious Earth-connection;
- Contemplative, mindful and appreciative practices, originating in the meditative traditions of major religions;

- A spectrum of art therapeutic modalities grounded in archaic human faculties and cultural practices; hunter-gatherer, foraging-type activity such as scanning, picking up, handling, selecting and combining found and/or natural and discarded materials for art-making, using techniques of binding, weaving, aerial hanging and placing constructed artefacts in natural, animal or human-made 'sacral spaces';
- Imagined and visualised potential creations, their location, construction, symbolic meaning, cultural resonances and wider social impact.

> *I hung my green 'angel' doll (with leaf-wings, 'antennae' and long, swinging legs, made following a mindful walk) in the window. She reminds me to walk & breathe, to keep a rhythm . . . look around and appreciate how interesting it all is, not be thinking all the time and get so tense and anxious.*
>
> (Psychology teacher, workshop participant)

Joanna Macy, in *World as Lover, World as Self* (2007), voicing our passionate, intimate and inter-dependent relationship with Earth and other beings, describes how, in an attuned mind state, we may experience the entire natural world, or a single leaf-blade, as a portal to connection, a source of support and artistic creative inspiration, subjectively experiencing the abundant, creative generativity of nature reflected in our own little 'garden', our body-mind. In classical tales it is often unexpectedly while out wandering or lost in nature, that the protagonist encounters their muse, often in the form of a liminal being, appearing like the personification of some natural force or element, who awakens and invites awe and devotion and in so doing stirs the creative faculties to poetry, song, painting and dance in honour both of the immediate and universal beloved. Intoxicating feelings of simultaneously specifically sensuous and transpersonal love open the doors of perception and creative expression. Walking is often instrumental in such encounters; both leading and following the protagonist (or ourselves as artists), attuned to the pace of the place and the body; the rhythm and flow of breathing, singing, thinking and imagining.

Therapists develop to differing degrees their potential to be attuned in body-mind to the client's psyche-soma, the field of the therapy process and surrounding natural world and I have used the walking activities described here in many therapy training workshops for this purpose. 'A Communion of Subjects' (Ch. 3 in Kopytin and Rugh, 2016, pp. 47–77) summarises my personal and professional journey towards integrating bodily/somatic awareness and systemic, field-inclusive approaches into art therapy, a rationale for this 'holistic' or 'earth-based' approach and how my attention was drawn to the role of walking as a supplementary and complementary form of bilateral activity and processing in art therapy, which is the primary focus of this chapter.

## Archetypal Walking, Walkers and Walks

Archetypal images of walks and walkers occur across cultures, from walking meditations to trans-continental hikes. From the wandering yogis and dancing yoginis of the Orient to mendicant Holy Fools of Russia, people have walked as an expression of power and vision, to find or assert affiliation or dedication to principle, people or place, making pilgrimage to show

**Figure 7.2** Explorations in embodied art-making

Artist: Paul Batten. Photo: Paul Batten, printed with permission devotion and discipline, as symbolic penance, purification and offering, or to rediscover and re-experience their place in the web of life unencumbered by the complexities and accoutrements of householder life. Walking is political, having historically marked campaigns of protest, of military conquest, enforced subjugation by a long, forced march, of persuasion as in the fashion industry's catwalk, that 'models' idealised body forms and walking styles, and the satirical 'cakewalk' dance of plantation slaves, creatively parodying their bosses by turning their walk into a wildly exaggerated, enjoyable dance.

The forms of walking I have observed occurring spontaneously in eco art therapy, or have adapted for specific purposes, have their origins in these archetypal walks and historical and contemporary traditions. Clients recognise such resonances during sessions and workshops, recalling walks made by their ancestors and often report that they feel empowered to take this work outside the therapy context, back into their creative and cultural life.

> *With each step we rise, pull away from the Earth, against gravity, then fall back to Earth, repeating a pattern that has metaphoric resonances.*
>
> (Feldenkrais teacher workshop participant)

## Green Studio

Eco therapy invites clients to enter into sensitive contact with nature and their own embodied life, to support trust in their own sensory and intuitive bodily experience, within the larger containing body-mind of nature. Nature contact or immersion can of itself prompt feelings of safety, belonging and empowering appreciation of one's place in the web of life and unique personal agency, all supportive components of trauma recovery. The urge to bond, to gain oxytocin-enhancing proximity and attachment to a safe person or place, to reduce anxiety in the face of perceived threat, is a natural survival mechanism, reflected in our hormonal system function (Heim et al., 2009). Inviting clients to venture outdoors to seek out mirrors of their suffering, to look for comfort, 'allies' or 'remedies' for that suffering, or sometimes challengers and questioners, within the immediate natural environment, is a complementary, resource-based, self-care skill. It offers a positive, actively creative alternative to a repeated, compulsive return to harmful, addictive substances or abusive relationships. While formal research is needed to make claims regarding evidence, anecdotal feedback from my clients often focuses on their having found 'something better to do' (art with nature) long term than their old habits.

As well as feeling held, affirmed and connected, some clients respond to sensory contact with nature with an intense 'opening' and accompanying vulnerability, which in turn may awaken deeper, sometimes negative, experiences of boundary loosening, permeability or violation. One role of the eco therapist is to be awake to such existential sensitivity and the risk of destabilising, re-traumatising or evoking defensive hostility and armouring and to provide appropriate pre- or post-activity grounding in, or supportive focus on, somatic and creative self-care skills.

> *We made a little art-paradise here in the garden.*
>
> (Participant, Youth Empowerment Project)

## Rediscovering the Body as First Ground: Somatic Awareness

> *I liked drawing on the floor, on the ground, it helped a lot to have somewhere to hold me. I felt safer. I wanted to lie down and press my whole body into the paper where I had painted, and rest like a child, maybe for the first time since I was a child.*
>
> (Psychologist, training workshop participant)

**Figure 7.3** Gestural drawing. Drawing from the breath and inner rhythm

Artist: Kaori Igarashi. Photo: B. A'Court, printed with permission

It is a premise of much holistic health care that, given the correct conducive environment, natural living systems tend to be self-regulating, often capable of self-repair. A challenge for therapy is how to co-create with our clients a therapeutic environment such that people's natural psyche-somatic self-healing capacities are activated, consciously engaged with and supported. To facilitate this, as summarised by Moshe Feldenkrais and core practices in the meditative movement disciplines of Scaravelli Yoga and Authentic Movement, we 'need to create the conditions that enable us to feel ourselves' (Adler, 2002; Feldenkrais, 2009, 1972, 1977, 1990; Scaravelli, 1991, 2011), thereby freeing ourselves from a 'psychopathology of insensibility' (McIntosh, 2008). Muscular effort creates a kind of intensity, 'noise' that obscures subtle bodily changes, and can mask our sensitivity to somatic signals as to who we really are in body and mind (Kurtz, 2008, p. 9). Just as mindfulness relaxes our efforts towards self and emotional containment, suppression and management, so that we can perceive without constriction whatever emotion is arising in that moment (Kurtz, 2008, p. 9), so movement and activity with minimum effort and without strain to reach a preconceived pace or posture relaxes bodily defences, so that we can open to conscious awareness of our body's structure and functioning. We may feel blissful, streaming sensations of life in our body, the 'sound of biological optimism in our bones' (Dellinger, 2016) as well as sensing ways in which we have grown, through conditioning, to embody societal concepts, beliefs, values and constricting taboos.

> *I was drawing on the floor and it was as if my whole body was humming, really happily humming, and 'drawing' felt easy, like I don't have to struggle so much in life, I'm ok, really, I'm alive, humming with life and I like the circles and swirls I made, lovely lines criss-crossing, patterns everywhere.*
>
> (Workshop participant)

**Figure 7.4** Embodiment. Gestural drawing from authentic movement

Artist: Laura Pickerill. Photo: B. A'Court, printed with permission

Similar awakening shifts often occur during authentic, gestural movement and mark-making expressive of subjective experiences, where we can observe the body's natural and acquired functioning, without criticism or interference. Clients often describe these as 'liberating' as they bypass or override pre-existing conditioned strictures about playful freedom of movement and authentic, exploratory expression we might call forms of social 'nakedness'. Earth-based art therapy encourages art-making as inquiry into experience; as an uncontrived, potentially relatively effortless process of non-doing, as natural as breathing or meditation, that can unfold under our relaxed gaze and transform as clients learn to trust the therapist, the art therapy process, their own physical capacity and the surrounding field, to allow spontaneous expression to arise, be safely witnessed, contained and responded to.

## Body Contact With Art Works

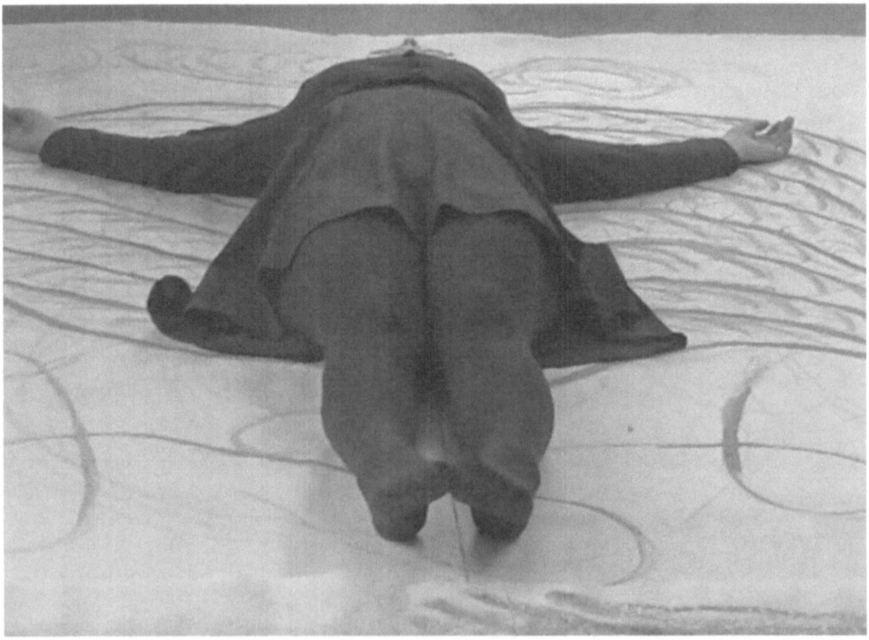

**Figure 7.5** Somatic sensing: Lying across a gestural 'lung' drawing

Photo: B. A'Court

The embodying of art works is now familiar within the creative therapies, as is the opportunity offered by some therapists to work outdoors, take outdoor walks, talking while walking and making art (Berger, 2008; Jordan, 2013; Kopytin and Rugh, 2016). Less recorded is body contact with art works in art therapy—touching, standing, lying or sitting on, or close beside, an image to somatically experience its impact. Walking from one image towards another is, to the best of my knowledge, relatively unexplored as part of the art therapeutic process, as is the restorative power of spontaneous, improvised creation of ritual pathways from art works (A'Court, in Kopytin and Rugh, 2016, pp. 47–77), which are then walked and reflected upon. The power of contact came to my attention initially while working with visually impaired clients who could sense colours through their skin. When other group members tried this, not only could they distinguish the colours, but sensed other qualities as well and their somatic systems registered many other sensations and gross bodily reactions in response to the art, often illuminating personal issues or autobiographical material.

Sitting and standing on art works often occurs spontaneously when clients make larger than body size paintings which they then feel an impulse to enter. Direct bodily contact typically facilitates sensory awareness, enabling attention to specific body parts or symptoms, often bringing surprising comfort and relaxation to these problematic body areas. Full body contact with, and movement within, large-scale art works has also facilitated, among my clients, awareness of personal space, boundaries and identity, status and role, rights of self-expression and movement, while also aiding visualisation and enhancing somatic sensing.

**Figure 7.6** Somatic sensing: Finding my place in the painted landscape

Artist: Workshop participants. Photo: B. A'Court, printed with permission

*As soon as I'd painted it I knew I had to lie down . . . pressed my stomach to the picture and just lay. The painful tense feeling in my abdomen went away. My belly liked pressing into the floor, the earth I had painted. I felt a really big woman, what a great feeling!*

(Training workshop participant)

In group sessions, spontaneous or invited combining and placing large images made by sub-groups into whole-group fields can call up the desire to directly, physically engage by sitting on, or laying, body areas on the art, catalysing many strong body-mind, insightful experiences able to shift traumatic perceptions. In other sessions, the group's impulse, or task, is to intentionally create a path from their images and to travel through it. Walking the painted path or landscape, in groups or individually, each person is held within a safe gaze and boundary, witnessed by the others. This Pathworking process evokes both very personal stories, and collective, cultural narratives, and can reveal and 'move' psychological states, as described more fully later.

## *Solvitur Ambulando*: Walking as Part of a Resource-Based Approach

We have vivid, imagistic linguistic idioms to express body-mind states such as shock and defeat, as when life has 'swept the rug from under us', 'the ground from under our feet' and circumstances have 'brought us to our knees'. Committed walking clubs and programmes aspire to getting unhappy, sedentary people 'back on their feet', supporting their 'steps to recovery' from illness, injury, surgery, addiction or to alleviate the ailments of ageing, helping people to once more 'stand tall' 'on their own two feet.' Gait is also being recognised as a predictive indicator of, as well as a remedial resource for, changes in brain structure, psychological health issues and dementia (Holtzer, Wang and Verghese, 2012).

Walking involves direction and agency and implies willingness and energy for change, all significant qualities in therapy and 'is a sort of living symbol for taking the initiative; the body reminds the mind that together they are in control and not passive victims of circumstance' (Ford, 2011, p. 107). Lawrence (1999) describes Eye Movement Desensitization Reprocessing (EMDR; Shapiro, 2001) as a special form of Ego State Psychotherapy (Watkins and Watkins, 1997) which loosens traumatic reaction-patterns, allowing new possibilities to simultaneously arise in the mind. He suggests that during mindful and/or relaxed walking we also enter a special ego-state, where the therapist facilitates the 'integration of needy ego states with resource states and mediation of conflicts between ego states' as well as 'communication, cooperation, and mutual appreciation within the family of parts, increasing their ability to work as a democratic team' (Lawrence, 1999, p. 1).

Historically, visionary artists, writers, inventors, composers, mathematicians and scientists have testified to the integrative effects of walking and its contribution to creativity, and inventiveness 'outside the box', the 'resource'-ability of this basic life activity to bring together and harmonise diverse areas of the body-mind. 'Learning to think in patterns of relationships, in sensations divorced from the fixity of words, allows us to find hidden resources and the ability to make new patterns, to carry over patterns of relationship from one discipline to another' (Feldenkrais, 1981, p. 35).

Typically, walkers experience body-mind and imagination coming into synchrony. Walking appears to both calm and slow abstract thinking, bringing the mind present to embodied reality while also freeing the imaginative mind, allowing it to take flights of imagination and open to eruptive new thoughts. Such subjective synchrony of body-mind-environment is expressed in feelings of 'attunement'; connection and harmonious belonging. Walking often brings a spaciousness to the thinking mind, in which feelings may intensify, flow freely, be more fully experienced in an embodied way, as this client so eloquently describes:

> *It was only when I walked from my painting that I really got what those feelings were, as if they were there living in the space between the two paintings, the two states. Only when I slowed right down and walked could I feel them (the feelings) something dark hiding there, I'm sweating. [client shivers and shakes body]*

Walking is also recognised as a way to loosen repetitive cycles and vortices of negative rumination (Bratman et al., 2015), colouring our thoughts more optimistically via the functioning of endorphins and oxytocin, amongst other physiological processes. 'Problems', from the emotional to the mathematical, have long been observed to unravel and self-liberate in natural, seemingly effortless, intuitive ways as new, unexpectedly relevant information arrives from the whole field of our body-mind-environment.

Walking, particularly in rural, green environments (Roe and Aspinall, 2011) may be regarded as a component of a resource-based approach (Schmidt, 1999) to bring simple, appreciative awareness to the life of the body, its radical potential for self-regulation, to illustrate the nature of dissociation and pain and the habits and correlates of mental suffering, while simultaneously drawing attention to, and providing inspiring resources from, the immediate surroundings, the client's present, physical reality. Walking has a role in facilitating clients to engage with positive resources prior to, and alongside, exploring traumatic experience: providing somatic experiences of balance, familiar ease, repetitive, rocking, rhythmic comfort (Chown, 2014), feedback from the moving-forwards body parts in a sense of simple autonomy, in the context of a reciprocal relationship with the changing surroundings, even indoors, all contributing to an overall state of body-mind, providing new information, and potential inspiration (Paulsen, 1994, 1995, 1996),

When we practice disengaging from immediately expressing our experience in words, which also delineate and define our experience, and engage in sensory thinking, we may experience our

> *personal life-force, energy or power as it is seen in many cultural traditions as a flow – called Prana, Chi or which is utterly connected to the flow of life force from the Earth we walk on and our well-being dependent on harmony within our ecological field.*
>
> (Dellinger, 2016, p. 1)

My session observations appear to support the traditionally recognised complex, multi-faceted power the simple act of walking has to simultaneously;

- Relax and loosen fixed familiar concepts, facilitate cognitive fluidity, enhance receptivity and openness to new forms of thought, imagination and feeling, allowing syntheses of familiar elements into new meaning constellations, in particular being a catalyst for experiences of connection and inter-being.
- Temporarily free our minds to wander free from defined agendas and aims, allowing memories, dreams/visions, knowledge to fluidly mingle with current somatic experience, leading us to find and follow trails of 'clues' in our environment; patterns and synchronicities subtly and obliquely relevant to our concerns, as scryers and diviners reading the signs we meet.
- Allow us to intentionally alter our focus of attention, away from complex or painful concerns towards the sensory, here and now, to attend to, and feel re-connected with sensuous, pleasurable, uplifting and inspiring somatic experiences and the objects which evoke these.

'The idea is to find your own pathway to bliss' (Campbell and Kudler, 2004, p. xxvi).

Art-making often forms a phased narrative; of accessing imagery, absorbedly engaging with it and emerging from it as from a journey or daydream.

Art itself has been called a 'map to self-discovery' (Roth, quoted in Cameron, 1997, p. 87). The image of 'the way', the journey of life, is ancient and ubiquitous throughout cultures and religious traditions. Its archetypal qualities, resonances and the wisdom embodied in associated archaic practices can inform and support our creative-expressive therapy.

> *It can be very satisfying to discover that one can indeed walk through sadness and out of it.*
>
> (Davidson, 1995, p. 76)

Walking slowly from one painted image to the next, feelings associated with learned patterns of behaviour and expression can arise and be felt, sometimes for the first time. Integration is enabled by the slow, rhythmic walking, as the body-mind loosens its grip on resistant over-control. Relaxed, uncontrived or intentionally mindful walking may also catalyse the two different types of insight within Buddhist psychology and in psychotherapy, as identified by Fulton and Siegel (in Germer, Siegel and Fulton, 2016, pp. 41–43).

- Insight as psychological understanding of thought forms and feelings as they arise, their content and possible origins in prior attitudes developed out of trauma and conditioning.
- Insight into the nature and process of the thinking mind itself; thoughts moment-to-moment, spontaneously arising, changing and dissolving, the 'groundless' nature of our existence and how we contribute to suffering when we expect, crave for and habitually strive to create permanence and demand that life fit our fixed idea/mental concept.

Just as 'each moment arises anew from a multiplicity of contributing factors' (Germer et al., 2013, p. 71), mindful walking, with each step, yields a new view and creates and reveals new dynamic relationships with surrounding life.

> *I don't know how I would have found them (the feelings) without the slow walking. I would have just switched to the next picture, been in the next state, I'd have missed how I got there, how I always get there, what I do inside to myself.*
>
> (Art therapy client)

## Bilateral Activity in Psyche-Somatic Healing

Research evidence is accruing for the role of bilateral stimulation in art therapy (McNamee, 2003, 2004, 2006; Shapiro, 2001; Talwar, 2007; Tripp,

2007; Urhausen, 2015). The alternating bilateral movement involved in play with objects and the use of art media has been observed to accelerate information processing and the neural network connections involved in psychological healing (Schmidt, 1999, pp. 1–2). Instead of left-right eye movement between positive and negative images, or art-making which involves lateral visual scanning, walking is also a potential trauma recovery resource: naturally bilaterally stimulating, it is correlated with a number of physiological processes contributing to overall well-being, cognitive flexibility and creativity in children (Hillman, Erickson, and Kramer, 2008), physical health and reduced cognitive degeneration/dementia (Erickson et al., 2011), improved psyche-somatic conditions and beneficial for disabling and some degenerative conditions (Bratman, 2015).

The photographer-therapist Shibata Bennett's *Structural Listening Touch* (2013) combines pendulation and tensegrity (Levine, 2010, pp. 74–78) in facilitating movement which mirrors the 'involuntary, internal rocking back & forth between expansion and contraction' (Bennett, 2011, p. 1), a rhythmic feature Levine considered evolutionary and saw in many human activities, physical and mental-emotional, and which is also a feature of walking: extending one leg, opening the pelvic area, followed by closing and then extending the other leg, creating lateral sway, spinal flexing and gentle pivoting of the torso.

Specific walking practices stimulate powerful cognitive and physical benefits for patients with Parkinson's disease and its associated movement impairments; marching, taking large strides with exaggerated bilateral extension of both arms and legs and Tai Chi, which works on axial mobility, also a feature of ordinary walking (Morris, Iansek, Matyas and Summers, 1996). Combining standing, walking and large-scale drawing, using the long muscles as done by pre-literary infants, can enable a person with advanced Parkinson's to create tremor-free, shapely forms and enjoy a degree of fluidity in smooth, balanced body movement (A'Court, 2016 unpublished). Embodied visualisation of walking with large strides along a straight path is also advised to help with actual mobility and reduce falls for some Parkinson's sufferers.

Slow, mindful walking brings a focus to the detail of our bilateral, embodied experience and can reveal to awareness dualities and polarities within our body-mind, cognitive attitudes expressed in body posture, gesture and other expressive qualities. Out of our bilateral movement linked with art-making emergent unconscious information arises, because, as one of my clients said, 'it has somewhere to go to be received and reorganised'.

In reviewing research that suggests clinical benefits, environmental enrichment of cognitive function or neurological correlates of walking (Erickson et al., 2011) we need to distinguish the components of walking:

**Figure 7.7** Drawing astride outside with impaired mobility

Artist: Chris Brown. Photo: B. A'Court, printed with permission

- The anatomical, kinaesthetic, bilateral and spatial motion of walking itself: the structurally diagonal and pivotal relationships between body parts as we walk and the relationship to deep brain stimulation and other processes affected by bilateral processing. General characteristics of balance, rhythm, fluidity, speed, size of pace and the many correlated physiological changes stimulated, such as effects on heart rate, the release of endorphins and neurotrophic factors.
- The specific setting and context of the walking and the walker's interactions with this, from therapy room, to city street, to rural wilderness, in particular, the health benefits of walking in close sensory and imaginative contact with nature, and the many numinous encounters it provides with non-human wild-life and processes.

Each of these has its specific and combined influence on the body-mind and symptoms of the walker (Holtzer, Wang and Verghese, 2012).

## Wandering Body, Wandering Mind: The Journey From Fragmentation to Wholeness

Western European education for problem-solving has historically involved two complementary processes; analytic de-construction and reduction of a complex phenomenon to discern and identify contributing elements and dynamics, followed by re-construction in new configurations, or integrating newly arriving information from the unconscious, from the wider context and field. Dismemberment and remembering, the return from fragmented or dissociated thought, into embodied presence and memory, appears in a many powerful and resilient ancient myths from the tale of Isis and Osiris to the Arctic tales of Sedna. Bodily and material disintegration can be a metaphor for the loss of a central organising principle, presence and sense of autonomy, as can occur in many anxiety, fear and psychotic states. In art therapy this is often visible in the art work, where, for example, the cognitive fragmentation of dementia and damage following a stroke often appear as loose, unattached lines strewn haphazardly across the page, with no synthesising pattern or coherent image to connect them.

Walking as a complexly co-ordinated activity seems capable of enhancing mental organisation and a remembering; a coming back into one's body with awareness and memory of continuity and connection. The linear flow of a walk mirrors the narrative flow of our cognition exemplified in story and our sense of a continuous identity, and the metaphor of the therapeutic or healing 'journey'.

> *A synchrony of body, mind and imagination producing creative synthesis occurs as we wander and simultaneously allow 'our ordinary, vagabond attention.'*
>
> (De Botton, 2005, p. 141)

### *Example: Walking in the Therapy Studio, Weaving a Path Between Painting and Paints*

I have described elsewhere (A'Court, 2016, p. 57) the client who spontaneously placed the paints and her art work at several paces' distance, necessitating a walk between them every few brush strokes, until, over several weeks, my own somatic impression of her sessions became one of constant movement back and forth, as she painted and walked to create large, dynamic paintings whilst intermittently speaking about her traumatic childhood abuse. Within six weeks she had dramatically reduced her anxiety, anguish, self-doubt and feelings of hopelessness and disempowerment, and felt free to return to her work, home and family.

Shortly after this, a paper was published by an American art therapist (since removed from circulation) describing her similar observations, and subsequently Talwar (2007) published her Trauma Protocol. I have used this setup since with many clients, and seen others choose it for themselves, appearing to facilitate the re-visiting and integration of long buried feelings.

## Passage: Stepping Beyond the Known

Much therapy involves healing the obstacles to freedom and flow in a life after disruptive, paralysing or compulsively repetitive trauma. Addictive repetition compulsion for familiar harmful states has to be met with commitment, as moving beyond the known is learned and practiced. Ritual aspects of creative art processes can offer a supportive vehicle for this and other transformative processes.

Walking may mark the shift from feeling trapped or stuck in post-traumatic freeze-appease mode, to experiencing some understanding, freedom of choice and movement, a shift from fearful immobility to the ability to move away from abuse or neglect. Some of my child clients would weave webs of coloured wool across the therapy room, tying door handles to chairs, table legs to window latches, making the room impassable, seemingly inescapable from within and impenetrable from outside, expressing the complex dynamics between powerlessness, safety, freedom of movement and control. This blending of profoundly painful experience and memories of danger, with physically trapping play, evokes archetypal fairy tales where children become lost, captured and imprisoned by dangerous adult beings while out walking. It seemed to mark a stage in the establishment of trust in me as therapist and the therapy setting itself. I could enter and survive inside the desolate and terrifying mind 'prison' with them and together we could, each week, find a way out.

Ritual, with which art therapy shares many roots, typically combines elements of:

- Self-, social- and contextual awareness in the individual;
- Vision and appreciation of the creative potential, as yet unborn, or undisciplined, undedicated, power of the person and their life to come;

- Sequences of creative, symbolic and physical action involving colourful and dramatic symbolic decoration, walking and dancing;
- Participation and witnessing by one or more closely involved others who support the person's progress and transformation.

Across many cultures, ritual is a traditional medium for maintaining and repairing humans' relationship with the field of Earth and our non-human kin. Ritual walks, marches, religious processions and ceremonial rites of passage embody long lineages of mythic significance, artistic heritage and spiritual power. The rite of 'passage', the stepping and walking away from, across a transition zone, towards another place, is a crucial spatial and psychologically metaphoric process, involving the approach to, standing at and crossing a potent threshold, entering a place of new identity, responsibilities, roles and potential, symbolically achieved by walking between representations, through actual or constructed doorways, gates, under built arches or green boughs, into water, across fire, by dark or light. In passing from one place or state to enter another, we forgo the possibility of return to pre-initiate status. We know too much and are changed.

Art therapists have for some decades integrated client-centred and therapist-client co-created rituals, into therapy as embodied, witnessed personal transformation. In the art-based constellations and ceremonial pathworking described here, this process of passage, conducted with sensitive attention to present body-mind-field qualities and dynamics, can be seen to contribute to, confirm and anchor in the body-mind shifts in awareness and the emergence of insight during therapy. Clients may spontaneously, or be invited to, stand on or closely beside an image they have made, become somatically aware of their systemic responses and then step off and begin to move away from this first image, towards a second or third in a series. Bringing mindfulness to somatic shifts, emergent memories and associations occurring with each move can bring a deepened embodied awareness of the significance of the images and their connections. Walking away from conflict is a theme that arises in work with couples. It may constitute essential self-rescue, but slowing down a fantasised 'walk-out' in a ritualised way, using images and symbolic paces, can bring to light subtle and complex workings of mind that enable insight and compassion to flow.

## Walking Constellations and Installations

This process is most effective where clients already have some somatic sensitivity, or are developing this through participation in other embodied activities. The client paints a series of images, or creates a series of installations outdoors, each an expression of an aspect of their situation. It is important that the client, whatever prior thoughts they may have had, selects in the present moment four or five features, persons or dynamics of the situation most emotionally charged and expressively represents these, allowing bodily experience and impulses to infuse the marks with energy. After the images have been placed around the space, the client visits each in turn, walks towards, touches, stands or sits on or beside them, and witnesses arising somatic reactions, noting any insights. Having heard from this part of the field, the client is invited to step off and away from each image slowly so that the subtle shifting in experience can be felt in the body and connected to other embodied experience. Sometimes this first step is repeated increasingly slowly to allow this to be fully experienced and then the client proceeds slowly towards the next image noticing somatic changes with every step.

The process is often dramatic, with facial skin colour, posture, temperature, flexibility, balance, apparent solidity, weight and coordination, all shifting visibly and significantly with each step. Memories and images spontaneously break through and unexpected connections are made. Aspects of the self or situational field we literally 'turn our back on', 'walk out on', literally 'overstep' or 'overlook' in passing, become accessible via our sensory and anatomical systems. Leaving an image of a seemingly dangerous situation or threatening person, we may feel the full bodily impact of our action, our latent power, our insecurity and fear of the unknown and experience a desire to retreat back to known danger.

This art therapy client describes a common phenomenon using an installation to resolve a complex situation:

> *I put one of my pictures near the door (to the corridor). I already felt something when I put it there, I nearly put it outside the room . . . wasn't sure I wanted to go there. Then I placed the other pictures. I'd had this problem, this decision, for months—which way to go? As soon as I stood and started to walk my body knew, it knew where to be, where to walk. It was easy.*
>
> (Art therapy client)

Several attempts may be needed to allow the body-mind to shift, re-align and feel congruently able to walk on. Following this, grounding art-making can anchor the revised body sense and positive orientation. Such witnessed walking from art works, both indoors and outside, can reveal and reconnect us with our embodied knowledge and the larger field of our self in gentle and natural ways beyond simply looking at, and verbally reflecting on, our art.

### *Example: Walking the Chakras*

An art therapist supervisee made a series of paintings, in the colours traditionally associated with each of the body's energy centres or chakras. On each image she placed an accompanying, colour-matched, handmade clay pot. She worked with these using embodiment techniques, initially arranging the pictures with their pots in the room. The linear structure of standing on each image in sequence, with somatic awareness, then walking from this to the next image seemed, we agreed, to mirror the alignment of the chakra energy centres in the body and was an appropriate modality to use to explore her professional work and related home-life issues.

Stepping from the first base chakra image, she felt 'loved, connected' to her tribe and family but identified a 'heavy sticky feeling' as the 'holding power' of conditioned roles and expectations regarding her work life and a degree of 'masculinising' herself to 'keep doing and make things happen' out of fear and the difficulty of stepping out of and away from this. Her left leg suddenly appeared to me as insubstantial, uninhabited, and I found it difficult to focus my eyes or see it clearly. She reported that her legs felt dead, limp, unable to hold her up, and she felt and appeared unbalanced, one leg longer and stronger than the other, as if she might fall. This led to an exploration by stepping ever more slowly forwards and back again, to discern in detail the precise sensations, emotions and associations evoked by this situation. The emergent insight was accompanied by her being able to step forwards in a totally different way, her legs suddenly appearing full, alive with substance, gravity and balance. She commented that this 'could not have happened without the walking'. The spatial embodiment had felt 'pivotal' in creating the shift in her understanding. For myself as witness, this was a dramatic experience of visual shape-shifting.

In subsequent sessions she repeated this procedure of standing on an image, becoming aware of the somatic reactions and then sensing when the impulse came to move to the next image. Standing on the red base chakra painting, she glowed, felt strongly grounded and rooted, adopted a pleasurable hip-swaying 'skiing posture'. However, stepping off this image she experienced two very different sets of feelings, depending on which leg she led with. By repeatedly stepping away and returning she was able to identify, as she led with her right leg, this shadow tendency to identify as a doer who 'left the ground behind' and left herself 'cut off from the earth' with her whole right side lacking in energy. Leading with her left leg, she 'took the ground' with her and grew taller as she described feeling her spine flexing and energy flowing smoothly up her whole body. She walked between the base and sacral chakra images, occasionally picking up either image and holding it against her body, noticing the sensory experiences and repeating the steps until she felt a shift towards how she wanted to be. Over several sessions this process revealed embodied knowledge, sometimes via unexpected, apparently obtuse, metaphoric images and word-play that erupted during a single or few slow steps. The somatic responses facilitated accessing and feeling her inherited, conditioned, conceptual world, and the slow walk was crucial to discovering the connections between aspects of herself, enabling these to be integrated and moved beyond.

Feldenkrais teacher, Ruthy Alon, articulated this aspect of our neural plasticity, using movement to

> *challenge the non-supportive habits that reside in our subconscious minds . . . awaken in the nervous system that innate, primal wisdom which enables it to correct its own actions. . . . re-educating adults' neuro-motor functioning towards restoring innocent grace, efficiency and ease.*
>
> (Alon, 1996, p. 5)

Combining this with mindful art-making and the intimate truths embodied in personal art works we have a rich, trans-disciplinary approach to uncovering the seeds of our conditioning, our shadow selves, in the spaces between breaths, marks and walked steps.

## On Insecure Ground: Transitions

It has long been recognised that a certain insecurity or ungrounded-ness accompanies transitions from one place to another, one activity to another (Sivertsen, 1978). Self-soothing, personal and cultural rituals or addictive, obsessive behaviours often arise to fill the uncertain space with known activity. Mindful walking between images allows clear experience and observation of such intervals between aspects of the personality, identity and biography, and provides opportunities to fill them with embodiment, awakening sensory pleasure or pain, witnessing awareness, acceptance and understanding. In therapy, the edge of change is often a risk point accompanied by feelings of external insecurity or threat. Fear, avoidance, loss and emptiness often follow our release or ejection from a status quo and precede our arrival at a new state and can trigger reversion, regression or immobility (Sivertsen, 1978 and personal communication, 1977).

### *Example: Edges, Thresholds and Portals; 'Nailed to the Doorstep'*

Thresholds therefore are often a valuable environmental metaphor and those within the zone of the therapy may take on special significance: images of portals, rainbow arches, doorways, gates, rivers, shorelines and walls often occur spontaneously in the art during such times. Embodying these, a client may stand or begin to walk under an imagined or constructed arch or approach and step over a threshold which may be simply a drawn line on the floor, the door to the outside from the therapy studio or an installation created for this symbolic purpose. In 'Communion of Subjects' (A'Court, 2016, p. 57) I describe how this embodiment and walking an image can liberate frozen conceptualisation and catalyse insight in the client via somatic memory.

A client, who recognised a current situation was stimulating memories of a painful childhood dilemma, used the bodily metaphor of being 'nailed to the doorstep'; immobilised between painful alternatives. Embodying this, she stood, 'swaying and amplifying her movements in tiny increments, she explored possible directions of movement, risking extending her body and her play the space behind and ahead of her' (A'Court, 2016, pp. 55–56).

After many repetitions she was able to take a single step, simultaneously loosening a new way of seeing, re-framing the 'doorstep' as a 'springboard for action' and creative engagement, 'the safe harbour or home-base I could safely return to and earth' (A'Court, 2016). From this new position and perspective on her situation, her past acquired a revised meaning, and her future a sense of creative potential, which she then expressed and grounded in an art-work she called 'Goddess Feet'.

## Pathworking

The process I have called Pathworking (A'Court, 2016, p. 58) developed over many years, evolving from observed instances of the path arising as a potent image in art therapy and the perceived benefits to individual clients, students and groups of taking this into body-sized, walked form. Collectively constructing a path from art works or found, gathered materials and objects to hand, each person has the opportunity to walk the path, in silence or to commentate aloud on their subjective flow of feelings, thoughts, associations and imagery. A vital component of this ritualised process of movement and transition is the witnessing by fellow group members, who mirror and may amplify, in their own somatic and emotional experiences and, if invited to, in physical and verbal feedback, as in traditional Greek drama, the inner life of the walker. Witnesses are encouraged to monitor their own authentic responses—somatic, emotional and physical—and to offer feedback at the end, or participatory support if invited to, during the person's walk. As with the dramatic chorus, witnesses may experience urges to accompany, offer support, push someone along or off their path, obstruct or playfully divert them, mirroring for the walker some inner process usefully brought to their awareness.

In essence this process brings the body and environment to the fore within art therapy. Some groups take their painted paths outdoors or construct paths outside in nature, often integrating some natural feature to include archetypal symbols such as a climb, a threshold, portal or obstruction and a zone to be entered and crossed. Participants in therapy and personal development courses have used Pathworking outdoors to create their own ceremonies of passage, using the location's natural and man-made features; trees, ponds, slopes, steps, archways, doors, gates and wild, uncultivated areas to create a route to be walked, symbolic of the process they are either embarking on or graduating from. This has the added dimension of nature's responses during each person's walk and especially noticeable are the activities of wind, sun and rain, rainbows, birds, deer and insects in behaving in ways that resonate with the participants' subjectivity and trigger perceptual and emotional shifts.

**Figure 7.8** Assembling paintings into a path

Artists: Waldorf Teachers Group. Photo: B. A'Court, printed with permission

### *Example: Training Completion Ceremonies*

Eco village trainings invite students to create personal talismans for their future work, embodying what they hope to contribute or for a specific natural location. Following this, one such group constructed a path on the communal green of the Findhorn eco village and each student took time to walk it. Despite being a young group in a public area, the process took on a solemnity as each person made their own deliberate, mindful rite of passage, walking symbolically from student status to emergent activist empowered with an academically acknowledged skill-set. An apple tree near the start of the walk took on significance as a resting place, its fruit offered round to all at the celebratory finish. Similar completion and graduation walks have been made by art and art therapy students, counsellors, social workers, women's groups, teachers, managers needing to see a spatial representation and experience ritual embodiment of their roles, team dynamics and future planning process, clients facing decisions between alternative 'life paths' or at the end of a period of therapy. The 'path' may be constructed by the group but the materials take on vividly unique appearances and meanings for each individual as they walk with full presence of mind and body.

Where a severe obstacle appears to be blocking a client's further progress, a path may be made which includes, towards its end, a gap, an empty zone, appearing as a place of unknown to be stepped into, entered and crossed to arrive at the desired destination. This has been used to represent a whole life story, or a specific situation. Clients may face painful inner voices approaching the 'gap', manifesting visible somatic signs at the edge; sweating, fearful facial expression, muscular tension, trembling or tears. Finally stepping off the known edge into this now highly emotionally charged, symbolic empty zone, and crossing it to arrive at a longed-for destination, becomes a powerful body-mind experience for most participants, reflected in dramatically visible somatic and emotional transformations witnessed by the therapist or rest of the group.

With some preparatory training to develop somatic awareness, this process can also be done 'virtually' using miniature sculpted self-figures, who are 'walked' mindfully along the path by hand, meeting and traversing obstacles. This can have an equivalent somatic potency, resonance and effectiveness in catalysing transformative insights for the client into their body-mind state and life.

In other mindful walks within the studio, clients may follow clues, allowing their attention to be led by 'flirts' (Mindell, 2000, p. 215) and other subtle inner promptings, drawn to objects in the studio that 'call' them, or they may go in active search, venturing outside the studio into nature, finding something that resonates with their current mind-state or symptom in a form of mythic quest. All the while walking in a swaying rhythm, gently cradling

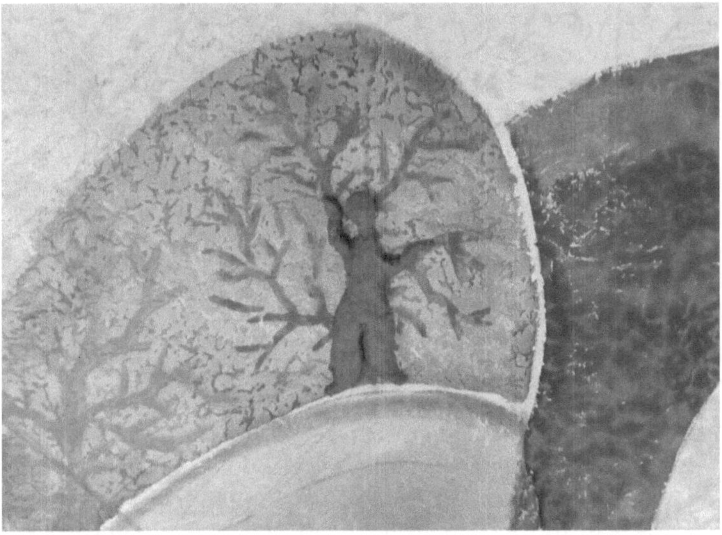

**Figure 7.9** Mini pathworking

Photo: B. A'Court

their 'problem' situation in mind, they may choose to let it, or its bodily expression in symptoms, guide them. This closely resembles the resource-focused approach Schmidt (1999) describes and can have similar results; in a changed perspective, reframing a new, more optimistic view of the 'problem' as an opportunity for growth, learning or greater freedom. Similarly, in Mindell's (2007, 2010) vector walking, a structured form of walking meditation used in Process Work, slow walking in and between directions representing different experiences, facilitates awareness of the stream of spontaneously arising shifts in movements, sensations and feelings and the emergence of deeper knowledge (Mindell, 2007, p. 62). The walker then walks a direction corresponding to a deeper or more inclusive 'meta-view' or 'superposition', described as 'mythical knowledge accessed through inner work practices' (Mindell, 2007, p. 63). Vector Walking is described by Murphy (2008) in her master's paper, 'Lorn and Loan and Oansome: An Exploration of Myth and the Tools to Elicit Mythic Potential':

> *by allowing the body to choose its own direction in answer to questions and problems that disturb the mind, path walking shifts attention from deliberate mental processes to emergent forms of consciousness through sensing, feeling, and moving. This gives rise to spontaneous experiences which are in some way answers to the problems or questions of the everyday mind.*
>
> (p. 62)

Murphy also describes Diamond and Jones's (2004) use of walking different paths between problems. Finding a meta- or super-path revealed strongly charged and denied personal power dynamics, and in this technique the person's 'superpower' was found to be directly related to their problem area (Diamond and Jones, 2004, unpublished course programme). In this way walked passage between a series of art works, or through an installation formed of dismembered art works indoors or out, becomes a journey in which awareness unfolds as much, or more vividly, in the transitions as in the individual art works.

### *Example: School Students and Youth Empowerment Programmes*

Walking became part of sessions with school students and young adults with histories of abuse or deprivation, who have grown up in care homes and/or experienced foster placement breakdown, educational difficulties and law-breaking. Sometimes the only art a child or adult initially feels able to make is to use their own hands or feet as templates to be painted and decorated: making a footprint or drawing the outline, creating a background and filling the forms and surrounding area with symbolic pattern and imagery. The often spontaneous desire then is to step onto the painted feet and play with standing in and walking from them, trying them on as a metaphor for trying out new identities and ambitions. Rescued teenagers in a children's refuge in Nepal, culturally familiar with images of decorated feet, were enthusiastically responsive to this activity and used it to express strong and complex feelings about their lives and future. A typical spontaneous choice in early sessions is to paint their own or each other's feet and walk, making footprints across the paper, creating a pattern or path effect to link parts already painted or to create the starting structure for a painting. The image may then be hung vertically to be completed, or kept on the floor to be developed into a more explicit path which can then be walked again when dry.

Sometimes a painting or painted pair of feet may be taken outside to be placed in a symbolic location that extends creative possibilities. A therapeutic ritual walk may begin inside on the painted soles and pass through the door to an archway, pool or steps outside, providing the basis for ritual procession of transition, completion and safe crossing of a threshold to a new state. Children and young adults get pleasure and affirmation from these simple processes, more adventurous than hand-printing, needing footwear to be shed and whole body involvement, as they step onto their art, often amidst laughter and dancing around. Their comments express recognition, explicit or subliminal, that with every step we separate, depart, transit, fall, land and arrive, we make a journey, passing from one place and state to another:

**Figure 7.10** A collaged path of feet and leaf prints

Artist: Gabrielle Haworth Buist, printed with permission

> *I feel brilliant, like I have left that old self I was behind, I'm not going back to him.*
>
> *I walked right out of it. I'm going my own way. Every step felt like a long way, like I was really moving on.*
>
> *I like the pattern with the lines and my feet—I'm climbing out of a cage. Even if I go back there I know I can just walk out, I didn't know that before.*
>
> *I like my path I made, it's like nature, with all the leaves stuck on, a nice place I'd like to be with all my family, I feel really proud I made something, a place of my own. I feel physically brilliant—my body feels fit, how does that happen?*
>
> (Workshop participants)

## Everyday Pilgrimage

Walking is part of almost every ordinary life maintenance activity, providing perfect opportunities to witness ourselves in body and mind and develop awareness. Inspired both by Buddhism's focus on the breath and ordinary life tasks as opportunities to practice mindfulness, and the art work of Merles Laderman Ukeles (1992) to 'honour and confirm the dignity of maintenance work as a life sustaining, life enhancing activity' (Phillips, 1995, p. 183), I devised a ritualised activity (A'Court, 2016, p. 60) for transforming walks into daily self-care. Clients often arrive into therapy longing to feel more alive, to emerge from absent, disembodied, unaware states in which many routine walks and maintenance tasks are carried out and which leave them unmoved, untouched by details, overlooking and not receiving nourishing, sensory delight from life. Bringing fully embodied presence to everyday walks, we can ritualise our routines and reframe them as ceremonial; discovering how it is to walk with attentiveness, in receptive, appreciative awareness, touched, able to be moved and inspired by all we encounter. Embodied intuition may inform us as to right action; as when a client was painting her daily walk to school with her child along a busy road and with breath and observation it became a playful, educational adventure well before school started, where the urban trees, patterned pavements, curious roadside hedges and window boxes were all met with presence, emptied of judgement as dull, boring, ugly. Awareness of 'nature' and 'wildness' in the body, mind and environment equips clients with the ability to take embodied imagination and mindfulness into their routine life-maintenance tasks, completely transforming some clients' habitual, numb, depressive, bodymind states with long-term positive effects on their relationship with their everyday locality.

> *My whole work week has been transformed by this exercise—I see so much green now that I missed before. It's the city but there's so much growing . . . and flowers, I just didn't see it or smell it before.*
>
> (Administrator, workshop participant)

There is a long literary, mythic, cultural history to the eruption or return of feral urges to 'vagabond'; in the vigour and restless youthful and mid-age desire to pit one's body and mind into and against the elements in an endurance sporting challenge, the need at times of intense psychological challenge, growth, change and traumatic loss, to walk away, the religious calling to retreat into an intentionally renunciate lifestyle, to embark on a walking pilgrimage to mark transition to the 'third' age of life, entering eldership, and to reconnect with our root Earth-connection. Earth-based art therapy workshops for professionals, intensives and retreats for personal development allow space for such feelings to surface and be received and responded to by others and the surrounding, witnessing natural world. Walking rituals provide a framework for playful and serious exploration of, and practice in, walking away from, through and beyond into personally new, uncharted territory. In the process they may become authentic rites of passage for participants.

*I discovered a lot on my tiny mini-pilgrimage (mindful walk), mainly that it is up to me how I experience the world, & my everyday life, that was empowering. I feel excited to go home & try it out.*

(Teacher, workshop participant)

Earth-based art therapy invites the client to turn both inwards to subtle sensations and out towards the shimmering, responsive non-human world, and to make unique and spontaneous syntheses from their explorations. Clients often make walks out into the garden or woods and dunes close to my studio, and return having discovered places and had numinous encounters which are then explored further in their art work. They may take a 'story string' in which to tie a knot, marking each significant moment or encounter on their walk. This typically brings into brighter focus their awareness of events in the immediate vicinity and field of synchronicity of all that is occurring at this same time as part of their walk. In one client's words: 'everything became significant, became part of the story of my walk . . . I couldn't leave anything out.' The natural world and human creative imagination are synchronised in such moments and meaning resides in the interplay between these two expressions of Nature. Abram has described how language serves to 'renew reciprocity with the surrounding powers of the Earth and sky, to invoke kinship in which the vitality of each place, moreover, is rejuvenated by the human enactment and enchantment of the storied events that crouch within it.'

*Intelligence is no longer ours alone but is a property of the Earth . . . each ecology seems to have its own particular intelligence, its unique vernacular of soil and leaf and sky.*

(Abram, 1997, p. 262)

Art-making 'on the hoof' with the invitation to nature to participate achieves a similar sense of shared intelligence and reciprocity, where the client experiences direct, precise, immediate feedback on their intimate relationship with all that is, often in challenge to their cognitive paradigm of individuality and separateness. Permission to include spontaneous walking alongside art-making invites clients to enter a world of infinite materials, numinous encounters and a 'magical', non-ordinary, but very ordinary, opportunity; to give respectful attention to intuitive, embodied perceptions which they may typically ignore, marginalise or override. Old habits of thought and action, witnessed as walked, can be re-worked in somatically anchored ways. Working 'outside the box' of language, in the plastic arts we can practice open-ended exploration and the self-reflection our species needs.

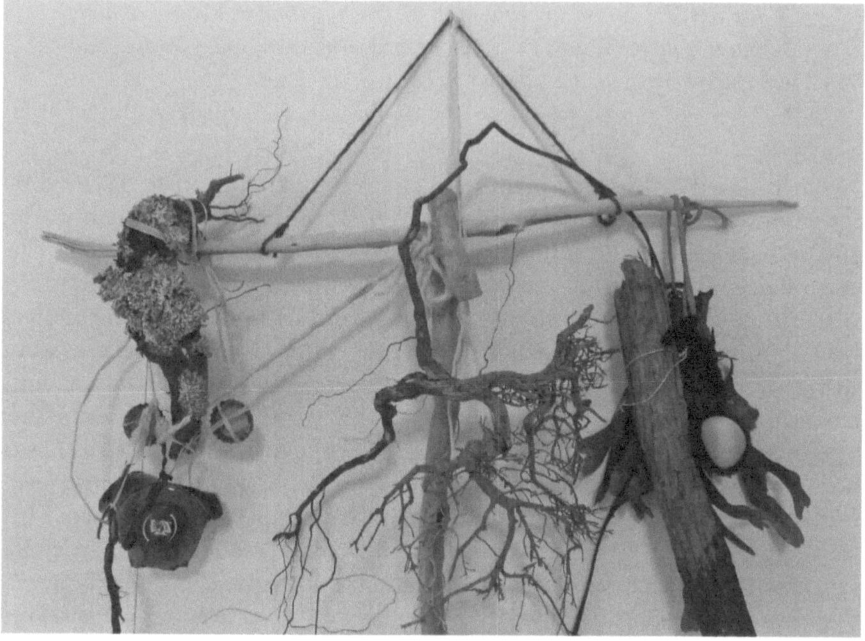

**Figure 7.11** Natural beach-combed media

Artist: Jane Rasbash. Photo: B. A'Court, printed with permission

## Intimate Cosmos

The aims of ecopsychology are ambitious; to develop theories and practices which enhance human relationship with the Earth, which in turn enhances vitality within natural systems. Where we cultivate appropriately for the ecology, vegetation and wildlife thrive sustainably. While the industrialised world spends billions on medical technology to see inside our bodies, we may have dormant, undeveloped, natural faculties for inner seeing, listening and imaging, just as our 'physical' body's neurological and biochemical processes are known to be influenced and transformed by how we use our mind. Millennia of spiritual and health practitioners concerned with fundamental questions of liberation from suffering perceived that our own body-mind has its own tendencies to ensnare us in compulsively repeated harmful acts and past pains, as expressed in this question: 'What is the climate which enables our nervous system to reach an updated decision, free of past conditioning? (Alon, 1996, p. 35).

All therapy engages with our innate neuroplasticity via processes which facilitate the updating and transforming of distorting, self-destructive habits. Eco psychology and nature-based therapies often highlight the grave consequences of our collective 'habits' of mind and body and have a role to play in

**Figure 7.12** Somatic exploration of a developing theme in a sequence of art works

Artist: Training workshop participant. Photo: B. A'Court, printed with permission

awakening and sustaining respectful, embodied, inquiring awareness in all aspects of our experience, if we can create 'the conditions which return us to the primal state of mind characterised by open-ended exploration' (Alon, 1996, p. 35).

Indigenous and traditional forms of health care and medicine struggle for credibility alongside allopathic medicine and its scientific models. However, the World Health Organisation's Traditional Medicine Strategy, 2014–2023 recommends a global strategy of respectful integration between these diverse cognitions' associated coherent approaches to healing. Eco therapies with their origins in Earth-based, cultural traditions have a role to play in bridging this polarity and developing practices based in traditional, more embodied and ecologically sensitive knowledge systems.

Buddhism- and quantum science–informed systemic therapies acknowledge that each individual sentient being has power via its mode and quality of embodiment and what this inevitably transmits and radiates. In her sensitive work with the body-mind in movement, Alon (1996) aspired to restore three qualities inspirational in our pursuit of ecological harmony and dynamic peace and often apparent in authentic, embodied art making, responsive to our deepest interdependent nature; 'innocent grace, efficiency and ease' of movement in body and mind. The transformation of an illusory 'individual' impacts the entire field of life, via nature's deep continuum of being, as we breathe and move in unavoidable intimacy with all beings. In this context, mindful arts therapies, embedded within, and informed by nature, provide opportunities for connecting deeply radical, subversive and

**Figure 7.13** Restore the Earth Conference workshop

Artist: Conference delegate. Photo: B. A'Court, printed with permission creative impulses with both our immediate locality and social and practical activities, and the wider field of global, ecological processes.

It is traditionally said that enlightenment is 'as close as the nose on our face', yet we cannot recognise it. A growing body of research across diverse fields from neuroscience to public health suggests that there is wisdom inherent in the act of walking (like breathing) which is similarly accessible. It is my hope that the examples in this chapter contribute to recognition of and respect for Earthed, embodied knowledge, and wiser ways to sustain and heal our body-minds via the creativity of our naturally imaginative body within the web of creation.

## Note

* I refer readers to Shibata Bennett's work on the myofascial network, hypothetically one of our highly sensitive bodily systems for attuning inner-to-outer events.

## References

Abram, D. (1997). *The spell of the sensuous: Perception and language in a more-than-human world.* New York: Vintage Books.

A'Court, B. (2016). 'A communion of subjects': Holistic eco-art therapy: Integrating embodiment and environment in art therapy. In A. Kopytin and M. Rugh (Eds.), *Green Studio: Nature and the arts in therapy* (pp. 47–76). New York: Nova.

Adler, J. (2002). *Offering from the conscious body: The discipline of authentic movement.* Rochester, VT: Inner Traditions.

Alon, R. (1996). *Mindful spontaneity: Returning to natural movement.* Berkeley, CA: North Atlantic Books.

Bennett, H.S. (2011). Myofascial Mechanoreceptors. Retrieved from https://firstofnine.wordpress.com/2011/09/23/myofascial-mechanorecptors/

Bennett, H. S. (2011). Tensegrity got rhythm [Blog post]. Retrieved from https://firstofnine.wordpress.com/2011/07/16/tensegrity-got-rhythm/

Berger, R. (2008). Building a home in nature: an innovative framework for practice. *Journal of Humanistic Psychology, 48*(2), 264–279.

Bohm, D. (1980). *Causality and chance in modern physics.* Philadelphia: University of Pennsylvania Press.

Bratman, G. N., Hamilton, J. P., Hahn, K. S., Daily, G. C., and Gross, J. J. (2015). Nature experience reduces rumination and subgenual prefrontal cortex activation. *Proceedings of the National Academy of Sciences of the USA, 112*(28), 8567–8572. doi:10.1073/pnas.1510459112

Cameron, J. (1997). *Vein of gold: A journey into your creative heart.* London: Pan Books.

Campbell, J., and Kudler, D. (Eds.). (2004). *Pathways to bliss: Mythology and personal transformation.* Novato, CA: New World Library.

Chevalier, G., Melvin, G., and Barsotti, T. (2015). One-hour contact with the Earth's surface (grounding) improves inflammation and blood flow—A randomized, double-blind, pilot study. *Health, 7,* 1022–1059. doi:10.4236/health.2015.78119

Chevalier, G., Sinatra, S., Oschman, J. L., Sokal, K., and Sokal, P. (2012). Earthing: Health implications of reconnecting the human body to the Earth's surface electrons. *Journal of Environmental Public Health*. doi:10.1155/2012/291541

Chown, A. (2014). *Play therapy outdoors*. London: Jessica Kingsley.

Davidson, R. (1980, 1995). *Tracks: A woman's solo trek across 1700 miles of Australian outback*. London: Vintage.

Dellinger, S. (2016). What does it mean to feel the sound of "biological optimism" in your bones? [Blog post]. Retrieved from https://movelikeachild.wordpress.com/2016/03/03/feeling-the-sounds-of-biological-optimism-in-your-bones

Diamond, J., and Jones, L. S. (2004). *A path made by walking: Process work in practice*. Portland, OR: Lao Tse Press.

Erickson, K., Voss, M.W., Prakash, R.S., Basak, C., Szabo, A., Chaddock, L., . . . Kramer, A.F. (2011). Exercise training increases size of hippocampus and improves memory. *Proceedings of the National Academy of Sciences of the USA*, *108*(7), 3017–3022. doi:10.1073/pnas.1015950108

Feldenkrais, M. (1972, 1977, 1990). *Awareness through movement: Health exercises for personal growth*. New York: Harper and Row.

Feldenkrais, M. (1981). *The elusive obvious*. Cupertino, CA: Meta.

Feldenkrais, M. (2009). *Awareness through movement: Easy-to-do health exercises to improve your posture, vision, imagination, and personal awareness*. San Francisco: Harper One.

Ford, A. (2011). *The art of mindful walking: Meditations on the path*. Lewes: Leaping Hare Press.

Germer, C. K., Siegel, R., and Fulton, P. (Eds.). (2016). *Mindfulness and psychotherapy* (2nd ed.). New York: Guilford Press.

Heim, C., Young, L. J., Newport, D. J., Mletzko, T., Miller, A. H., and Nemeroff, C. B. (2009). Lower CSF oxytocin concentrations in women with a history of childhood abuse. *Molecular Psychiatry*, *14*(10), 954–958. doi:10.1038/mp.2008.112

Hillman, C., Erickson, K., and Kramer, A. (2008). Be smart, exercise your heart: Exercise effects on brain and cognition. *Natural Review of Neuroscience*, *9*(1), 58–65.

Holtzer, R., Wang, C., and Verghese, J. (2012). The relationship between attention and gait in aging: Facts and fallacies. *Motor Control*, *16*(1), 64–80.

Jardine, D. (2002). Speaking with a boneless tongue. *Philosophy of Mathematics Education Journal*, *16*.

Jordan, M. (2013). *Taking therapy outside – a narrative inquiry into counselling and psychotherapy in outdoor natural spaces*. PhD thesis, University of Brighton, UK. http://eprints.brighton.ac.uk/13232/1/Final%202014%20pdf%20PHD%20.pdf

Kopytin, A. (2016). Environmentally and eco-based phototherapy: Ecotherapeutic application of photography as an expressive medium. In A. Kopytin and M. Rugh (Eds.), *Green Studio: Nature and the arts in therapy* (pp. 155–178). New York: Nova.

Kopytin, A., and Rugh, M. (2016). Introduction. In A. Kopytin and M. Rugh (Eds.), *Green Studio: Nature and the arts in therapy* (pp. vii–xviii). New York: Nova.

Kurtz, R. (2008). A little history. *Hakomi Forum*, 19–20–21.

Laderman Ukeles, M. (1992, Summer). A journey: Earth/city/flow. *Art Journal*, *51*(2), 12–14.

Lakoff, G., and Nunez, R. (2000, 2001). *Where mathematics comes from: How the embodied mind brings mathematics into being.* New York: Basic Books.

Lawrence, M. (1999, March). EMDR as a special form of ego state psychotherapy: Part two. *EMDRIA Newsletter* (reprint). https://www.emdrworks.org/Downloads/Ego%20state%20sfesp2.pdf

Levine, P. (2010). *In an unspoken voice: How the body releases trauma and restores goodness.* Berkeley, CA: North Atlantic Books.

Macy, J. (2007). *World as lover, world as self: Courage for global justice and ecological renewal.* Berkeley, CA: Parallax Press.

Malchiodi, C. (2016). Expressive arts therapy and self-regulation. Retrieved from www.psychologytoday.com/blog/arts-and-health/201603/expressive-arts-therapy-and-self-regulation

McIntosh, A. (2008). *Hell and high water: Climate change, hope and the human condition.* Edinburgh: Birlinn.

McNamee, C. (2003). Bilateral art: Facilitating systemic integration and balance. *Arts in Psychotherapy, 30*(5), 283–292.

McNamee, C. (2004). Using both sides of the brain: Experiences that integrate art and talk therapy through scribble drawings. *Journal of the American Art Therapy Association, 21*(3), 136–142.

McNamee, C. (2006). Experiences in bilateral art: A retrospective study. *Journal of the American Art Therapy Association, 23*(1), 7–13.

McNerney, S. (2011). A brief guide to embodied cognition: Why you are not your brain [Blog post]. *Scientific American,* November 4. http://blogs.scientificamerican.com/guest-blog/a-brief-guide-to-embodied-cognition-why-you-are-not-your-brain

Mindell, A. (2000). *Dreaming while awake: Techniques for 24 hour lucid dreaming.* Charlottesville, VA: Hampton Roads.

Mindell, A. (2007). *Earth-based psychology in shamanism, physics and Taoism. Path awareness in the teachings of Don Juan, Richard Feynman and Lao Tse.* Portland, OR: Lao Tse Press.

Mindell, A. (2010). *Process mind: A user's guide to connecting with the mind of God.* Wheaton, IL: Quest Books.

Morris, M. E., and Iansek, R. (1996). Characteristics of motor disturbance in Parkinson's disease and strategies for movement rehabilitation. *Human Movement Science, 15,* 649–669.

Morris, M., Iansek, R., Matyas, T., and Summers, J. (1996). Stride length regulation in Parkinson's disease: Normalization strategies and underlying mechanisms. *Brain, 119,* 551–568.

Murphy, A. (2008). *Lorn and loan and oansome: An exploration of myth and the tools to elicit mythic potential.* Retrieved from www.processwork.org/files/Finalprojects/AnneM.pdf

Ober, C., Sinatra, S. T., and Zucker, M. (2014). *Earthing: The most important health discovery ever?* (2nd ed.). Laguna Beach, CA: Basic Health Publications.

Paulsen, S. (1994). *Ego state disorders: Dissociative but not multiple.* EMDRIA Conference presentation.

Paulsen, S. (1995). Eye movement desensitization and reprocessing: Its cautious use in the dissociative disorders. *Dissociation, 8*(1), 32–44.

Paulsen, S. (1996). *Using internal dialogue to achieve maximum EMDR results.* EMDRIA Conference presentation.

Phillips, P. (1995). Maintenance activity: Creating a climate for change. In Nina Felshin (Ed.) *But is it art: The spirit of art as activism* (pp. 165–193). Seattle, WA: Bay Press.

Roe, J., and Aspinall, P. (2011). The restorative benefits of walking in urban and rural settings in adults with good and poor mental health. *Health and Place, 17*(1), 103–130. Retrieved from www.sciencedirect.com/science/article/pii/S1353829210001322

Scaravelli, V. (1991, 2011). *Awakening the spine.* San Francisco: Harper One.

Schmidt, S. J. (1999, March). Resource-focused EMDR: Integration of ego state therapy, alternating bilateral stimulation, and art therapy. *EMDRIA Newsletter* (reprint).

Shapiro, F. (2001). *Eye movement desensitization and reprocessing (EMDR).* New York: Guilford Press.

Shibata Bennett, H. (2013). Compassion arts PDX [Blog]. Retrieved from www.compassionartspdx.com/

Sivertsen, N. (1978). Obsessional construing as activity interacting with surroundings, actions and content: In transition, bridges and semi-emptiness. In F. Fransella (Ed.), *Personal construct psychology* (pp. 135–151). London: Academic Press.

Steinberg, E. (2010). Promotion of health and biodynamic psychotherapy. *Psychotherapist, 11*, 8–9.

Talwar, S. (2007). Accessing traumatic memory through art making: An art therapy trauma protocol (ATTP). *Arts in Psychotherapy, 34*(1), 22–35.

Tripp, T. (2007). A short term therapy approach to processing trauma: Art therapy and bilateral stimulation. *Art Therapy: Journal of the American Art Therapy Association, 24*(4), 176–183.

Urhausen, M. T. (2015). Eye movement desensitization and reprocessing (EMDR) and art therapy with traumatized children. In C. Malchiodi (Ed.), *Creative interventions with traumatized children* (pp. 45–74). New York: Guilford Press.

Watkins, J. G., and Watkins, H. H. (1997). *Ego states: Theory and therapy.* New York: W. W. Norton.

# 8

# MARBLE HOUSE PROJECT

## The Creative Process Inspired by Nature

*Dina Schapiro*

### Introduction

> *Earth is not some fixed condition, but a creative process activated by polarity tensions requiring a high level of endurance. This creative process is not a clearly seen or predetermined pattern of action; it is rather a groping toward an ever more complete expression of the numinous mystery that is being revealed in this process. Groping implies a disquiet, an incompleteness; it also has the excitement of discovery, ecstatic transformation, and the advance toward new levels of integration.*
>
> (Berry, 1988, p. 220)

As creative art therapists, we are often perplexed as to why people do not participate in more forums that encourage creative outlets because it cleanses our body and mind of what we have absorbed from our environment. The explosion of art therapy coloring books are maddening to some in the creative arts therapy community, because it minimizes the dynamism of art therapy to a simple activity that makes you "feel good." Yet, what is happening around the world that is attracting people to want to color in that structured environment? Should we be focusing more on what is happening in our environment that is moving people to seek out structure in that form? And should we be advocating to study how our environment is stifling our creative process?

Creative arts therapists value the creative process and understand what role it plays in elevating consciousness for the individuals and the communities we work with. We understand that the creative process can only occur in the present moment because it is an active process; it's the act of being. Making art only happens in the present moment, and it is only in that moment that change can occur. "There is only a single moment in which we can truly be alive, and that is the present moment" (Thich Nhat Hanh, 2010, p. 26).

Because art making can only happen in the here and now, any issues that arise in that moment, whether they are past events or future anxieties, are in the present moment. And in that present moment (where our past is explored in the present) we can address them directly and affect a different or new outcome for our future. It is for those reasons that the Creative Arts Therapy Department chooses to have their retreats at the Marble House Project. They immerse themselves in Nature and return back to the main house to process ways of making the faculty more cohesive. In the last faculty retreat, the faculty spread out into Nature where they reflected on what they observed as it related to how they felt about being a creative arts therapist and how it impacted their teaching methods. Being immersed in Nature and returning into the structure of the house gave them the opportunity to relax and then gather and structure their experience so that it can be addressed and used in the department. In the book, *You Are Here*, Thich Nhat Hanh eloquently describes why issues can be explored in the present moment: "If we look deeply at the present moment, we see the past and the future in it . . . The past is always there, accessible" (Thich Nhat Hanh, 2010, p. 45).

Nature offers us a similar experience with time. Nature is active and alive at every moment. Because it is active from moment to moment, it is in a perpetual state of being present, of being in the creative process. It holds the past in its earth and its future in its roots, but it exists only in the present moment. When we reflect on Nature's creative process with that of our client's, we realize that the same actions we would take for ourselves is how we also need to treat Earth. The only way to heal the earth is to do it now. Only if we act now can the damages of yesterday begin to heal so that the future could seem more hopeful.

Both in Nature and with our clients, when the background (past) pushes toward the foreground (future), the present is created and an awareness surfaces. In this moment of awareness, the environment enhances and defines what is here and now, making us more aware of ourselves in relation to, and as part of, our environment. In that moment, we become One, and the creative process emerges like a seed filled with possibilities. Through the creative process, the people I work with slowly move toward awareness and consciousness, so that they can carve out new choices for themselves in their life. "When we act in full awareness, of even small things, it's possible to notice the motivation" (Thich Nhat Hanh, 2010, p. 11). The choices we make when we are conscious and aware are motivated by a deep grounded understanding of the whole system it will impact.

When the residents at Marble House Project move out from within the comforts of their housing and studios, they move deeper into Nature where a similar process occurs. I have often heard the artists say how difficult it is for them to stay in their studios because they feel compelled to walk into the woods and just be. We will often find a sculpture or installation that someone has left in the woods and in the quarry. These installations become part of Nature and over time will change. The sounds, smells and sensations they feel when they are in Nature inspire them to create, often changing unexpectedly, the direction of the intended work they came in with. They become extremely focused and often create art with no particular goal allowing one moment to take over the next. They are present, connected and aware. As an Artist Residency Program, we are interested in learning what is it about the artists relationship with Nature that impacts their creative process.

## The Physical Journey: Exploring Boundaries

What we look at on a daily basis affects the way we perceive the world and how we interact with it. As creative art therapists, we experience this with our clients as they create images on paper, reflecting their perception of the world inside of them that was impacted by the world outside of them. When the artists first arrive at the main house at Marble House Project, they are often taken aback by the structure. It is not often one sees a house, literally, made out of marble from top to bottom, on that scale. The house is in focus and Nature is the background. The house is front and center, scaling over the artists, in a sense distracting them at first from the Nature surrounding the house. How does this experience impact their journey toward their creative process?

It is fitting to begin this journey exploring the impact the house has on the artists as they descend into three weeks of complete immersion into the creative process. When we first purchased the Marble House Project property, there was a distinct relationship the main structure held with Nature. The house seemed obtrusive, cold and impenetrable. For over a century, the main living quarters were maintained in a way that mirrored their relationship with their environment (see Figure 8.1). The house is made out of hard stone that is heavy, thick and cold to the touch. Light bounces off the uneven, hand-chiseled surfaces of the stone while heat is slow to penetrate. Sound remains contained within the walls unless there is an invitation through narrow windows to listen. When the house was first built in the early 1800s it was not an easy task to heat the house, so openings were kept narrow and to a minimum, to prevent any heat leaving the house in the winter and perhaps cooler air in the summer. The walls protect anyone that is inside and barricade any unwanted guests from coming in. There is no flow or tranquil connection between the outside world and the inside world.

**Figure 8.1** Main Marble House 2016

Photo: Dina Schapiro

When the house was built, the purpose was not to connect to the outside world, but to have a disconnection from it. The house was created to protect against the cold Vermont winters and the unpredictable Nature of the wilderness. If a natural disaster occurred, the safest place would be inside those walls. The structure almost took on a human quality for me, reminding me of the clients that often come into my office experiencing the world around them as a threat. "Sigmund Freud wrote in his essay, '*Civilization and its discontents*': Against the dreaded external world one can only defend oneself by some kind of turning away from it" (Berry, 1988, p. 208). Their walls, often thick and impenetrable, gave my clients the sense of feeling emotionally safe. These walls serve as a defense mechanism, a means to protect the Self, for the sake of survival, yet, at the same time, they cause emotional isolation.

Disconnection is a defense against a threat from the outside world. Although initially a protective mechanism, prolonged isolation will inevitably stifle any growth. Fear and the constant threat of it depletes us from the nutrients we need for growing. Fear—and surviving the fear—is what often keeps us disconnected from the world around us. For my clients and the first inhabitants of that building, prolonged exposure to external threat and the fear of it created an unhealthy state of being.

When life is viewed from a survival perspective, there is no time for self-realization, consciousness and awareness. Threat causes us to close up and protect what is left, which is the exact opposite of what is needed in order to become aware and conscious. Kenny Ausubel described fear and its costly effects on the environment and society in a very similar way:

> *Fear and rumors of war have led us to build vast military-industrial complexes that have caused environmental harm, the magnitude of which will shadow us for generations. The supreme irony is that our security anxiety has made the world perilously insecure.*
>
> (Ausubel, 2012, p. 144)

The structure of the house seems to reflect a protective stance, perhaps in response to external threats, which limits the connection to Nature. When the house was built, Nature was viewed as the Other, separate from the builders. This was a contradictory attitude considering how dependent they were on Nature for survival. Only in recent years, as we've become more conscious of our environment, have we recognized that if we depend on something for our survival, we actually need to take care of it and find sustainable ways to relate with it. Survival and the fear of Nature created thick walls that disconnected the outside from the inside. Having such a thick disconnection gave the residents at that time permission to ignore the actual devastation they were causing to the land around them.

At the time the house was being built, Vermont had been completely deforested (see Figure 8.2). Because of the residents' fear of Nature, a great

**Figure 8.2** Main Marble House 1908

Photo: Dina Schapiro

disconnect occurred, which allowed them to abuse the land around them without any immediate consequence. I find myself reflecting on how often our fears cause us to be internally preoccupied, distracting us from noticing anything around us. When we are disconnected, we have no awareness that we are part of a greater system, in order to maintain sustainable growth. We are unaware of the suffering of others and are too busy trying to keep up the disconnection. Often when we do notice the Other, be it Nature or anything other than the Self, we are so exhausted from the effort that we feel defeated and impotent in having any impact toward change. Unfortunately, feeling unable to cause change can push us further in, and that inward motion comes at a cost to our planet, communities and relationships. It also interferes with our natural ability to enter and develop the creative process.

Not being able to enter the creative process stifles any opportunity we might have to become aware of ourselves and the Other. "Awareness of motivation plays a central role in the path of liberation" (Goldstein, 2013, p. 12). Being able to enter the creative process opens us up to possibilities not seen before. It is empowering and motivating to find connections and reasons for integration. When we are aware of the Other, we can begin the process of reintegration that inevitably brings about change. It is motivating to know that we can impact change.

For close to 200 years, the house grew and expanded while still maintaining a separation between external and internal worlds. Contrary to the cold, sharp lines of the exterior, the inside of the house is warm and complicated. Made up of mostly wood, it absorbs the sound and holds the temperature of the house, acting as a buffer against the cold stone. The rooms move in and out of each other, creating a certain flow or momentum. A rhythm is created by twisting and turning from one space into the next. Each room is connected by an inviting threshold that pulls you into another completely different space. Yet, with all of the new additions made throughout the boom of the industrial age, no inviting thresholds were created between the external world and the inside dwelling. Nature was still viewed as a threat and no healthy connections to the outside world were made.

There was a missed opportunity to experience reintegration into the environment. There were no thresholds to stand on where awareness of the Other could happen. An awareness was missed by not having the consciousness to connect the external world with the internal world—a connection we all need in order to gain awareness of our Selves in relation to Other, so that better choices can be made and we can move forward into a more sustainable existence. "Restoring the environment is about creating and sustaining healthy, functional relationships—both between people and nature and between people and people. As in any long-term relationship" (Ausubel, 2012, p. 43). Because we believe our relationships with Nature impact our creative process, studying the structure the residents live in gives us an opportunity to re-evaluate what will work for our residency as we evolve.

## The Physical Journey: Moving Outward Toward Awareness

At Marble House, when you step out into the formal garden, you feel safe, contained and in control. There is a square pool at the front of the garden that seems to be endlessly supplied by the spring at the top of the hill. There is a marble tea house that can protect you from the heat or summer rain (see Figures 8.3 and 8.4). The garden is beautiful to look at, but a disconnection is still felt. Perhaps it is the formality and the structure that keeps the artists at a distance. The artists can look at the garden, sit on the grass or benches, but it remains separate. Perspective is limited because the presence of the house is still dominant compared to them. They are not fully integrated into Nature and perhaps not fully aware of their possibilities.

Berry (1988) states, "Any particular activity must find its place within the larger life systems itself. This change of scale is one of the most significant aspects in the change of consciousness that is needed" (p. 44). The scale of the house and the limiting (yet protective) garden fence restrict the artist's

**Figure 8.3** Formal garden

Photo: Dina Schapiro

**Figure 8.4** The outside tea house

Photo: Dina Schapiro

ability to place themselves in the larger context of Nature. Despite this limitation, it is not fully disconnected; the artist moves into a new space and begins to work toward reintegration.

The parameters of the garden are surrounded by heavy marble walls (see Figure 8.4). It is as if moving out into the wild needed some imposed structure, for fear something might happen. The marble was carefully laid out stretching across the lawn in horizontal and vertical lines. And then as you follow the lines through the gates and up the curving staircases, you reach the top of the hill, where a pergola is perched overlooking the garden (see Figure 8.5). As they leave the protective linear marble structures and begin to climb, they are physically challenged by the angle of the hill. They are breathing heavy and sweating, becoming more animal, more natural with each step.

At the top of the hill, overlooking the structures, they have ascended into a new threshold. The pergola (see Figure 8.5) is affixed between two places, that of the old (see Figure 8.6) and that of the new (see Figure 8.7). If they are facing the house, they see the more structured, protected self, if they turn around they face a lesser structured but wilder self. The pergola represents the pinnacle between letting go of our fear and moving toward it. At that point, the artist can descend into the protective comfort of what is known, or turn around and move toward the lesser known.

When the artist turns around and decides to move toward the lesser known, they are faced with a new perspective and a new context for Nature. No longer protected by the thick walls, they are bare and vulnerable against the flat land and the mountains. The mountains become the backdrop for the barn and farm and the artist can begin to experience scale and perspective

**Figure 8.5** Walking up to the pergola

Photo: Dina Schapiro

**Figure 8.6** Looking down at the formal garden

Photo: Dina Schapiro

**Figure 8.7** Farm and barns

Photo: Dina Schapiro

on a completely new level. Just a few steps back, the scale of Nature was familiar and in the context to the house and garden. On the farm and by the barn, the scale is entirely different and offers a completely new perspective for the artist as they attempt to figure out their place in the system. It is a less structured space so the artist can relax and let their guard down allowing for new experiences.

Being able to look at themselves in relation to the mountains, and look at the barn and farm in relation to the mountain, puts things into new perspectives. What seems to be grand now is Nature; there is nothing in between the artist and Nature except perspective. In that expanse, the artist experiences time and space in a whole new way, and begins to examine what it means to be a part of a system. Feeling part of a system is the beginning of integration.

The barn, farm and artist are working to integrate with each other and Nature. The barn, as the structure in the field, feels more part of Nature than separate because it is made of wood taken from the property; it is open and airy and inviting. Although the barn looks like it has always been there, we recently added it to the grounds to offer a gathering center that connects the greater community with the artist and the farm. The artists can move in and out through welcoming thresholds. The barn, farm and the artists are all shadowed by the great mountains; they are aware of it but not fully immersed in it. Their bodies and minds are exposed to the immensity of Nature, which reminds them of their vulnerabilities.

The distance and perspective gives them time to evaluate themselves against Nature. That crucial innocent vulnerability is the spark that sets off the journey toward the creative process. When the artists immerse themselves in the farm and look up at the open sky and across the tall mountains, they begin to internalize what they see. They can see the vastness inside of themselves is as limitlessness as Nature. They begin to look at themselves in context, comparing and contrasting, back and forth, who they are in relation to the Other.

This comparison could not happen if there was a disconnect from the Other. Comparison is an acknowledgment of the Other. When fear is a motivator to disconnect from Nature, there is no attempt to see Nature reflected in the Self. Fear prevents us from comparing and exploring differences, because exploring differences points out our vulnerabilities. Comparing only comes as awareness begins to grow. Comparing is only a small part in awareness but a crucial turning point in the creative process. Because when we compare we acknowledge diversity and diversity is essential for our survival. "Life . . . cross-pollinates and mutates. It builds resilience through diversity, decentralization, and redundancy, allowing for failure and building in safeguards to avoid the possibility of crashing the whole system at one" (Ausubel, 2012, p. 33). Comparing is often viewed as negative, but I believe a necessary act to go through as one begins to explore themselves.

For example: the preteen child who weeks before seventh grade did not care about what he wore or how he styled his hair, becomes hyper-aware and excruciatingly uncomfortable with his new awareness about himself. An uncomfortable awareness, that invites the boy to explore who he is. Once the artists begin to compare, they begin to explore themselves in a new way and try to express that creatively. "Creativity has been associated with a disequilibrium, a tension of forces, whether this be in a physical, biological, or consciousness context" (Berry, 1988, p. 217). Tension is needed in order to be pushed into awareness. Another key element in pushing the Artists into awareness is the farm.

Although the farm is structured, its beds are rounded and reflect a conscious effort on our part to mimic more organic forms found in Nature (see Figure 8.7). In this space the artists touch and play with the dirt, encouraged to let go further and connect with the earth. They begin the transformation of being separate to being a part of their environment. Being part of their environment comes with consciousness regarding impact and being impacted, cause and effect. By working in the garden, they are made aware of how systems impact each other. They feed the chickens who give them eggs, they pick tomatoes from a plant they just watered and dig into the earth to collect potatoes seeded by the previous residents. As they become aware of the systems put in place prior to that moment of picking, they reflect on the impact they will have on those who come after them. Time takes on a different mask in this perspective. By working on the land in the present moment, they become aware of what happed before them, and where it might lead. In that moment, they have become aware of a greater system. As Thomas Berry wrote: "We seldom get to our functional role within the creative intentions of the universe" (Berry, 1988, p. 25). On the farm, the artists begin to participate with Nature, gaining a clearer understanding of their part in the creative process that occurs in Nature at all times. The awareness of their part in Nature's creative process begins to mirror an awareness of their own creative process.

The barn and the farm also function as a space where other groups of systems merge. This part of the property hosts many community events that encourage non-residents to interact with the artists and the environment. It is in this space that the artists become aware that they are now part of Marble House Project.

> *In all of these societies spiritual movements took place, indicating that the ritual celebrations and codes of conduct needed to be supplemented by an interior intensity equal to the elaborate exterior enactments. At the center and along the margins of these classical ritual civilizations, spiritual movements appeared in order to intensify the energy resources of both the individual and the society and to enable them to function in a properly human mode.*
>
> (Berry, 1988, p. 26)

In this gathering space, artists and community members find themselves connecting to each other and to Nature in ways that bring the artist back from an individual experience to a collective experience. In that space, the creative process is inspired by the flow between inside and outside, the individual and the collective.

## The Artist's Final Journey

The goal of the residency program is to lead the artists through a transformative journey that is similar to the one we strive for with our clients. This journey is learned through observing our relationship with Nature and mimicking its natural systems that bring about a creative process. As the artists become more aware of themselves in Nature, they become more curious and are drawn to venture further into the wilderness. There is a path behind the first quarry that will draw the artists to venture into a new threshold. It is a kind of rite of passage that is not open to the public. It resembles a birth canal canopied by maple and birch leaves leading the artists into the most untamed part of the property.

When the artist emerges through the path, they find themselves in an abandoned quarry that has not been in production for over a century. The marble blocks lay untouched since the last day of production. The angular and horizontal lines have been brushed by time. They are chipped and seem less sharp. They no longer look out of place. Time, weather, oxygen and plants have transformed their colors from bright white to the now dark green brown and black earth colors (see Figure 8.8). The moss and ferns have

**Figure 8.8** Abandoned quarry

Photo: Dina Schapiro

found ways to get into the cracks and splits on the surface of the marble—sometimes completely covering it up. Nature has taken over and is breaking down the hard cold stone that a few hundred feet away seemed glorious and unbreakable. The melting snow and rainwater filter through the rocks and mountains settling and collecting where once a busy quarry production stood. The water encourages new life to form. The small fish are eaten by the bigger animals, who can find shelter among the blocks discarded by the quarry men.

The abandoned, overgrown quarry has developed a microclimate of its own—a wild and biodiverse space that is alive and present. There is a different sensation of time in this area of the property. The abandoned blocks are overtaken by Nature and create tension between past and future in the present moment. The enormous marble blocks that can withstand the test of time are slowly being taken over by growth. This tension creates an awareness unlike any other space on the property. In this space, there is constant movement between life and death; past, present and future. The blocks have been swallowed by Nature and slowly integrated into the whole system. The bold and obtrusive blocks are no longer the focus. Nature is neither in the background or the foreground, but all around and inside of the artist.

In this present moment, nothing is more important than the other. "Every being has its own interior, its self, its mystery, its numinous aspect. To deprive any being of this sacred quality is to disrupt the larger order of the universe" (Berry, 1988, p. 134). When awareness breaks through all life forms, systems are truly equal because there is a mutual dependence. This interdependent system is a cyclical and sustainable system where all impact and are impacted by it. As the artist travels from the familiarity of the linear and structured spaces up into the more fluid and experiential land, they are invited to shed the history they hold with Nature. Through every threshold they cross, another layer is released and vulnerability exposed—a vulnerability that is uniquely human and essential to our creative process. "Our only hope is in a renewal of those primordial experiences out of which the shaping of our more sublime human qualities could take place" (Berry, 1988, p. 4). The artist has shed the layers that have kept them away from the unpredictable wild world. They are beginning to realize that they are part of Nature, that they are Nature. "Awareness of all-pervading mysterious energy articulated in the infinite variety of natural phenomena seems to be the primordial experience of human consciousness" (Berry, 1988, p. 24).

In this space, the artist has entered into the creative process that occurs in Nature and sees themselves as part of Nature, not apart from Nature. In this space, they come face-to-face with an ancient stone covered in new life, and they see that inside of themselves. Like the marble blocks, the artist begins to reintegrate back into Nature, changing their colors and softening their lines. The artist becomes aware of the cycle of life, of what has been there before them and what will come later. It is a recognition of life that they are part of, part of the creative process. They emerge in the present moment, aware of themselves because they recognize the Other exists in them as well.

## Conclusion

The transformative quality that Marble House Project offers the artists is influenced by the structures and natural environments of the property. The transformation depends on the many systems that were put in place prior to the artists reaching the quarry. There is a gradual rhythm that occurs leading up to the creative process. The artists that attend Marble House Project are selected by the previous years' artists. They are accepted into the residency after being voted on by the artists who have already experienced being there. The artists who attend this residency will always be conscious of their impact toward the next group of artists and aware of the artists that have come before them. This experience can be found on the farm when one group of artists plants the seeds for the next group that will be harvesting them. This is a sustainable system that encourages all the artists to become aware. The artists are carefully curated into groups of 8 to 10 in a session. The sessions last three weeks, and will always have writers, musicians, dancers, performers, sculptors, visual and digital artists, poets, journalists, and so forth. We believe that creating a biodiverse group will help inspire and encourage connections that will manifest as a result of the artists' creative process. "The practice of biomimicry requires community, not just with other organisms, but with people in other disciplines" (Ausubel, 2012, p. 34).

We believe that once the artist enters the main house, a transformation begins to happen. The artists who were carefully curated and placed in the house together begin to define themselves and their art. They cook for each other and eat together, creating a momentum that pushes their vulnerabilities. Each discipline shares their perspective and enriches the space by contributing their experiences. Like a seed surrounded by rich diverse nourishment it is encouraged to go outward and venture into the world, the Other. The inspiration from others outside of themselves motivates them to search, and the searching leads them to go outside where they can slowly walk up the hill into higher consciousness. As they leave the safety of the house, they begin to open up to what is around them. They explore the farm, connect in the barn, and walk up the hill to the quarry where they stand on the edge. In complete silence and total humility, they are present in the moment, where no one knows they are there except them, where the self melts away because everything exists in the here and now. "In reality the human activates the most profound dimension of the universe itself, its capacity to reflect on and celebrate itself in conscious self-awareness" (Berry, 1988, p. 132).

As with a session, a connection must be made and trust must be established before diving into the creative process, because getting there requires losing oneself and connecting to the whole at the same time. Being a small part of the system and being the system, being here and everywhere at the same time. In the creative process, time moves backwards and forwards while they are standing present. Nature holds these qualities, and all one needs is a moment to reflect and become aware of how alive and present Nature is.

Awareness is needed in order to recognize the qualities that Nature holds. Awareness means the external already exists within. This is why they must go through a transformation, a journey of undoing and reconnecting with Nature before they reach the quarry. When they become present and aware, their creative process begins to take form and ultimately expressed through their own modality. They are inspired by Nature because they are Nature. Ausubel writes that as we become more aware we begin to take our lessons from Nature, and we

> *grow food like a prairie, harness energy like a leaf, weave fibers like a spider . . . compute like a cell and run a business like a redwood forest. Quieting human cleverness is the first step in biomimicry. Next comes listening, then trying to echo what we hear.*
>
> (Ausubel, 2012, p. 33)

The creative process is just another lesson to be experienced by and learned from Nature. And the artist and Nature mirror each other, where they are equal, part of the same system and part of the whole, integrating and reintegrating themselves and their ideas as they become one, in the present moment, "Until the human is understood as a dimension of the earth, we have no secure basis for understanding any aspect of the human. We can understand the human only through the earth" (Berry, 1988, p. 219).

## References

Ausubel, K. (2012). *Dreaming the future: Reimagining civilization in the age of nature.* White River Junction, VT: Chelsea Green.

Berry, T. (1988). *The dream of the earth.* Berkeley, CA: Counterpoint.

Goldstein, J. (2013). *Mindfulness: A practical guide to awakening.* Boulder, CO: Sounds True.

Hanh, Thich Nhat. (2010). *You are here: Discovering the magic of the present moment.* Boston, MA: Shambhala.

# 9

# MUSIC-NATURE-THERAPY

## Outdoor Music Therapy and Other Nature-Related Approaches in Music Therapy

*Eric Pfeifer*

### Introduction

> *She looked me up at the library and liked an article I wrote fifteen years ago discussing Jung's notion of inventing a new therapy language for each patient. [. . .] I took it even further than Jung. I suggested we invent a new therapy for each patient, that we take seriously the notion of the uniqueness of each patient and develop a unique psychotherapy for each one.*
>
> (Yalom, 1997, p. 6)

Reading Yalom's popular novel, *Living on a Couch*, one will find this very interesting passage introducing the idea of not only inventing a new therapy language, but, even more, developing a unique psychotherapy for each patient. Of course, the task of doing so is not an easy one, and the psychotherapist has 'to be bold and creative enough to fashion a new therapy for each patient' (Yalom, 1997, p. 7). Nevertheless, these words create a perfect framework for what will now be explored in detail within this contribution.

To some extent, it (still) requires a lot of courage for a therapist to choose to work outdoors and/or in nature. Some therapists even conduct their outdoor sessions 'secretly', keeping them 'hidden', as they doubt whether their colleagues, other professionals or the authorities would support or approve of what they are doing. Regarding the therapists' stories collected by Jordan (2015, pp. 103–104, 119), some claim that they felt like they were transgressing or breaking the rules of therapy. They were anxious, and feared being seen by another therapist from their community while working outdoors.

On the other hand, the late Hans Zulliger—a famous Swiss child psychoanalyst and educationalist—once commented that one cannot make children with neurotic disorders lie down on a couch for the purpose of performing psychoanalytical sessions. He argued that, according to their state of development, children have to be allowed to be in motion. Interestingly, the therapeutic process was much smoother and more effective if he and his young patients left the therapy room behind and headed out for a walk in the nearby forest.

Zulliger even suggested going out for walks with adolescents as a therapeutic method, resulting in a concept known as 'Spaziergang-Behandlung' ('treatment-/therapy-walk'). In relation to the aforementioned notions by Yalom ('new therapy language' and 'unique psychotherapy' for each patient), Zulliger adds one more in the sense that it ought to be a therapist's objective to find the most practicable/passable route or path for each patient according to their age (Zulliger, 1973a, p. 192, 1973b, p. 428, 1990, p. 72).

Regarding the preceding given statements, nature could possibly be an essential element in creating new and suitable (music) therapeutic languages, or even (music) therapies for each patient. As Zulliger recognized years ago, transferring therapy to locations outside in nature is sometimes a very helpful adaption to the unique needs of an individual patient. Although this process of incorporating nature is, most likely, not at all a new one to music therapy (as to be displayed in the next chapter), and despite the fact that there could still be thoughts and feelings of anxiety and transgression in doing so, it is among the core obligations of a therapist to guide the 'pathway' of a therapeutic process alongside the patient's needs and requirements. To be more precise, the word 'therapy' etymologically implies the tasks of 'curing, healing, service done to the sick' (Harper, 2016). Consequently, therapy means to act in service of a patient. In other words, it is about creating and applying the individually adequate therapy, therapy language and route for each patient. And sometimes such a therapy, language and route works best outside of the therapy room and instead in a forest, near a lake, in a cave, in a mountain meadow and so forth. A certain amount of bravery may be needed in this case. Although placed in another context, Pavlicevic and Ansdell propose what could be decisive for the given subject matter, too:

> *Perhaps this is the key: [. . .] their courage to throw theoretical concerns to the wind when appropriate, to follow the needs of people and circumstances, asking not 'what is music therapy?' and 'what is a music therapist', but 'what do I need to do here, now?' They dare to follow where people and music lead.*
>
> (Pavlicevic and Ansdell, 2004, p. 30)

## Music Anthropological Background—A Brief View Into Human History

Music is an indispensable part of human society. Throughout human history, human beings have produced music. No matter the different ways and manner this music happened (to be), the main point is that no civilizations, cultures nor tribes were without music. Singing, making and playing music fostered community-building processes, supported healing rituals and held a prominent role in spiritual welfare and mental hygiene. Regarded from this perspective, music and music therapy could almost be understood as a kind of culture therapy (Timmermann, 2008a, pp. 79–81, 2008b, p. 85).

What is more, it is not only that music itself seems to have been influential and important in relation to health-caring intentions among the history of humankind, but to take it one step further, considering current research activities and publications, it is already possible to demonstrate connections between music, nature and possible curing objectives. Researchers have reported on caves that were used for shamanistic and curative purposes due to their particular resonance phenomena and acoustic impacts. To be more precise, some of these caves comprised a selection of colored and painted rocks, stalactites, stalagmites and spots. Hitting these resulted in very special tones, sounds and effects. One might wonder how these stony drums—or lithophones—had to be beaten in order to cure some prehistoric patient's migraine or to create the sounds of a passing horse. In fact, there were 'guidelines'. Within some caverns, paintings had been created on the walls to function as user manuals or prescription/package inserts showing how to do it right (Devereux, 2005, p. 19; Montagu, 2007, pp. 5–6; Reznikoff, 1995).

To put it in a nutshell, history offers quite a few illustrations of how the idea of bringing together nature, environment and music for the purposes of health care neither appears to be uncommon, nor recent from a present point of view. But, apart from that, to know that there is rational historic approval behind this, may give reason, reliability and confirmation to pursue further approaches. Obviously, back in the old days, there were no academically trained music therapists, clinical music therapy rooms, electric guitars and pianos available. The shamans, healers or 'music-making neanderpists' (Pfeifer, 2016, p. 119, in print) had to use stalactites and rocks as their drum sets, caverns as their music therapy rooms, and cave paintings as music therapy manuals in order to cure suffering and to foster health. Of course, this historical experience allows us to recognize the conjunction of nature and (music) therapy as not to be something 'abnormal'. Actually, safe in the knowledge that such procedures have already existed a long time ago, this offers rich foundations on which theoretically and solidly argued models of nature-related music therapy can be generated.

## Defining Outdoor Music Therapy (OdMT)

To begin with, the following statements are mainly a summary of what has already been explained and published more thoroughly in other writings by the author of this contribution.[1] One of the most important perspectives is that Outdoor Music Therapy (OdMT) shall not be defined as a music therapy approach or school of practice in its own right, although there are some unique characteristics that will be dealt with later on. Perhaps a quote by Aasgaard originally describing 'musical environmental therapy' does good justice to summarizing the OdMT framework, too:

> *To regard musical environmental therapy as a school of practice in its own right is questionable, but it certainly has a focus which is unique.*
> (Aasgaard, 2001, p. 35)

OdMT is not a separate form of music therapy. It is a manifold and versatile idea within music therapy. OdMT still is music therapy with music therapy methods and interventions happening during the sessions. In this case, there seems to be no disparity or uniqueness. The differences lie in the material that is acquired, the surrounding and setting to be chosen for therapy and the expanded therapeutic relationship. There are particular options concerning space and time, the patients' needs, a therapist's skills and competences, as well as possible, enriching, multifaceted interdisciplinary collaborations with other therapeutic disciplines (nature, psycho-, physio-, occupational, body-oriented therapy, etc.). Above all, there is indeed an emphasis on nature, natural materials and surroundings. At this point, it is useful to focus precisely on the tag 'outdoor' in the compound 'Outdoor Music Therapy'.

OdMT can happen in the open—in nature, nearby a lake or on the beach, in forests, in caves—but not exclusively. And this is the essence when interpreting the term 'outdoor' here. The settings of OdMT are not restricted to the open country and nature. OdMT also occupies various other places and spaces to be found in the environment (underground car parks, mountain huts, caves, sports hall, etc.).[2] 'Outdoor' implies a kind of perspective and approach to just 'get out of the door', namely the therapy-room door. If we open this door (which sometimes is a real 'barrier') and step across the threshold, there is not only this open(ed) door, but also a whole new world of therapeutic possibilities and potentials opening up for the patient and the therapist. Therefore, OdMT shall be seen as, or act as, a sort of bolstering 'door-opener' (Pfeifer, 2012, pp. 10, 14), aiming to leave the common four walls behind, and exploring suitable and helpful places, rooms and space for our patients outside of the music-therapy room.

In short, OdMT may best be summarized as a generic or collective term describing a critical process of reflection and discussion concerning the application and acquisition of environmental, natural or outdoor settings and surroundings, materials and, therefore, altered therapeutic relationships in music therapy. Further details concerning these aspects will be discussed later.[3]

First and foremost, some key factors must be considered when working outdoors. Although OdMT offers various possibilities for extending beyond the typical setting of a music-therapy room, it is a definite must to keep in mind the needs of a patient. Whatever outdoor setting a music therapist chooses, she/he has to be aware that the patient should feel comfortable within the selected space. The surroundings shall be appropriate and not harmful to the patient's health, therapeutic process, personal development and personal state. Leaving the secure space of a music therapy room could evolve and lead into situations and atmospheres of sensory overload, overstimulation and anxiety. Imagine how frightening the extreme reverberation of a gorge, underground car park or the 'noisy' quality of a dark forest can be. Therapists must not put patients in such overwhelming and inundating settings!

Finally, it is not only about the patients—it is about the therapist's preferences and competences, too. If a therapist does not feel authentic and secure in outdoor settings (alpine meadows, mountain huts, big forests, etc.) this will, of course, not be supportive to a successful therapy process. Also, it does not really make sense if one starts to incorporate materials and instruments that one is unfamiliar with or does not like herself/himself, such as tools to create musical instruments, mossy tree branches as drum sticks, muddy stones as a percussion set. This could not just be counterproductive but also dangerous!

## Influences, Associated and Comparable Nature-Related Approaches in Music Therapy

Besides the aforementioned thinking required for OdMT in relation to outdoor settings, and the integration of nature and natural materials, there are other relevant developments and influences going on in the music therapy world. This chapter will name a few of them and provide a condensed overview. Among them are the works of Klar (2011, 2012). Calling himself an 'integrative-cinical-music-and-nature-and-mountaineer-forest-and-weather-water-meadow-fire-gorge-cave-therapist' (Klar, 2011, p. 6), Klar offers substantial descriptions of his music therapy outdoor activities in forests, on mountain sites, near riverbeds, at the bottom of gorges and so on. When conceiving similar projects, Klar's publications are informative and inspiring. Not only does he offer deeply touching insights of OdMT processes with children and adolescents, he gives advice and background knowledge of the therapeutic effects and application for specific natural materials, settings and elements (mountains, water, fire, wood, lakes, sea, etc.). According to Klar, nature has a strong influence on the therapeutic relationship and can support the self-healing powers of body, mind, soul and psyche. Experiences gained in outdoor music therapy differ significantly from those happening in the therapy room. Being part of a music therapy session outside in nature creates a different space of 'inter-natural' and interpersonal contact, bonding and relationship. When this occurs, there happens to be space for whole-body/holistic resonance, perception and listening (Klar, 2011, pp. 35, 37–38, 2012, p. 166).

Another approach to interlinking nature and music therapy can be found in the application of 'nature recordings'.[4] 'Nature recordings' are an attempt to faithfully depict and record the sounds of nature or the sounding environment. According to Fasser (2012, pp. 26–27), the application of 'nature recordings' in active and receptive music therapy supports various issues. The recordings can, for example, be used as an accompaniment during music therapy relaxation techniques. Moreover, parts and elements of the recordings may correlate with or mirror passages or challenges a patient is currently undergoing in her/his period of life. While listening to the recordings, these emerging experiences could work as a stimulus for further processes and therapeutic steps. Finally, Fasser also practices therapeutic 'harkening-hikes' in the mountains with his patients (Domogalla, n.d., p. 1; Fasser, n.d.).

To a certain extent, conceptualizations and thoughts formulated in Community Music Therapy (CoMT) also establish some relevant nature-related aspects. For instance, citing Stige (2005, p. 128), CoMT aims to unlock new arenas from clinical and discrete settings to more open and inclusive settings. Why not implementing nature and environmental settings as new arenas into CoMT? In addition, there is a noticeable emphasis on ecological interests and attitudes in describing music therapy and music, as well as music therapy intentions and the underlying humanistic worldview (Simon, 2013, pp. 297, 304; Stige, 2005, p. 128; Stige and Aarø, 2011).

Interesting outdoor concepts in music therapy can also be found in the publications and projects of Kern. She designed the 'Sound Path' and the 'Music Hut' as therapeutic 'interventions' and focused on outdoor play of children with autism on playgrounds and so on (Kern, 2002; Kern and Aldridge, 2006; Kern and Wakeford, 2007). Aigen (1991) too puts forth an interesting experience in one of his older publications. Although his thoughts are not exactly what could be understood as a nature-related approach in music therapy, there is a tangible connection and inspiration. He writes about an experience in the desert, the 'voice of wisdom in nature' (Aigen, 1991, p. 92), rituals and shamanism, and the nature of music—in fact, there is a lot of interaction between nature and music therapy in his article. Following Aigen's contribution, the writings of Kenny (2006) cover traditional aspects. Kenny, who has a Native American background of Navajo, outlines the relation between music therapy and traditional healing rituals, myths and wisdom in Native American cultures. She also describes what she calls 'Ecological Music Therapy' in her publications.

Other relevant efforts include works by Bogataj (2015) discussing intersections between music therapy and nature based on a survey of case examples, Rachinger (2016) exploring silence in adolescence as part of an Outdoor Music Therapy project, Deuter (2009) with 'listening walks' and 'listening workshops', and Virtanen (2010) examining music therapy in nature as a concept for burnout prevention.

## Relevant Current Research, Forthcoming Publications and Ongoing Projects

On the one hand, this chapter acts as a kind of retrospective of what has already been conceived and released in nature-related music therapy. On the other hand, there is also a prospect of what is happening at the moment in this field, or of what is going to come. To be realistic, it is obviously not possible to name and know all OdMT or other nature-related music therapy projects taking place globally. The previously listed publications at least prove that a couple of inspiring ideas have already been realized and discussed. Using nature-based terminology, OdMT seeds have been sown and spread somewhat. However, not many research projects filed under the flagship of 'Outdoor Music Therapy' seem to be pursued these days. But what can be noticed is a growing number of publications, academic theses and congress lectures and workshops on nature-related aspects in music therapy (Pfeifer, 2012, pp. 18–20, 2016, p. 123). This positive development possibly reflects what Jordan calls a noticeable growing interest in recent decades 'in the relationship between our contact with the natural world and its effect on our emotional well-being' (Jordan, 2015, p. 1).

It is fascinating that especially in the academic field more and more theses seem to be realized that explore the topic practically as well as scientifically. A valuable example is the one already commented on by Bogataj (2015). She reviewed relevant literature and case examples and finally focused on the approaches of Klar, Pfeifer, Fasser, Virtanen and Community Music Therapy (all named in the preceding chapter). When analyzing these case examples and approaches, she concluded that only the concepts of Fasser, Klar and Pfeifer have nature serving as an integral part/element in theory and practice of music therapy. Furthermore, she delivered additional details referring to nature's functions as setting, co-therapist and material in music therapy.

Another academic thesis showed that OdMT practiced in nature is an effective way to help adolescents experience silence more consciously and become comfortable with it. Rachinger identifies the characteristic features and resources of OdMT as possible crucial factors in achieving this. Her investigation included an analysis of literature, interviews with participating adolescents, and a survey of professionals (Rachinger, 2016).

In his master's thesis Fasser examined the effects of applying 'nature recordings' (*Naturhörbilder*) in music therapy practice. Among other outcomes, there seems to be a significant effect of 'nature recordings' on brain activities positively affecting relaxation reactions and emotional involvement. An EEG spectral analysis had been used for the process of collecting and evaluating the data (Fasser, 2012, pp. 59–60).

Some years ago, Pfeifer conducted a small, qualitative survey (Pfeifer, 2012). It barely deserves the classification of 'scientific,' although it is of relevance and provides some surprising outcomes. As part of the examination, six sound files were sent to several music therapists around the world (from Australia to the United States, from Norway to Austria, etc.). These sounds represented excerpts from music therapy sessions with a group of boys. Although all of the sound files included the same group of boys, the recording dates were different. The kids were between 9–12 years of age and suffered from various disorders and diseases (trauma, bullying, ADHD, anxiety states, etc.). Four of the six sound files were of music therapy sessions that happened outdoors in nature (in a cave, on the terrace of a mountain hut, in a forest, etc.), while two took place indoors (in the music therapy room of a clinical institution). The music therapists were asked to listen to the sound files as often as they preferred to and to determine whether they happened 'outdoors' or 'indoors'. Furthermore, they had to justify their decisions and—if possible—note down possible advantages and disadvantages of OdMT projects, specific characteristics relating to the sound files, and so forth.

Astonishingly, the 'hit rate' was approximately 68%. In other words, more than two-thirds of the sound files were correctly detected as being 'indoors' or 'outdoors'. Even though the survey had only been a small and 'semi-scientific' one, a cautious hypothesis could be raised that music therapy sessions happening outdoors may have a unique sound, characteristic or atmosphere.

This is what has already been realized regarding nature and OdMT-related (academic) research projects in the past. So, what is going on at present? Currently, the first leg of a study by Pfeifer, Sarikaya and Wittmann (in print) has been completed and submitted for publication. Silence lasting for 6 minutes and 30 seconds, preceded by two different conditions consisting of either a university seminar or a session of Depth Relaxation Music Therapy (DRMT), developed by Decker-Voigt (2007), were the two arms of this study carried out at a university with students as subjects. Outcomes show that silence combined with DRMT is effective in fostering relaxation, reducing the sense of space, slowing the perception of time and modifying the perspective of the future. Participants also felt the period of silence following DRMT to be significantly longer compared to the equally long period of silence after a seminar. The subjects' individual levels of impulsiveness and mindfulness did not affect the aforementioned effects. In the DRMT condition, participants judged the duration to last longer than in the control condition. Whereas an overestimation of duration is typically related to negative affects, such as boredom or depressed mood (Wittmann, 2015), Pfeifer, Sarikaya and Wittmann were able to show that a relative overestimation of duration can also be related to a more relaxed state of being in the present moment. Consequently, the second leg of the research project is already in progress. This time, both conditions take place outdoors, in the natural surroundings of a city park. In other words, there is an interconnection of Depth Relaxation Music Therapy, silence and nature functioning as the core element of the practical part of this study. The project itself may well be filed under the denotation of Outdoor Music Therapy.

Last but not least, Pfeifer and Decker-Voigt (in preparation) are currently preparing two compilations addressing the field of nature in psychotherapy and arts therapies. Book one will focus on theory and research, while book two provides a rich selection on practice, methods, interventions and case examples. A selective choice of professionals from all over the world and various backgrounds (psychoanalytical psychotherapy, analytical psychology, systemic therapy, music therapy, art therapy, nature therapy, behavior therapy, dance/movement therapy, horticultural therapy, expressive arts therapy, Gestalt therapy, humanistic psychology, existential analysis and logotherapy, etc.) will be represented. The intention of these books is to supply the necessary scientific, empirical and practical groundwork to support further developments in what might carefully be called an emerging, nature-related movement among therapists and therapies.

## Nature in Music Therapy—Music Therapy in Nature: Justification, Essential Components and Factors

The process of transferring music therapy sessions into outdoor settings and nature, as well as inviting nature, nature materials and phenomena into therapy has, of course, an influence on the therapeutic process. There is movement, development, expansion and extension, metamorphosis, modulation, growth—in other words, something is evolving and changing, music therapy is not the same anymore. Like music in music therapy, nature too can be an important and efficient, beneficial factor in therapy. This does *not* mean that it is always appropriate to include nature in music therapy or to conduct music therapy sessions outdoors. Besides the advantages and positive effects, there *are* risks which need to be assessed for and kept in mind. Some of them have already been mentioned in this contribution (sensory overload, overstimulation, frightening surroundings, unfamiliarity with the material, etc.).

The following chapter with its subsections extracts and describes a few of the inherent and essential nature-related components of Outdoor Music

Therapy. Furthermore, there will be a critical discussion regarding a lack of experience with nature among today's populations, and its possible adverse effects. This may encourage an inclusion of nature in (music) therapy offers.

## Why Moving Music Therapy Outdoors?

*Responding to the question of why she prefers to play at home, instead of playing in the woods, a child says: 'There aren't any sockets in the forest!'*

(Klar, 2011, p. 19)[5]

On the one hand, this statement sounds quite amusing, but viewing the context of this statement in light of contemporary expert literature, it rather calls for vigilance. Recently, two 'new' terms have emerged on the surface: the 'Nature Deficiency Syndrome' (Weber, 2008, p. 19) and the 'Nature-Deficit Disorder' (Louv, 2008). The Nature Deficiency Syndrome (or NDS), as described by Weber, occurs especially in children whose life is happening in front of a TV or computer screen. These children are not playing outside in nature anymore. As a result of this, symptoms such as hyperactivity, melancholia and stumbling while walking across flat lawns and meadows are to be observed (Weber, 2008, p. 19).

Nowadays, an increasing number of children experience nature only artificially through TV and similar forms of media; nature is reduced to some kind of backdrop function surrounding a sports event broadcasted by a TV channel. Klar agrees that more and more children have problems in walking along tarred grounds, not to speak of mountain terrain and forests. They do not have any experience or skills climbing up trees. They feel disgusted by touching sand and digging their hands and fingers into clumpy soil (Klar, 2011, p. 19).

What does that mean in terms of possible consequences? Jordan comments on that: 'It is clear that our relationship with nature (or lack of it) has an effect on our emotional and psychological well-being' (Jordan, 2015, p. 1).

In other words, a shortage of nature might cause, or be co-responsible for, the development of maladies, illnesses or disorders. Although today's younger generations increasingly become experts in mastering technical and digital tasks, they concurrently seem to be developing a growing 'undernourishment' in other areas. The zeitgeist mirrors and indicates a lack of space, time or even possibilities for real person-to-person communication, physical experience and exploration, adventures in nature, tactile, sensual and emotional experience, creative, assessment-free developing and designing processes (Pfeifer, 2016, p. 125).

It seems like the child's 'exploratory system' (Stern, 1998, p. 94) is asked more and more to unfold at home, and for the child to experience the world and nature in front of a tablet or smartphone. The world and societies are gaining speed, and there seems to be no more time left for visiting real nature. Innumerable TV spots, web ads and guidebooks tell us what is good and healthy. Simultaneously, they directly sell us the necessary natural products with the click of a mouse. Advertising and 'selling' nature for the purpose of promoting health certainly is a profitable business in worldwide economy. But, nature itself drastically differs from such a misuse in economy. Neither does she[6] advertise nor praise, nor does she offer—she invites us (Pfeifer, 2011, p. 24)! While being in nature we are allowed to touch, to listen, to smell, to move, to feel . . . According to this, nature is accessible to almost everyone. Incorporating nature and various outdoor settings into music therapy adds a good deal of materials, sounds, surroundings and possibilities to a music therapist's and music therapy's palette.

Consequently, there are new ways of meeting the needs and resources of our patients, to react to their diseases and symptoms, but to also foster prevention—especially in regards to the increasing number of people suffering from burnout, exhaustion, depression and so on. Nature allows us to recover in silence, to collect individually beneficial sounds and silences, to rest while listening to the archaic concert of a mountain river concerto, to take part in a stone percussion call-and-response improvisation across a mountain meadow, to jointly move barefooted in a morning rhythm group dance ritual in the sandy beaches next to the sea. Nature also provides enough space and places where we can work off feelings of aggression and anger while hitting big rocks with tree branches as part of a wild percussion battle. In such surroundings, nobody will be harmed or judged by his or her letting go of emotional tension. As Strittmatter (1997, pp. 118, 122) once wrote, the inclusion of nature in psychotherapy implies a devotion toward the living, and she can help us get a therapeutic process started or going.

## Different Aspects and Functions of Nature in Music Therapy

To begin with, let us focus on one of the most important elements of (music) therapy: the therapeutic relationship. In music therapy, this relationship may be seen as a kind of triad, consisting of the patient, the therapist and the method/medium (namely the music, the instrument, etc.). Inviting nature into music therapy favorably changes and affects this system. The triad actually develops into a tetrad. Klar (2012, p. 168) states that the common dialogical principle between patient and therapist evolves into a polylogical one by adding nature. Berger and Lahad (2013, p. 44) believe that this extension allows nature to be(come) an active partner in the therapeutic relationship—one that has an influence on the design of the setting and on the process itself. According to Kreszmeier (2012, pp. 43–44), after the therapist has set the framework, allowing the patient to get into closer contact with himself/herself and the natural environment, his/her task is to carefully assist the emerging processes. The therapist remains in an attitude of trust and empathy, but his/her role moves a bit more into the background. Subsequently, this 'upgrading' in the therapeutic relationship also affects the 'potential space' of therapy. Winnicott (2006, pp. 49, 52, 62, 76–77) defines the 'potential space' to be the space where two areas of play (playgrounds) are to overlap—the therapist's and the patient's. Psychotherapy happens where two persons play with each other. Playing is already psychotherapy.

Potential space as a kind of 'playground' is available in manifold varieties in nature and OdMT:

> *OdMT offers (almost boundless) space so as to experience sensuous 'experiencings'—to sense and feel oneself, to have a presentiment of one's own being as a 'being-with' or 'being-in' a surrounding world (e.g. the therapy group, flora and fauna in nature), to recognize and discover mindfulness and carefulness regarding oneself, nature and environment.*
>
> (Pfeifer, 2012, p. 16)[7]

Going back to what was previously stated, it is also possible to name nature as a 'co-therapist' in the music therapy process. Nature is not just an abstract or passive something in the tetrad of therapist, patient, method and herself. She is an active fourth within this compound. She vibrantly participates and contributes to the process. Nature as a co-therapist sometimes even acts as a signpost or guide along the road of a therapeutic process. She paves and directs the route, and shows a way out when being stuck in a dead end. For example, the birds' singing unconsciously introduces and leads over to the next segment in the therapeutic process; the murmuring of the leaves suddenly reminds a patient of his almost forgotten grandfather's peaceful voice while talking about his family matters. A heavy thundering summer storm in the mountains perfectly reflects and closes a highly emotional cathartic process.

This example also exposes nature's resources as setting. There are limitless places and spaces in nature where we can explore and access music therapy, as already mentioned. Nevertheless, it is important to mention not only the visible and concrete ones, but the invisible ones as well. In a particular way, the very special atmospheres and phenomena of nature are of rare quality too. Imagine the steady change of seasons, the regular shift from dawn to dusk, the continuous flowing of a river, the enduring sound of breaking sea waves . . . There is movement and stillness, ritual and tradition, continuity and recurring change. These phenomena provide possible beneficial applications for therapy. They may be used as metaphors for processes in our lives and can mirror them (regeneration of immune system, sleep-wake rhythm/cycle, etc.). On the other hand, they could carefully contain, reflect, assist or initiate awareness or exploration of unconscious and hidden material. The phenomena-settings of nature can give sound to the soundless and wordless, meaning to the inexplicable and incomprehensible and light to the hidden and submerged. But one should never forget that—within the therapeutic relationship and these settings—it is always the therapist's task to be attentively present and to accompany. He has to take care of whether or not a setting is helpful to the patient's needs and to the therapeutic process!

As nature as co-therapist and setting have already been focused on, a few words shall now be put forth dealing with nature as material. In reference to music therapy, we can find a lot of materials in nature that work very well as instruments and sound-producing objects. Just imagine the varied tuning of different rocks and stones, a handful of muddy riverbed sand slapped on water, the warm crackle of a fire and the dry bang of moldy tree branches hit against each other. Furthermore, in nature, and even nearby outdoor-environments, we can often find and collect various materials in order to create and construct our own instruments. Therefore, it is a wonderful additional advantage if you have access to a workshop with tools.

Of course, the therapist should be familiar with these tools and the workshop room, but if she/he is, this opens up some more possibilities and 'arenas' within the ways of thinking and practicing music therapy outdoors. The activity of handling the materials and creatively letting one's own instrument

**Figure 9.1** Creating a bull-roarer

Photo: Eric Pfeifer

emerge is a highly therapeutic one. There is a process of the self that is deeply involved in the act of genesis, as well as with finally being able to listen to one's own and individual self as a crucial part in the sound of the instrument (Pfeifer, 2011, p. 25). Actually, it is a transitional shift and process. In other words, these self-constructed instruments could—in a therapeutic sense—be interpreted and applied as transitional objects (Winnicott, 2006, pp. 10–11, 13, 24).

In explaining and reasoning the involvement of nature in therapy and counseling, Jordan points out the aspects of transference, countertransference, transitional objects and attachment (Jordan, 2015, pp. 45–57). As will be outlined later, these elements are existent in OdMT, too. But the way they are to be applied and included into the therapeutic process may be slightly different. Regarding all this,

> *it must be said that Outdoor Music Therapy is not better or more effective than other approaches or schools of practice in music therapy. Its effects, too, do not evolve faster or more intensively, nor are they of better diagnostic capacity—it is simply different. OdMT is unique in the way that it tries to acquire and to provide new and different paths for therapeutic work and objectives. OdMT happens in settings most probably different from conventional models. Certainly, it makes a difference whether you perform a drum session with a group of kids in a music therapy room situated on the third floor of a clinic or using stones and rocks as drums nearby a wild and roaring mountain river. A vocal improvisation with a bunch of adolescent psychiatric patients on the terrace of a hut, high in the mountains and sparkled with warm rays of summer sun, sounds and feels freer and lighter than one happening within the social institution.*
>
> (Pfeifer, 2016, pp. 125–126)

## Diagnostic Potentials

By reference to Oaklander (1993, pp. 210, 217) and Winnicott (2006, pp. 62, 101), observing play and playing allows a therapist to see, learn and recognize a lot concerning for example the state, creativity, strategies, problems and skills of a patient. As a matter of fact, play and playing are effective diagnostic instruments. Klar (2011, p. 49) comments that as diagnostics alters, therapy does too. Therapy and diagnostics intermingle, leading into what might be called 'theragnostics'. Moreover, existing nature therapy approaches even seem to resemble popular and standard diagnostic methods, such as 'house, tree, person' (Berger and Lahad, 2013, p. 53).

Quite a few interesting ideas can be deduced by transferring and interlinking these concepts with Outdoor Music Therapy. The multiple functions of nature, and the combination of play, music, instruments and materials in various settings and environments, affects and supports the diagnostic view of a therapist. Heading out into nature, touching, collecting and incorporating materials (stones, branches, saws, hammers, rasps, clay, soil, etc.), being in motion and creative—all of this opens up a whole new palette of diagnostic possibilities for a therapist. In this way she/he is able to get to know more about a patient or to initiate contact with her/him that is beyond the sometimes hindering and sterile conditions of clinical settings. Moreover, interesting diagnostic questions and perspectives may be raised: How does a patient walk across uneven paths in a forest? Is she/he solidly grounded within her/his body? How about taking part in a call-and-response improvisation spread across the woods? Is the particular person more or less exploring the situation and the setting, or is she/he staying close to the therapist? Has she/he taken great pains to put together a set of instruments made of natural materials from nature or has she/he just randomly picked up stuff that was lying around? What about working on her/his instrument? Does she/he spend much effort and imagination in creating her/his own bull-roarer, using hammers, files, rasps and a soldering iron to decorate and shape it in an individually unique way? How does she/he react to the sound coming out of the handmade instrument? Is she/he disappointed or enthusiastic about it?

Synergistically merging these diagnostic and therapeutic possibilities, thoughts and current alterations, a unique terminology could be suggested or introduced: OdMT as a form of 'music- and nature-assisted theragnostics'.

## Case Examples

The following case reports hopefully allow the reader to dive a little bit deeper into what could be OdMT reality and practice. The selected examples were taken from the author's therapeutic work and portray different therapy processes. What unites all of them is the fact that they represent OdMT sessions with children, adolescents and adults in natural settings and surroundings. Some of these examples have already been printed in other publications by the author.[8]

### *Case Report 1*

Jim,[9] nine years old, is going through hard times at school. His classmates bully him and refuse to accept him. More and more he is pushed into a state of being the outsider. A year ago, Jim's mother suffered from a massive burnout syndrome resulting in a depression and a suicide attempt. While his mother was away due to a necessary hospital stay, Jim experienced this absence as traumatic and threatening. For some time Jim has been affected by several disorders (e.g., insomnia). Within the group of our new OdMT project, Jim is becoming increasingly more lively, humorous, socially engaged and thoughtful. Moreover, he is very swift, fit and really keen on romping around in nature.

One day the whole group is performing a freak-out drum session under a rock ledge. Suddenly Jim cannot hold back anymore and has to let go. Still singing and dancing, he is wandering around the group circle and jumps up on top of two rocks, stretches his legs and creates some kind of bridging rooftop across both rocks. The next that happens is that all the other group members are dancing their way underneath this rooftop-bridge. With a happy smile on his face, Jim gets to experience how it feels being 'the bridge on top of an entire group' and 'the protecting rooftop' shepherding the group. Jim has gotten an energy boost within this session. Afterwards he began to behave more confidently.

**Figure 9.2** Freak-out drum session under a rock ledge

Photo: Eric Pfeifer

## *Case Report 2*

Ivy is a young, 15-year-old, smart and 'typical' teenager, but her outgoingness toward adults contrasts her inner state of being. Ivy struggles to manage life, school, barriers and expectations. She lives in an apartment-sharing community, which is part of an assisted-living project for young people. Ivy's way of life so far has not been easygoing for her. She suffered sexual abuse in childhood and other traumatizing situations. For example, her father set fire to the flat and left the house, while Ivy and her sister were asleep in their bunk beds. An attentive neighbour was able to enter the flat and tried to save both kids from the spreading fire. Unfortunately, Ivy got her head stuck in the ladder of her bunk bed. In the end, they were able to escape, but one can only imagine the (invisible) wounds Ivy carried. Ivy did not really engage with music therapy and psychotherapy when in a regular therapy setting. Feelings of rigidity, constriction, motionlessness and stillness were evoked. I got the impression that the room suppressed Ivy's movement and suffocated her expression. I suggested to Ivy that we go outside for a walk. She seemed to be relieved and accepted quickly. As it is autumn and the session is held in the evening, it is already quite dark outdoors. We decide to just have a walk, being careful and curiously attentive toward the sounds and acoustics surrounding us on our way. While taking one step after the other, next to each other, we get into a joint rhythm and a state of unconscious sharing. Suddenly, Ivy starts to talk, hesitantly at first, and the darker it gets, the more easily she shares her life. A few sessions later she explains that the surrounding silence of nature, which was so prominent during our walk, appeared to reflect the silence and speechlessness inside herself that hindered her from verbalizing what she had experienced back then. But the securing anonymity of the cocooning darkness and the joint walking rhythm provided enough confidence and stability for her to let her thoughts go.

### *Case Report 3*

When Robert (11 years of age) joins our OdMT group I do not know that much about him. He only had a few single sessions before. What I know is that he seriously suffers from being bullied by his classmates and he hardly has any friends. According to what his mother has told me, he avoids getting into conflicts, fearing them.

To me, Robert seems to be rather rigid concerning his emotions (in both gestures and facial expression). There is no smile, no anger, no happiness in his face. Already at an early stage I recognize a certain aggression in Robert that is firmly kept under lock and key. I feel that this, above all, deserves and requires attention and room first.

While taking part in an OdMT project, we decide to check out a forest up in the mountains. Armed with wooden tree branches we begin to wildly beat tree trunks, rocks and bushes. Doing so, I am situated quite closely next to Robert.

The other members of the group use their percussive sounds and voices in order to communicate with each other across the forest. Robert is not participating in this and is solely playing for himself. He hits the wooden drums very hard. With forceful and powerful strokes, Robert is blasting away dead and dried-out branches from the trees. For quite some time he is doing so, smashing several died-off trees. At a certain point he ceases his 'drum opus'—obviously tired, soaked with sweat but relaxed and easy.

The following day we are determined to visit the woods again. We intend to put together a freaky 'forest-drumming-orchestra'. On the way to our destination I suddenly recognize that I left the branch drum sticks, which I had picked up in the woods the day before, at our mountain hut. With a smile in his face Robert holds out his saying 'Look! You can have mine. I do not need them anymore!'

The next session involves a somewhat different, changed Robert. He is drumming together with the others and joining them in search of material and instruments. From time to time there are even one or two emotions sneaking onto Robert's face.

Most likely the wild, powerful, angry and loud drumming in the forest enabled some kind of cathartic process for Robert. Within this process he

**Figure 9.3** The tree as a drum set

Photo: Eric Pfeifer

was able to give way to his locked aggressions. From this moment on, Robert increasingly and actively participated in group activities.

## *Case Report 4*

Nancy (21) loved to sing during her childhood and adolescence. She was very gifted and attended a junior high school with a special emphasis on music. Then, when she was 15, she fell victim to a car crash where she was the passenger, and the driver and perpetrator himself was a good friend of hers. She suffered a massive traumatic brain injury that entailed years of rehabilitative measures and frequent stationary and ambulatory clinic treatments. Today, Nancy is very proud that she has managed to recover surprisingly well on many levels. She is an office employee at a protected workplace, and she is able to almost completely organize her life independently.

However, Nancy's vocal chords have not fully recovered from the car crash and the subsequent surgeries. This has affected her voice and singing capabilities, which is very hard for her. She is very sad about that and identifies that when trying to sing, it feels like there is something forcing her vocal chords to stick together tightly. No movement, no resonance or vibration is possible. Finally this leads to a state where her entire body is totally cramped and there is an abrupt interruption to her singing.

At the very beginning of one of our weekly sessions, when we are still in the joining phase, Nancy comments a bit regretfully and humorously: 'The weather is so beautiful outside and the poor two of us have to sit in this cool and distant clinical room.' I am happy to suggest to her that we pick up our stuff and move outdoors, which she accepts delightedly. Having a guitar and a bunch of the lyrics of Nancy's favorite songs with us, we unhurriedly walk up a hill. At a certain point during our short journey we are exposed to a wonderful view over lush meadows, trees and a herd of cows mooing from time to time. Nancy kind of reaches out, takes a deep breath and, in the same breath, announces loudly and clearly that she would like to sing a song right here on the spot in this sunny loneliness. We decide to go for 'What's Up'—a famous song that she really likes. What happens next is Nancy singing so joyfully and freely. She seems to want to move beyond the constrictions preventing her from singing the way she used to back before the accident. Moreover, I get the impression that she is shaking these barriers down to their foundations as she pushes through them for the very first time! Afterwards, Nancy smiles proudly and tiredly, and we do not speak a word for quite a while, still remaining in the echo of this powerful experience.

Importantly, it is not that Nancy's voice sounded so much better from a technical perspective, but that the way she approached and actually *was* (in) the singing, was very much different. From this particular session onwards, Nancy's attitude toward her voice began to change, and her vocal chords seemed to be allowed to conquer more and more space to breathe and to sound. Looking back, I am quite convinced we would not have met this therapeutic turning point by staying indoors.

## *Case Report 5*

Daniel (11 years old) is heavily suffering from dyslexia. He describes himself to be the scapegoat of his class. Some time ago things had been quite alright in school, but recently there has been a new headmaster and things have gotten worse and worse. Daniel is also undergoing intense bullying at the hands of his classmates. In such cases, he sometimes cannot hold back and he responds aggressively toward the perpetrators, scratching their faces, for example. In kindergarten, Daniel experienced a situation that had been rather traumatic to him. He held this inside himself, not showing anything until three years ago when he burst into tears, perhaps due to a retraumatizing event. Recently, Daniel and his parents decided to switch him to another school. Daniel is looking forward to doing so. What is more, he seems to be a young boy who is fascinated by a lot of things going on in the world. He knows a lot, but when he starts reporting on what he knows, he does so in a very rigid way.

Daniel especially seems to be in his element when we perform OdMT sessions in nature. Even though it is hard for him to establish contacts with other group members, he expectantly participates in a 'solo-tutti-improvisation' on the terrace of a mountain hut. After the group as a 'tutti' has responded and reproduced Daniel's solo improvisation, he is standing in front of the group—amazed, wide-eyed and with a happy smile, and he puts forth the following comment: 'Mirrored way down as far as to the tips of my toes!'

The terrace is one of Daniel's most favorite places anyway. Again and again he is spontaneously, actively, and happily creating musical improvisations with other group members and myself at this pleasant and sunny spot. Titles such as 'joyful mood' are generated by him describing the performances. Following one of these terrace improvisations, Daniel started to talk about how he feels about being the scapegoat in class and not having any friends. Immediately, he receives replies from other group members who understand and share his experience.

The feeling of being a welcomed member of a group is a very important first step for Daniel, a step leading into a 'new' direction. Within further terrace improvisations, receptive listening-walks through the forest, percussion performances nearby a riverbed, Daniel carefully and tentatively starts to disclose more and more.

**Figure 9.4** Improvisation on the terrace of a mountain hut

Photo: Eric Pfeifer

### *Case Report 6*

Mark is 11 years old. He has already gone through years of tragedy and chaos in his family of origin. A while ago he got adopted by a very solicitous and attentive family. Things improved visibly. Unfortunately, this did not last for long. Soon after, a teacher at Mark's school became violent toward him. This was greatly traumatic for Mark and, already suffering from ADHD symptoms, insomnia 'returned', too. Just as Mark had started to gain a foothold and to develop trust, those filigree means of support and networking collapsed.

So, while in the forest Mark sets out alone when all of the other group members are constructing a handmade hut of wood and so forth. He is deeply busy developing and creating impressive defence facilities and mechanisms. By the time the group is ready and has finished building the hut, Mark is showing me around, describing his facilities in detail. For this purpose, he is using his voice and branch drum sticks as sounds, melodies and rhythms for each mechanism. He introduces me to all functions and declares that everything is to be navigated with the help of a remote control. After this, we are all together and safely packed in our handmade hut.[10] Using his remote control, Mark gets his defence facilities into action. The whole group is supporting this with sounds produced by their bodies, voices, and forest instruments while the countdown quickly approaches zero—implying the ultimate ignition. At the same time, Mark explains: 'This rocket is going to kill all people, no, it is going to kill all evil people.' But immediately following, he corrects this and adds: 'No, the rocket is going to kill the evil in all people so that there is only the good in people left over!'

After we get out of our shelter Mark appears to be pretty pleased and evidently relaxed, and he passes over the remote control for his defence facilities to me.

### *Case Report 7*

Mr. Hillman is in his early sixties. He suffered a stroke and is now participating in a music therapy group as part of an ambulatory neurologic rehabilitation treatment. The stroke did not so much affect Mr. Hillman's physical state as it changed his cognitive skills and (emotional) behavior. His wife sadly lamented that he started to behave sexually invasively toward her on several occasions. But most noticeable is that there is no personal initiative coming from Mr. Hillman, a man, who used to be highly creative and active in his days before suffering the stroke.

Due to Mr. Hillman's devotion to music—he played piano and guitar—we hope to find a way to rediscover his creativity and self-initiative. Unfortunately, after quite a few sessions, the therapeutic team has to face a resistant stagnancy.

Then, at the beginning of the music therapy group session in the morning of a very cold January day, I ask the members if there are any preferences for the day's session. By the time it is Mr. Hillman's turn, there is silence at first—as to be expected, but suddenly I hear a 'We could go outside!' This is the very first time Mr. Hillman made a suggestion by himself. Still surprised by his response, I start thinking about how we could do this as the whole group on a bitter cold, winter's day, where one patient is sitting in a wheelchair, one person is seriously suffering from multiple sclerosis and needing a special medical walking stick, and so on. I fear that this will remain the sole suggestion made by Mr. Hillman if we do not go outside. As all of the other therapy group members are curious about moving outdoors, and with the help of some colleagues of the therapeutic team, we finally manage to get outside. We agree to perform a short 'listening-walk' during which we intend to be attentive toward pleasant sounds surrounding us. Everybody is invited to collect such sounds and store them in an imaginary bag for further usage.

Weeks later the group is still speaking about this jointly shared outdoor listening experience. By the time it is Mr. Hillman's turn to let the group know what his preferences are for the particular therapy session, he always grins broadly and answers—much to the pleasure of the other group members: 'We could go outside and collect some sounds!'

## Conclusion

> *They say the seeds of what we will do are in all of us, but it always seemed to me that in those who make jokes in life the seeds are covered with better soil and with a higher grade of manure.*
>
> (Hemingway, 1994, p. 91)

Picking up the wonderful sentence from Mr. Hillman and the happiness he most likely felt each time he was able to place 'his' sentence as a running gag at the very beginning of the group therapy sessions, humor and jokes could indeed be good nutrients for the seeds of therapy too. At least, the preceding patients' stories and reactions may give reason to believe that moving music therapy outdoors and inviting the 'outdoors' into music therapy proves to be effective and supportive. But it is not only the patients' voices that should be taken into account. The increasing number of academic theses, research projects and writings on the topic too emphasizes possible advantages. Not to mention that there is an apparent lack of contact and interaction with nature in today's societies, co-existing with a rising demand and awareness concerning the health-fostering benefits of nature.

In any case, Outdoor Music Therapy may likely be a versatile and valuable contribution to a therapeutic community that is rediscovering nature as a major impact and integral element among a complex holistic system. Whereas, back in ancient days, there have been the shamans and perhaps 'music-making neanderpists' (Pfeifer, 2016, p. 119, in print) practicing such a fruitful interconnection of music, therapy and nature, it is currently and prospectively necessary to critically consider possible approaches within this field from a scientific, practical and theoretical point of view. Perhaps, going back to Yalom's words at the beginning of this contribution, this will also lead to new ways of creating unique therapies and therapy languages for our patients. Sometimes it is necessary to leave common grounds and (indoor) settings behind in order to discover innovative people, and, of course, therapeutic pathways:

> *This song put me in the middle of the road. Travelling there soon became a bore so I headed for the ditch. A rougher ride but I met more interesting people there.*
>
> (Young, 1994)

## Notes

1. See relevant publications for additional insights Pfeifer (2011, 2012, 2014, 2016, in print).
2. Paying attention to the title and main intentions of this book, there shall be a focus on the nature-related aspects of OdMT within this contribution, not so much covering therapeutic work in 'non-nature' outdoor settings (underground

car parks, workshops, etc.) and 'non-nature' materials (waste, construction site materials, tools, etc.).

3. See publications mentioned in note 1 for further information.
4. 'Nature recordings' is a somewhat poor English translation of the German original term *Naturhörbilder*, but due to a lack of a more appropriate alternative the mentioned translation had to be used.
5. Annotation: Translation by the author as the original text is written in German language.
6. Although grammatically it would be correct to use 'it', therapeutically 'her' seems much more adequate in this context ('Mother Earth' as the origin of all life on earth, etc.).
7. Annotation: Translation by the author as the original text is written in German language.
8. See list of references.
9. All the patients' names got anonymized.
10. The hut being much more a therapeutic 'safe-place' in this case.

## References

Aasgaard, T. (2001). Music therapy as milieu in the hospice and paediatric oncology ward. In D. Aldridge (Ed.), *Music therapy in palliative care. New voices* (pp. 29–42). London: Jessica Kingsley.

Aigen, K. (1991). The voice of the forest: A conception of music for music therapy. *Music Therapy, 10*(1), 77–98.

Berger, R., and Lahad, M. (2013). *The healing forest in post-crisis work with children: A nature therapy and expressive arts program for groups*. London and Philadelphia: Jessica Kingsley.

Bogataj, L. (2015). *Wo Musiktherapie und Natur sich begegnen. Eine qualitative Untersuchung musiktherapeutischer Fallbeispiele*. Diplomarbeit, Universität für Musik und darstellende Kunst Wien, Wien.

Decker-Voigt, H.-H. (2007). Methodology of music therapy and depth relaxation (DRMT). In I. Frohne-Hagemann (Ed.), *Receptive music therapy: Theory and practice* (zeitpunktmusik, pp. 239–251). Wiesbaden: Dr. Ludwig Reichert Verlag.

Deuter, M. (2009). 'Hör-Werkstatt': Ein musiktherapeutisches angebot in einer suchtklinik. *Musik und Gesundsein (MuG), 16*, 19.

Devereux, P. (2005). Tempel der Ahnen: Eine Einführung von Paul Devereux. In J. Groht, *Tempel der Ahnen. Megalithbauten in Norddeutschland* (pp. 11–26). Baden und München: AT Verlag.

Domogalla, S. (n.d.). *'Winter-Stille'—eine Horchwanderung*. Retrieved from www.wolfgangfasser.ch/Winter-Stille,%20eine%20Horchwanderung.doc

Fasser, W. (n.d.). *Die Kunst des Hörens: Horchen und lauschen mit hilfe der Musiktherapie*. Retrieved from www.wolfgangfasser.ch/00%20Die%20Kunst%20des%20Hoerens.doc

Fasser, W. (2012). *Naturhörbilder in der Musiktherapie. Theoretische Hintergründe und Implementation von Naturaufnahmen in die musiktherapeutische Praxis*. Masterarbeit, Zürcher Hochschule der Künste in Kooperation mit der Interkantonalen Hochschule für Heilpädagogik, Zürich.

Harper, D. (2016). *Online etymology dictionary: Therapy*. Retrieved from www.etymonline.com/index.php?term=therapy

Hemingway, E. (1994). *A moveable feast*. London: Vintage Books.

Jordan, M. (2015). *Nature and therapy: Understanding counselling and psychotherapy in outdoor spaces* (Dual First). East Sussex and New York: Routledge.

Kenny, C. (2006). *Music and life in the field of play: An anthology*. Gilsum: Barcelona.

Kern, P. (2002). *The sound path: Finding my way in the playground*. Retrieved from www.musictherapy.biz/Dr._Petra_Kern/Publications_files/Kern%202002_Sound%20Path.pdf

Kern, P., and Aldridge, D. (2006). Using embedded music therapy interventions to support outdoor play of young children with autism in an inclusive community-based child care program. *Journal of Music Therapy*, *43*(4), 270–294.

Kern, P., and Wakeford, L. (2007). Supporting outdoor play for young children: The zone model of playground supervision. *Journal of the National Association for the Education of Young Children*, *62*(5), 12–18.

Klar, S. (2011). *In ko-respondenz mit dem Heilenden der Natur: Reflexionen und Konnektionen: Integrative Therapie—integrative Musiktherapie und Natur-therapie*. Retrieved from www.fpi-publikation.de/images/stories/downloads/polyloge/klar-in-_ko-respondenz-_mit-dem-heilenden-der-natur-reflexionen-polyloge-21-2011.pdf

Klar, S. (2012). Wir hören nur mit dem Herzen gut: Hören und Wahrnehmen in ko-respondenz mit der Natur. In Deutsche musiktherapeutische Gesellschaft e. V. (DMtG) (Ed.), *Jahrbuch Musiktherapie. Music therapy annual. Das Hören des Therapeuten* (Vol. 8, pp. 157–176). Wiesbaden: Dr. Ludwig Reichert Verlag.

Kreszmeier, A. H. (2012). *Systemische Naturtherapie* (2nd ed.). Heidelberg: Carl-Auer Verlag.

Louv, R. (2008). *Last child in the woods: Saving our children from nature-deficit disorder* (Revised and updated ed.). Chapel Hill, NC: Algonquin Books.

Montagu, J. (2007). Origins and development of musical instruments. Retrieved from http://chapters.scarecrowpress.com/08/108/0810856573ch1.pdf

Oaklander, V. (1993). *Gestalttherapie mit Kindern und Jugendlichen* (8th ed.). *Konzepte der Humanwissenschaften. Angewandte Wissenschaft*. Stuttgart: Klett-Cotta.

Pavlicevic, M., and Ansdell, G. (2004). Introduction: 'The Ripple effect'. In M. Pavlicevic and G. Ansdell (Eds.), *Community music therapy* (pp. 15–31). London: Jessica Kingsley.

Pfeifer, E. (2011). Vom 'Bio-sound' der 'Öko-Instrumente' in der Musiktherapie—ein emphatisches Sinnieren über das klanglich Instrumentale angebot der Natur. *Musik und Gesundsein (MuG)*, *20*, 24–26.

Pfeifer, E. (2012). *Outdoor Musiktherapie: Musiktherapie jenseits des klassischen Settings. Zeitpunkt musik. Musiktherapie Universität Augsburg: Band 1*. Wiesbaden: Dr. Ludwig Reichert Verlag.

Pfeifer, E. (2014). Naturverbundene gedanken als Resümee einer synergetischen Begegnung—Ergotherapie und Musiktherapie. *Praxis ergotherapie*, *27*(1), 24–28.

Pfeifer, E. (2016). Outdoor music therapy with children and adolescents: Sounds from the wood? In A. Kopytin and M. Rugh (Eds.), *'Green Studio': Nature and the arts in therapy* (pp. 117–136). New York: Nova Science.

Pfeifer, E. (2017). Outdoor Musiktherapie mit Kindern und Jugendlichen: Die Berghütte als exemplarischer Praxisbezug. In T. Timmermann and H. U. Schmidt (Eds.), *Zeitpunkt musik. Musiktherapie Universität Augsburg. Förderung von Kindern und Jugendlichen durch musiktherapeutische Vorgehensweisen. Ausgewählte Schriften zur Musiktherapie der Universität Augsburg.* Wiesbaden: Dr. Ludwig Reichert Verlag.

Pfeifer, E., and Decker-Voigt, H.-H. (Eds.). (in preparation). *Nature in psychotherapy and arts therapies: Theory and research* (Vol. 1). Wiesbaden: Reichert Verlag.

Pfeifer, E., and Decker-Voigt, H.-H. (Eds.). (in preparation). *Nature in psychotherapy and arts therapies: Practice, methods, interventions, case examples* (Vol. 2). Wiesbaden: Reichert Verlag.

Pfeifer, E., Sarikaya, A., and Wittmann, M. (2016). Changes in states of consciousness during a period of silence after a session of depth relaxation music therapy (DRMT). *Music and Medicine*, *8*(4), 180–186.

Rachinger, M. (2016). *Stille erfahren im Jugendalter. Am beispiel eines outdoor musiktherapie Projekts.* Masterarbeit, Universität Augsburg, Augsburg.

Reznikoff, I. (1995). On the sound dimension of prehistoric painted caves and rocks. In E. Tarasti (Ed.), *Musical signification* (pp. 541–557). Berlin: Walter de Gruyter.

Simon, C. (2013). *Community music therapy—Musik stiftet Gemeinschaft: Heilsame Wege in einer sich wandelnden Kultur* (Library of Healing Arts. Bibliothek der Heilenden Künste: Vol. 11). Klein Jasedow: DrachenVerlag.

Stern, D. N. (1998). *Diary of a baby: What your child sees, feels, and experiences.* New York: Basic Books.

Stige, B. (2005). Toward a notion of community music therapy: Synopsis and contextualization of (parts of): Stige, Brynjulf (2003): Elaborations toward a notion of community music therapy. In Berufsverband der Musiktherapeutinnen und Musiktherapeuten in Deutschland e. V. (BVM) (Ed.), *Jahrbuch Musiktherapie. Music therapy annual. Forschung und Entwicklung* (Vol. 1, pp. 107–134). Wiesbaden: Dr. Ludwig Reichert Verlag.

Stige, B., and Aarø, L. E. (2011). *Invitation to community music therapy.* New York: Routledge.

Strittmatter, M. (1997). Synergiewirkung der Verbindung von verbaler und nonverbaler Sprache durch den Einbezug der Natur in die psychotherapeutische Arbeit. In G. Pulverich (Ed.), *ADP-Schriftenreihe: Band 5. Psychologie und Therapie bei Kindern und Jugendlichen. Beiträge der 5. Brixener Tag für Psychologen* (pp. 117–122). Berlin: Deutscher Psychologen Verlag.

Timmermann, T. (2008a). Anthropologische und ethnologische Aspekte. In H.-H. Decker-Voigt, D. Oberegelsbacher, and T. Timmermann, *Lehrbuch Musiktherapie* (Vol. 3068, pp. 79–84). München: Ernst Reinhardt Verlag.

Timmermann, T. (2008b). Historische Aspekte. In H.-H. Decker-Voigt, D. Oberegelsbacher, and T. Timmermann, *Lehrbuch Musiktherapie* (Vol. 3068, pp. 85–93). München: Ernst Reinhardt Verlag.

Virtanen, M. (2010). *Musiktherapie in der Natur. Ein Konzept gegen Burnout.* Diplomarbeit, Westfälische Wilhelms-Universität Münster, Münster.

Weber, A. (2008). *Biokapital: Die Versöhnung von Ökonomie, Natur und Menschlichkeit.* Berlin: Berlin Verlag.

Winnicott, D. W. (2006). *Vom Spiel zur Kreativität* (11th ed.). *Konzepte der humanwissenschaften*. Stuttgart: Klett-Cotta.

Wittmann, M. (2015). Modulations of the experience of self and time. *Consciousness and Cognition*, *38*, 172–181. Retrieved from http://s3.amazonaws.com/academia.edu.documents/38342971/WittmannConscCog2015.pdf?AWSAccessKeyId=AKIAJ56TQJRTWSMTNPEA&Expires=1470835582&Signature=l%2BPemESEjmgFC%2FjWev4Sy2OzfAA%3D&response-content-disposition=inline%3B%20filename%3DModulations_of_the_experience_of_self_an.pdf

Yalom, I. D. (1997). *Living on the couch: A novel*. New York: Harper Perennial.

Young, N. (1994). *Decade: A 3-record set on 2 compact discs* [CD]. Reprise Records, Warner Bros. Records.

Zulliger, H. (1973a). Die deutungsfreie psychoanalytische Kinderpsychotherapie. In G. Biermann (Ed.), *Handbuch der Kinderpsychotherapie* (3rd ed., Vol. 1, pp. 192–198). München: Ernst Reinhardt Verlag.

Zulliger, H. (1973b). Die Spaziergang-Behandlung: Eine Form des psychotherapeutischen Umgangs mit gefährdeten Jugendlichen. In G. Biermann (Ed.), *Handbuch der kinderpsychotherapie* (3rd ed., Vol. 1, pp. 428–434). München: Ernst Reinhardt Verlag.

Zulliger, H. (1990). *Heilende Kräfte im kindlichen Spiel* (Ungekürzte Ausgabe). *Geist und Psyche*. Frankfurt: Fischer Taschenbuch Verlag.

# 10

# EXPRESSING THE FULLNESS OF HUMAN NATURE THROUGH THE NATURAL SETTING

*Lia Naor*

## Introduction

In this chapter, we will focus on the concept of *human wholeness* as a key component of healthy human development, cultivated and nurtured through the natural environment. In contrast to common notions in psychology that view good mental and physical health as the elimination and repair of negative symptoms or cure of ailments, we will present a more holistic approach to health, involving the awareness and expression of human wholeness.

From this perspective, the 'ailment' in need of healing has a great deal to do with the fragmented, unfulfilled self, expressed by the human yearning for wholeness. In this respect, good health involves cultivating awareness and an intimate, meaningful relationship not only with personal aspects of the self but with wider aspects and dimensions of life represented by nature that foster human wholeness.

Wholeness may be better understood by it's absence, experienced as not belonging to self or world, leading to an underlying sense of indifference, emptiness or meaninglessness. These are common ailments in modern society even when the individual is considered 'successful' by social standards, such feelings can be unsettling and evoke a gnawing feeling in the individual that something important is missing. Goldfried and Davila (2005), in their study of critical moments in an individual's life, describe exactly this—individuals who have lead 'unlived lives' that, whether realized or not, they found to be a major instigator for profound change and development.

Without a doubt, people will go to great lengths to find a solution to such unsettling feelings. A healthy search may include therapy, workshops, mindfulness developing, nature walks, arts and physical activity. Conversely, unhealthy ways to momentarily subdue these feelings often lead to addictive behavior or consuming material goods as a means of 'feeling fuller'. For many individuals, however, neither scenario leads to a definite solution, because the focus is on reducing, calming or eliminating the painful symptoms. While by our point of view the symptom holds the key to the cure.

From this perspective, deep unsettling yearnings—even when painful and dismantling among healthy humans—are an inner calling to live a fuller life. These yearnings, when dealt with therapeutically, may be utilized as a life force, pushing one to experience deep relationships including meaningful connections to other humans and the wider natural world. In this way wholeness is cultivated, giving the feeling that one is an intrinsic part of the 'web of life' and becoming aware that one's existence is worthwhile.

This notion has been theorized by the field of ecopsychology (Roszak, 1992, 1995, 2009)—a philosophical, evolutionary-based approach that integrates the environment with psychology. Ecopsychology seeks to re-examine the human psyche as an integral part of the web of nature holding that awareness of the interrelatedness of all systems of life on earth serve as a necessary aspect of good psychological health. Just as the goal of previous psychologies was to recover repressed contents of the unconscious, the therapeutic goal of ecopsychology is to awaken an inherent sense of environmental reciprocity within the core of the mind, termed the ecological unconscious (Roszak, 1995). Ecopsychology calls for an expansive psychological understanding of the self, often referred to as our *ecological self*. This term, coined by Naess (1973), denotes the development of a more mature authentic self that is aware of the physical-emotional and spiritual interdependence that humans and non-humans share and the inevitability of fate and future that are common for all of them (Drengson, 2005; Seed, Macy, Fleming, and Naess, 1988). It is a very different perspective from anthropocentrism and human-centeredness that, it can be argued, are limited and misguided in the way they see and relate to life, sometimes even provoking vicious cycle of exploitation and violence (Zimmerman, 1997). From an ecopsychology position, remembering and reconnecting to nature is a form of 'cure'. In a psychotherapeutic sense, it means redefining mental health as a 'green psychotherapy', which focuses health within an environmental context (Conn, 1995; Roszak, 1995).

Ecopsychology has contributed greatly to the growing awareness of the implications of humans distancing themselves from nature from a psychological perspective. While used by therapists to describe their worldviews and philosophical notions in clinical practice, this approach has not yet developed an operational therapeutic framework, nor has significant research been carried out to date on its effectiveness within a therapeutic setting (Rust and Totton, 2012; Sevilla, 2006). It follows, then, that while these theories are clearly important, at present they have a more philosophical/theoretical basis, lacking operational application. This is where expressive therapies contribute greatly, by providing actual and embodied creative means by which these significant ideas can be manifested in a concrete form.

The field of expressive therapies has emphasized the significance of creative human expression in its many forms for fostering psychological health and wholeness. This connection between creative language and therapy has elicited various means for healthy expression, whether through the visual arts, music, movement, drama and so forth (Atkins et al., 2003). In contrast to the more common verbal means of expression in traditional therapy, expressive therapies implement an experiential means of communication by which various opportunities to express the many aspects of the self are offered, contributing to human wholeness.

Through the conceptual lens of expressive therapies, nature is often implemented as an experiential, symbolic and multidimensional setting and therapeutic partner, suitable for enticing creative self-expression. In the spirit of this book, wishing to examine ways to deepen the human relationship with nature through integrating the expressive arts, this chapter will focus on the unique opportunities for creative self-discovery and expression offered by nature contributing to human wholeness.

The expressive arts are a means by which various aspects of self may be creatively expressed and worked with in the therapeutic process. Integrating nature takes this process a step further, viewing nature not only as a therapeutic partner, physical setting, but as an actual partner offering abundant concrete and embodied situations by which one can experience human wholeness. From this perspective, nature is not only a means for experiential expression of self but an innate and core construct of human wholeness. This conceptualization of nature steers the therapeutic process involving the cultivation of human wholeness in a new direction. This new direction goes beyond the expression and development of self to an expansive dialogue, experience and connection with all that exists.

## Nature

Nature's role in the process of healthy development has been attributed to our human's biological, psychological and evolutionary-based design and is reflected in several theories (Kellert, 2005; Kellert and Wilson, 1995; Oliver and Ostrofsky, 2007; Wilson, 1984). The 'biophilia' hypothesis was one of the first theoretical constructs for later conceptions that viewed nature as central to human flourishing (Wilson, 1984). This theory maintains that there is a fundamental, genetically based human need and propensity to affiliate with the natural world as representing life. It contends that the human species has evolved within the natural environment for over millions of years and, as a result, 'prefers' natural landscapes that hold biological, adaptive significance for human development. The biophilia hypothesis presented later by Kellert and Wilson (1995) goes beyond the biological connection to nature. It underscores the psychological importance of direct human experience with nature as a means of attaining personal knowledge and environmental values that foster the development of human identity and personal fulfillment.

Inspired by these theories, Ulrich (1993) presented the psycho-evolutionary theory (PET), putting its emphasis on human evolutionary preference for natural landscapes. It claimed that humans have an immediate sensory and emotional response to nature, well before their cognitive skills kick in. From this perspective, humans experience nature in a way that may enhance adaptive behavior and reduce health-related problems (especially stress and anxiety), long before they have been analyzed cognitively.

Soon after, and based on a series of studies dealing with the effect of nature on human psychology, environmental psychologist Kaplan (1995) presented the attention restoration theory (ART). This theory hypothesizes that natural environments enhance psychological well-being by enabling the recovery of a limited and fatigable cognitive resource, necessary for self-regulation and cognitive functioning. According to ART, everyday activities that involve focusing on uninteresting stimuli and focusing attention in the face of external and internal distractions require an effortful form of attention. The capacity to voluntarily employ or direct such attention is limited, however, and as this capacity becomes depleted, it becomes increasingly difficult to remain focused, keep distractions at bay and regulate behavior. In order to regain the capacity to direct attention, one must let it rest. Natural settings seem particularly well-equipped to facilitate this restorative process, because they allow a different form of cognitive functioning to take over, a form of effortless, involuntary attention, termed 'fascination'. This form of cognitive perception stimulates self-reflection, helping individuals to cope more effectively and function more successfully (Kaplan, 1983).

Based on these theories, a growing body of empirical evidence and research in various fields links nature to humans' psychological and physical well-being (Berto, 2005; Gatersleben, 2008; Herzog, Maguire, and Nebel, 2003; Kaplan, 1983, 2001; Pretty, Peacock, Sellens, and Griffin, 2005; Ulrich et al., 1991). Additionally, new research has uncovered neurobiological factors shown to be adaptive to nature (Bratman, Hamilton, Hahn, Daily, and Gross, 2015). They have assessed the influence of nature on rumination, a neural mechanism associated with heightened risk for depression and other mental illnesses. Their results show that a mere 90-minute walk in nature decreased rumination and subgenial prefrontal cortex activation, in contrast to the same walk in urban surroundings. They concluded that the lack of exposure to nature may help to explain the link between urbanization and mental illness.

Additional studies show a correlation between living spent purely in human environments characterized by extensive artificial stimulation and exhaustion and lack of vitality (Katcher and Beck, 1987; Stilgoe, 2001). Byrnit (2006) has argued that postmodern social and working practices demand that we adapt to conditions far removed from those of which our developmental history prepared us to cope with. She concludes that although we can survive in our rapidly evolving cultural environment, our chances of thriving in it are small.

Understanding the importance of nature as a partner in the process of healthy human development has instigated the search to reveal the unique characteristics and ways by which nature contributes to human flourishing. This process involves connecting the existing theories with empirical evidence to extract the basic healing constructs in nature including a distant, restorative, metaphoric and sensory setting providing new and expansive ways of being and connecting.

## Nature's Unique Characteristics

The natural environment, far removed from the personal and social stimuli encountered in daily life, offers us time and privacy to relax, contemplate and reflect on oneself and life. This is imperative if one wishes to cultivate self-awareness and personal growth as shown by empirical evidence (Boyd, 1994; Boyd and Myers, 1988; Hammitt, 1982; Hartig, Evans, Jamner, Davis, and Gärling, 2003; Kaplan and Kaplan, 1989; Korpela, Hartig, Kaiser, and Fuhrer, 2001; Ulrich et al., 1991). It is in these natural surroundings, often unfamiliar and usually devoid of everyday stimuli, that habitual patterns of behavior and avoidance strategies are challenged, allowing the individual to experience different ways of being and doing. This, in turn, raises the possibility of broader definitions of the self (Trace, 2003).

For example, Sarah (aged 38), who described herself as a 'doer', was uneasy, kept constantly active and had a very short attention span. While sitting with her in a garden, I turned her attention to a hill of ants. This had her full attention within minutes. She sat there calmly, gazing intently at it, for a long time. Halfway into the session, I asked her how she felt, and then informed her that 20 minutes had gone by. She was surprised that she had stayed calm for so long and told me that while watching the ants she was amazed at how busy they were. Out in nature, Sarah had discovered the ability to be still and calm, while reflecting on how it looked to be so busy. In this encounter, she discovered a new and surprising aspect of herself, which brought her to contemplate new ways of being.

Results of different qualitative studies carried out among hikers, nature lovers and so forth found wilderness immersion to be a unique way of experiencing time and space. Through its various forms (Hammitt and Brown, 1984), including canoeing (Swatton and Potter, 1998), hiking (Fredrickson and Anderson, 1999) and long periods of solitude (Coburn, 2006; Ellison and Hatcher, 2007), participants felt able to reconnect with themselves. Not feeling judged and being distant from cultural/social norms and daily duties offered them an opportunity for deep reflection and contemplation. Furthermore nature evoked in them a new awareness of interconnectedness, which was described as the 'dissolving of boundaries' between the self and nature. In these instances, experiencing a connection to a greater whole contributed to their sense of connectedness with self and the world (Terhaar, 2009; Williams and Harvey, 2001; Wood, 2010).

The significance of the natural environment lies not only in its ability to slow down the body and calm/open the mind, but also in enticing challenging and sensory aspects. McDonald and Schreyer's (1991) book provides an integrated, critical synthesis of empirical studies relating to the spiritual benefits of leisure that have been published in the last 18 years. They conclude that nature provides a "unique combination of extreme states of consciousness and increased sensory acuity" (p. 23). They also state that visual, gustatory, olfactory, auditory and kinesthetic senses are enhanced within a wilderness setting, concluding that "wilderness-like settings heightens one's level of sensory awareness, resulting in profound personal experiences" (McDonald and Schreyer, 1991, p. 23).

Such experiences, which may occur spontaneously in nature, involve feelings of absorption in the moment in which physical borders of body, time and space may dissolve leaving one feeling at one with the environment (McDonald, Wearing, and Ponting, 2009; Terhaar, 2005; Williams and Harvey, 2001; Wood, 2010). In many instances they contribute to an expanded consciousness and may lead to major self and life transformations (Csikszentmihalyi, 1997; DeMares and Krycka, 1998; Grady, 2009; Maslow, 1971; Naor, 2014; Wood, 2010).

For some individuals these significant effects are related to nature's vast and diverse landscapes that provide rich opportunities for metaphoric projection, especially when the receiver is, in some way, susceptible to accepting the projection (both negative and positive) (Wilson, 2011; Terhaar, 2009). This was true in the example of Jack (aged 43), who was overwhelmed at work by the many responsibilities imposed on him as a high-ranking officer, but before resigning decided to come to therapy. Out in nature I asked him to find a spot that was most reflective of what he was feeling at the moment. Jack chose a very enclosed and small patch of bushes and thorns and lay down. After a while we sat to talk and he told me that lying there feeling so enclosed and alone brought up long forgotten memories from his childhood. When he was three years old, his parents moved to a foreign country, he did not have friends and did not know the language; this resulted in his spending most of his childhood alone in the attic. While talking Jack began to make the connection between his upbringing and current situation in which he never considered passing on responsibilities and always tried to do everything on his own. This resulted in an immense overload and most of his free time enclosed alone in his study.

Experiencing these aspects in an embodied and symbolic way enabled Jack to deal with personal issues that he had formerly avoided, by which he gained new awareness especially in regard to his personal relationships, opening the opportunity to make significant changes in his life.

From this perspective, the positive side of nature and its harsher, sometimes threatening and not easily accepted aspects become part of the experience of wholeness, whereby all facets of human nature are mirrored. Dufrechou (2002) touches on the significance of experiencing deep emotion in his study on psycho-spiritual transformation. His results point to nature as symbolizing and enabling in participants' experiences of deep emotion and grief, elicited as a response to nature. Expressing such deep emotions was described by the participants as a 'coming home' from a lost way of experiencing the world or a 'healing of the splits,' which resulted in personal wholeness and transformation.

These unique aspects of nature, which have a profound beneficial effect, have led to the concept of nature as a *transformational space*. Grady (2009), in his qualitative study on nature as a transformational space, summarized its effects in four key ways: (1) feeling connected to something bigger than oneself, which evokes a spiritual experience; (2) feeling attuned peacefully with the environment, reminiscent of the primary object relationship (similar to that of being held by another); (3) having a sense of awe and elevation in the face of the intensity and power of nature; (4) being free from the need to be compliant with societal expectations, when immersed in nature (allowing the connecting with and expressing of one's true self).

The aforementioned theories and other extensive research reveal various human characteristics (biological, psychological, evolutional, etc.), as well as environmental aspects and attributes that contribute to healthy human development and flourishing. And while these understandings are of great importance, there seems to be an additional element, stemming from a more holistic and effulging approach to the human connection to nature. From this perspective nature's contribution to human health is not assessed by specific environmental or human characteristics or outcomes but the way nature fosters human wholeness. This may be one of the reasons why people resonate, synchronize and benefit profoundly from connection with nature in ways that cannot be replicated by other means (Brymer, Cuddihy, and Sharma-Brymer, 2010; Ulrich et al., 1991). The conceptualization of nature as a mechanism of human wholeness has yet to be defined or described as earlier, but seems to be critical in understanding its significant contribution to human health.

## Wholeness

The ancient Indo-European root *kailo* means 'whole' and is related to words such as wholesome, health and holy, as well as hollow (which all lend themselves to a more holistic perspective of health) (Hufford, Sprengel, Ives, and Jonas, 2015). From this perspective, cultivating wholeness involves the integration of physical, psychological and spiritual aspects, all of which contribute to being a fully developed human being. In contrast, the dominant perspective of health in contemporary medicine and psychology is one of separation. Health care is segregated into numerous fields, all focusing on specific aspects of health rather than applying a holistic view; Medicine focuses on specific aspects of health (psychiatry focuses on mental health and pathology, internal medicine on physical health and pathology, etc.).

Therapeutic approaches are also segregated by focusing on different theories of human development and health (e.g., psychodynamic therapy focuses on unconscious thoughts, transpersonal therapy takes a spiritual perspective, and behavioral therapy looks at actions). Although most of them view good mental and physical health as the mere absence of symptoms, but not as quality of wholeness (Hufford et al., 2015), a deep yearning for wholeness may persist in human beings.

The notion that individuals sincerely seek and need wholeness, internal and external fulfillment and deep meaning for healthy development and growth is not new, and is found in the writings of classic humanists. Rogers, for example, came to believe that there is one single, basic human motive that he termed 'the actualizing tendency'. He also specified "the human underlying and inherent tendency, to move towards the constructive accomplishment of its potential" (Thorne, 1963, p. 26). This humanistic perspective involves delving into unconscious motives and developing a capacity to be able to fulfill one's unique identity (Mearns and Thorne, 2000).

Maslow (1968) referred to fully developed (self-actualized) individuals motivated by something beyond basic needs, that is by values that transcend the self. He argues that it is self-actualization that signifies hidden potential—talent or competency that has not, as yet, come to the surface and is made actual in a continuing, unfolding process, with no clear end in sight. The notions of well-being, self-actualization and the flourishing of the self have gained serious attention within the field of positive psychology (Seligman, 1998).

Furthermore, second wave positive psychology (SWPP) has gone a step further, taking a more inclusive perspective of these attributes. SWPP argues that full human development can best be described as the joining and appreciation of conceptual opposites, holding the complexity and paradox of life in its totality (Lomas and Ivtzan, 2015; Ryff and Singer, 2003; Wong, 2011). It is a dialectical view, characterized by a more integrative approach toward the concepts of positive and negative. Indeed, it argues that flourishing includes the appreciation and even embracing of the complex and ambivalent nature of life, while also finding meaning and virtue or *eudaimonia* (Greek for 'happiness,' 'welfare' and 'flourishing') (Held, 2004; King, 2001; Wong, 2011).

From this perspective, then, cultivating human wholeness involves a process of knowing or uniting with various unconscious and even contradictory/irrational aspects of the self and, when nature is involved, may include being in a relationship with the more-than-human world as well.

## The Catch

Up until now, the concept of personal wholeness has been described in terms that make it seem worthwhile attaining, but there is a catch. To gain wholeness, one needs to be aware of, in touch with and responsible with yet-unknown aspects of self and the world. Now in certain instances, experiencing these new aspects of one's self lead the individual to breakdown or disrupture when these newly discovered aspects do not 'fit' one's current identity. In other instances the experience may lead to the feeling of great joy and understanding while when not challenging may not instigate change. For example, let us take Erik (age 68) who recalled a profound moment in nature when gazing at the void between the stars on a dark night in the desert. Lost in time and space, he experienced what he called 'a unifying force' and gained an understanding of how monotheism came to be. As an atheist, experiencing the irrational space and power of nature on that starry night expanded his awareness regarding belief in a higher force.

However, although Erik's experience was significant, it did not contain dissonance nor did it change his perception of self or the world, and did not leave a lasting impression. It seems that in the cases in which this new information brings about dissonance and rupture, the opportunity for significant change occurs. Perhaps this is because newly revealed aspects have to do with the very characteristics and personal issues that one has done everything (both consciously and unconsciously) to hide, avoid and even eliminate in order to maintain a coherent identity.

Our lifestyles, social groups, working methods and intimate relations are usually structured in a way that maintains the equilibrium of our basic beliefs and perceptions of ourselves and the world. In this way, being open to significant new aspects and knowledge of self and the world that may expand consciousness and contribute to personal development and wholeness are avoided or buried in the unconscious, so one's personal equilibrium and identity are disturbed as little as possible. Of course, in the process of maintaining our identity, personal beliefs and current lifestyle, we will end up avoiding situations that may be disruptive to us and even beneficial in the long term.

Expanding consciousness and integrating significant new perceptions necessarily involves changing one's general patterns of experiencing and relating to oneself, others and the world (Vieten, Schlitz, and Amorok, 2009). So while we might think wholeness and full development are wonderful ideas, the process is a risky one and we need to be willing to turn away from our basic human inclination to maintain our equilibrium. Indeed, if we do decide to expand our personal beliefs and notions of the world, in an endeavor to become whole, we risk a "rupture [or breaking] in the knowing context" (Loder, 1989).

This, then, may be the reason that, in many cases, personal transformation comes about in the aftermath of unavoidable situations. Traumatic events and major life challenges often act as a catalyst for significant, even dramatic, life transitions, in which former beliefs and worldviews are severely shaken (Baumeister, 1991; Linley and Joseph, 2004; Tedeschi and Calhoun, 2004).

Mezirow (2003) describes these situations as profound opportunities for a transformational learning process, involving the destruction and reconstruction of basic identity structures. These descriptions are in line with dynamical systems perturbation studies that describe the destabilization of a system as an opportunity for new form and evolution (Jeka and Kelso, 1995). Experiencing profound rupture and destruction of inner structures is, of course, extremely uncomfortable and will, in most cases, be avoided or rejected by the individual. As Quinn puts is so well (2004): "We are all masters of claiming we want change, while doing all we can to avoid it" (p. 25). Luckily for many of us seeking to live full and meaningful lives, personal comfort and harmony are not enough to sustain us and our personal need for wholeness will be constantly sought motivated by a gnawing soul yearning.

This inner motivation is clearly expressed by Milner (1969), who seems to capture the process of change well in the following statement:

> *Certainly, some patients seemed to be aware, dimly or increasingly, of a force in them to do with growth, growth towards their own shape, also as something that seemed to be sensed as driving them to break down false inner organizations which do not really belong to them; something which can also be deeply feared, as a kind of creative fury that will not let them rest content with a merely compliant adaptation; and also feared because of the temporary chaos it must cause when the integrations on a false basis are in process of being broken down in order that a better one may emerge.*
> (pp. 384–385)

## The Cure

Change or development, from the perspective of wholeness, moves away from problem-solving or a planning-based approach toward something that focuses primarily on personal growth, essentially a process of becoming (whole) (Williams and Irving, 1996). "The literature abounds with papers and discussions of resistance, yet little we study the vagaries of the force that is on the side of psychic healing, the impulse to grow, to surrender, to let-go" (Ghent, 1990, p. 5). In this chapter, we are moving forward in this direction by looking at the deep, human yearning to feel complete, connected and actualized. And not as an ailment in need of correction or a behavioral problem, either; rather as a significant motive for human wholeness. Furthermore, we are looking at ways this process may be cultivated through nature as offering embodied engaging and challenging situations that foster new and expansive ways of being and perceiving, hereby contributing to wholeness without a traumatic pretense.

For example, let us take Rachel (aged 57), who participated in a workshop in the desert. For the first time in many years, she was confronted with her fear of not having her regular facilities, feeling exposed and frightened by the prospect of sleeping out in the open. She had just left her husband of 35 years and was overwhelmed by feelings of loneliness and insecurity in the prospect of being alone. Her feelings were mirrored in a concrete manner by nature, in the vast and desolate desert landscape she confronted feelings of loneliness and fear. But, in contrast to her regular behavior at home (inviting friends, keeping busy, being on the phone or watching TV), in nature she was confronted with a situation she could not avoid. Devoid of a means used to keep uncomfortable feelings at bay, nature gave her the time and place not only to grieve the end of her partnership but also to get touch with her inner strength and ability to cope with her needs, alone.

Whether through physically challenging situations, distant and unknown landscapes, aesthetic forms or in the presence of overpowering mountains, nature is a multidimensional setting offering endless opportunities by which formerly unconscious or avoided aspects of self and the world are revealed through experiential engagement. Gaining awareness and ultimately integrating newly discovered personal aspects of ourselves (both conscious and unconscious) as well as infusing spiritual and existential understanding into our lives contributes to our personal wholeness. In fact, nature in its entirety is deemed a vital life source, through which one connects to the fullness of human potential, leading to healthy development (Bratman et al., 2015; Kellert, 2005; Kellert and Wilson, 1995; Oliver and Ostrofsky, 2007).

Let us take the case of Ran (aged 42), a successful businessman who came to therapy because he felt that something in his life was missing. Although he had a family and a thriving business, he admitted "I have everything, but . . . I don't feel alive." After spending a few hours in a forest, at night, he became aware of feelings he had repressed for a long time. Alone there, Ran let himself feel weak and scared, and sought human warmth and comfort, and although these feelings were uncomfortable, he succeeded in feeling connected to inner aspects of his self. Revealing these allowed him to deepen his relationship with significant others and feel more connected and alive, which ultimately led to his feeling more complete.

The natural environment engages us multidimensionally, by connecting us to our bodies, senses, emotions, instincts and environments simultaneously. In such embodied, concrete experiential situations, one may deeply connect both on an internal and external level to various aspects of what it means to be human. Joseph Campbell (2008) described these experiences in relation to the human search for what is true, significant and meaningful. Resonating within our own innermost being and reality contributes to the actual feeling of being alive. No wonder nature is perceived as "one of the most basically important ingredients of human psychological existence" (Searles, 1960, p. 27).

## The Basic Constructs of Human Wholeness as Cultivated by Nature

Wholeness is cultivated when we acknowledge, express and feel in relationship with the many aspects of being human, both internally and externally. In this way a fragmented self, or way of being, may develop into something more connected and whole. This is important, even while the precise ways it operates remains a mystery. Therefore, our research on peak transformative experiences in nature is crucial, because it reveals the main constructs of human wholeness and personal transformation within nature. Phenomenological analysis of our research has enabled us to explain transformational experiences in nature. They involve the discovery of formerly unknown aspects of the self, as well as the world, both of which are significant factors in the transformative effect. I will now present the main findings of our research, focusing on the basic constructs of the process.

In-depth interviews were conducted with 15 participants aged 28–70 years (5 men and 10 women), all of whom identified as having had a peak transformative experience in nature. Phenomenological analysis of these interviews highlighted the 'essence' of the peak experience in nature as a revelation of significant new knowledge, inseparable from the participant's life story. Despite the wide range of both the participants and experiences, the essence of the peak experience remained the same—a moment of insight; a knowing. The revelation often concerned personal lifelong issues that were provoked by nature. On a personal level, the discovery was of formerly unknown or rejected aspects of self, all to do with development, authenticity and self-actualization. At an external level, the discovery involved a new and expansive way of perceiving and relating to the world.

For example, Tamy (aged 55), who is a second-generation Holocaust survivor, described herself as living in constant fear, up until her experience on a boat excursion in the Arctic. While at sea, temperature fell to freezing, eliciting common feelings of helplessness and fear of death. At a certain moment, she realized that she was cradling herself and had calmed herself down. The profound realization that she had overcome her fear, entirely alone, was empowering and instigated a journey of personal actualization.

In another example, Sarah (aged 39), who described herself as a 'people-pleaser', was hiking up a mountain and told her group that she intended to climb to the top. Halfway up, when the group stopped to rest, Sarah turned her head and the most magnificent view appeared before her eyes. She found herself in deep awe and felt no need go any further. "I had everything I needed in that moment; I felt complete." For a short while, she fought with her initial inclination to ascend the mountain, because that was what was expected of her, but soon decided against it. Taking a chance to change her regular 'way of being' was very significant for her. It triggered a deep process, whereby she felt more in touch with herself and understood her wants and needs. This, in turn, helped her pay less attention to social norms and put other people's needs before her own.

In the case of Judith (aged 42), her inability to ask for help or to be supported was mirrored by nature while hiking. At the end of a group of hikers descending a hill, at some point, she felt unstable and stopped. She stood 'stuck' for over an hour until someone came back to aid her, and was shaken by the revelation that it had not crossed her mind to ask for help. The situation in nature projected her inability to ask for help in a concrete way. As a result, she gained a new understanding of her loneliness in life, about which she was previously unaware.

Developing full potential requires both the knowing and accepting of yet-unknown personal perceptions. These often contradict the individual's self and world perceptions, up until that moment, and are therefore put aside or avoided. In nature, lifelong personal issues and worldviews tend to be projected through mostly unavoidable situations. In such concrete situations, participants could not remain neutral or stuck and were able to face previously avoided issues directly.

These newly discovered aspects of the self are not yet consciously part of who we are in life and, in many instances, cannot even be described in words. They have to do with rejected aspects or unresolved personal issues in our lives. In both cases, however, this new knowledge is a threat to our current identity and way of being. In this state, therefore, one strives to find a balance in one of two ways—either by ignoring the new information (in which case no transformation occurs), or by changing/expanding one's perception in a way that can incorporate the new information.

Choosing to reclaim and integrate such newly discovered aspects of the self may expand one's current perceptions, resulting in personal transformation. These findings support previous research, showing that a peak experience involves self-discovery. The way these transformations manifest themselves vary but all evoke an expanded perception of self and that, in turn, leads to a deep change in one's worldview (C'de Baca and

Wilbourne, 2004; Hollander and Acevedo, 2000; Miller and C'de Baca, 1994; Yair, 2008).

The choice to take apart an old perceptional structure and replace it with a new one involves a process of destruction and construction. In turn, this leads to the establishment of a completely new mental structure that changes the person's outlook (Laski, 1961). This is an unsettling process, threatening the individual's current identity, and can lead either to fragmentation or wholeness. Therefore, to fully develop and transform, one needs a guide to help one go beyond current boundaries of consciousness and to begin to know oneself and the world in an expansive and wholesome manner. Usually, this happens with the help of another person (facilitator) by which new insights may be rejected or related to the 'other person's' wisdom. Results of our research, and years of therapeutic work in nature, however, present a whole new system for cultivating inner knowledge and wholeness, that is letting nature take this role. By discovering such new aspects of self and gaining profound insight through nature, the wisdom revealed was not attributed to another's knowledge but to one's inner truth. Maybe this is why participants perceived their insights as an authentic, inner truth, enabling them to internalize the insights as integral aspects of their self.

To conclude then, nature's role in the transformative process was quite significant, enabling a deeper knowing of self and the world while offering new and original ways of being too. Participants recounted that they then made a choice to embrace that part of their experiences that had been projected onto nature. This led to an expansive and more authentic identity, and subsequent personal transformation. These results are attributed both to the symbolic and concrete ways in which significant knowledge is made conscious.

Nature, in its infinity, symbolizes and enables the projection of the unknown, the ungraspable and the unconscious that through nature's concrete embodiment become tangible. For example, Ruth (aged 32), who described herself as 'a leaf in the wind', lacked self confidence and trust in the world, and never feeling rooted. She participated in a workshop in nature and one of the activities involved walking blindfolded in the forest at night. After walking for a while, she stretched her hand out to touch a tree and was shocked to realize that, in some strange way, she already knew a tree was there. As a result of this incident, she began trusting her instincts, feelings and abilities in such a significant manner that she felt transformed by the event.

These concrete, physical and sensory experiences in nature reveal new ways of being in the world. For many, such 'earthly' means of connecting to the expansive dimensions of life enable one to be open and accepting of such new perceptions. As a result, the embodied experience validates these newly discovered perceptions and aspects, which may have been there all along but did not make sense until nature embodied them in graspable form.

Such examples express the way nature enables one to discover and connect with one's self and the world in a new, expanded manner. This process of becoming more whole has proven to be profound for the individuals who acted on their new understanding, pointing to the significance of wholeness for human development. Therefore, when assessing the therapeutic means, tools, settings and interventions by which human wholeness may be expressed, nature should be regarded as a key component.

## Discussion

The understandings presented here offer a new perspective on nature as an encompassing way of knowing self and life contributing to wholeness. To know nature fully we must go beyond specific definitions that have to do with geography and environmental characteristics and the feasible, physical setting of our world we live in. Nature is greater than our logical/rational mind can grasp, holding within it many paradoxes and mysteries that have influenced human development over thousands of years. Through nature, we can develop a relationship with the many aspects of our being human and 'more than human' aspects, both seen and unseen. In this way we may learn to acknowledge not only the natural setting but also discover a deeper knowing of our intimate relationship and place within the web of life represented by nature.

Nature evokes new and expansive *ways of knowing* by reflecting and embodying the great paradox of existence; sustaining life and destroying it, while encompassing what is within us and around us simultaneously. Its vast and uncontrollable forces arouse profound awe and amazement within us, as well as deep fear in life-threatening situations. Experiencing these abstract and paradoxical aspects can help us expand our current state of knowing far beyond current conceptions. And when we let nature arouse, mirror and engage us through its unknown and uncontrollable elements, one is triggered to personally discover and develop, offering new and expansive opportunities for knowing one's self and the world. By uncovering the vast and at times incomprehensible quality of nature, while expanding consciousness to know something in a new way, we need to discover what we do not yet know of it.

I use the verb *to know* not as the acquisition of factual knowledge but as a discovery of knowledge that has profound impact on the way one perceives self and the world. In this way, to know nature is to experience deep rapport and relationship with nature's many facets. Contemplating and experiencing nature's ambiguity and allowing ourselves to feel perplexed is a unique means of letting ourselves succumb to the element of mystery (i.e., that which is greater than us). Simultaneously, this may assist us in letting go of former notions, being open, curious and accepting of new realms and aspects of nature.

Often, when we acquire significant self-knowledge, we are changed in some meaningful way (Boyd and Myers, 1988). It follows, therefore, that being in relationship with something greater than us, while becoming aware that we are also part of this greatness, may evoke an expansion of self and contribute to a sense of meaning and belonging to the world in which we live. Of course, this does not stand true for every encounter, but through this lens it is possible to become more aware of opportunities for personal wholeness that nature offers.

The basic constructs presented here regarding nature's unique characteristics, as well as the process of wholeness as manifest in nature, give way to various means by which these understandings may be implemented. Expressive therapies provide infinite ways by which these personal aspects as well as natural richness can be harnessed for connecting and cultivating human wholeness. Whether through drama, arts, movement, photography, poetry or stories, the natural environment is an infinite and ever changing source for metaphoric material just waiting to be cultivated. These may include creative dialogue with natural elements, as in writing a love letter to the stars in which that aspect of romantic yearning and love may be expressed. In other instances one may be offered to get in touch with aspects of the child by an invitation to get into the mud and play around. For another, being in touch with one's wild part may be most important by getting naked, coloring one's body, moving like an animal and so on. When helping one connect to inner aspects of strength and courage, climbing a mountain, crossing rushing waters or roaring out loud and deeply from a canyon cliff can help one to connect and express these aspects. When we dialogue with the wind, animals or moon we become aware and connected to the greater world and its wisdom, hereby cultivating a belonging to the world we live in.

When we are aware of the movement of light from sunrise to sunset we may begin to be more in touch with inner as well as outer movement, connecting to all that is temporary and passing. This could be done by being out in the different hours of the day, connecting with the feeling in the body and enacting the movement of morning, noon, sunset and night. Nature's cycle can also be harnessed by ritual when one is called to mark or enact a meaningful passing or life change that ceremonially gains recognition by making a ritual of goodbye when the sun sets or welcoming the new at dawn. Natural elements are also used metaphorically through nature's elements, for example making a fire and consuming what we need to live or connecting to aspects of courage and strength; bathing in water to cleanse and start anew or kneading the earth and creating something by feeling the earth. One may be invited to build a shelter while fostering that aspect of being able to care for oneself. And sometimes the creative implementation is simple and comes naturally, as by just being aware of the feeling when walking barefoot and seeing the mark you leave with every step, which can trigger a feeling of meaning and connection to the whole of life.

These examples show various creative ways by which different aspects of wholeness may be evoked in order to elicit a more connected and whole way of being. Alternatively one may work with the whole as in Dr. Bill Plotkin's Soul-centric Developmental Wheel (2010). His theory of human development is based on 25 years of nature-based 'soul guiding' and vision quests, traditional shamanic wisdom and contemporary depth and archetypal psychologies. As a heuristic framework he suggested the Soul-centric Developmental Wheel (SDW). This life-span circular model portrays human development as ecocentric stages of life that lead to psychological maturity, true adulthood and elderhood in congruence with nature's cycles (e.g., the seasons). Utilizing this model involves deciphering the individual's place in the process of personal growth on the SDW while developing means for integrating the different parts to cultivate full development (Plotkin, 2008, 2010). For example identifying with the north aspect of the wheel involves discipline and responsibility and according to his model refers to adulthood or the winter. If a person has this identification, he or she is encouraged to find and cultivate all the other aspects for developing wholeness (e.g., develop the wild child in the south, the spiritual aspect of the elder in the east, and so forth). This model is very helpful in assessing a client's current position in the process of wholeness as well as offering a base from which various creative interventions can be fabricated. Whether through specific preplanned interventions or spontaneous connections, nature can be harnessed as a gateway through which one may pass to experience expansive ways of knowing oneself and the world.

## Conclusion

In light of the research discussed here, the process of personal transformation and wholeness through nature is very much like a pilgrimage (to one's self). Sites of pilgrimage have been defined by Edith and Victor Turner as "places where miracles once happened, still happen, and may happen again" (Dubisch, 1996, p. 70). Pilgrims seek a truth and an understanding in their travels that is beyond their reach in their everyday lives. They are, as a result, inhabiting a subliminal space, an 'in-between' their former and future selves, and their former and future ways of life. Pilgrims engage in the experience of losing their old identities as a crucial part of their rite of passage of their journey (Coleman and Elsner, 2002).

Nature is a wonderful guide in the pilgrimage to human wholeness, providing endless opportunities to discover who we are, while connecting to the greater world. And, at the end of this long journey, the greatest discovery is that nature is about discovering the profound within us. As T. S. Eliot remarked:

> *We must not cease from exploration and the end of all our exploring will be to arrive where we began and to know the place for the first time.*

## References


Atkins, S., Adams, M., McKinney, C., McKinney, H., Rose, L., Wentworth, J., and Woodworth, J. (2003). *Expressive arts therapy: Creative process in art and life.* Boone, NC: Parlway.

Baumeister, R. F. (1991). *Meanings of life.* Guilford Press.

Berto, R. (2005). Exposure to restorative environments helps restore attention capacity. *Journal of Environmental Psychology, 25*, 249–259.

Boyd, R. D. (1994). *Personal transformations in small groups: A Jungian perspective.* New York: Psychology Press.

Boyd, R. D., and Myers, J. G. (1988). Transformative education. *International Journal of Lifelong Education, 7*(4), 261–284.

Bratman, G. N., Hamilton, J. P., Hahn, K. S., Daily, G. C., and Gross, J. J. (2015). Nature experience reduces rumination and subgenual prefrontal cortex activation. *Proceedings of the National Academy of Sciences of the USA, 112*(28), 8567–8572.

Brymer, E., Cuddihy, T. F., and Sharma-Brymer, V. (2010). The role of nature-based experiences in the development and maintenance of wellness. *Asia-Pacific Journal of Health, Sport and Physical Education, 1*(2), 21–27.

Byrnit, J. (2006). Primate theory of mind: A state of the art review. *Journal of Anthropological Psychology, 17*, 5–48.

Campbell, J. (2008). *The hero with a thousand faces.* Novato, CA: New World Library.

C'de Baca, J., and Wilbourne, P. (2004). Quantum change: Ten years later. *Journal of Clinical Psychology, 60*(5), 531–541.

Coburn, M. J. (2006). *Walking home: Women's transformative experiences in the wilderness of the Appalachian trail.* Unpublished doctoral dissertation, Institute of Transpersonal Psychology, Palo Alto, CA.

Coleman, S., and Elsner, J. (Eds.). (2002). *Pilgrim voices: narrative and authorship in Christian pilgrimage.* Oxford: Berghahn Books.

Conn, S. (1995). When the earth hurts, who responds? In T. Roszak, M. E. Gomes, and A. D. Kanner (Eds.), *Ecopsychology: Restoring the earth, healing the mind* (pp. 156–171). San Francisco: Sierra Club Books.

Csikszentmihalyi, M. (1997). *Finding flow: The psychology of engagement with everyday life.* New York: Basic Books.

DeMares, R., and Krycka, K. (1998). Wild-animal-triggered peak experiences: Transpersonal aspects. *Journal of Transpersonal Psychology, 30*, 161–177.

Drengson, A. (2005). The life and work of Arne Naess: An appreciative overview. *Trumpeter: Journal of Ecosophy, 21*(1), 5–60.

Dubisch, J. (1996). Anthropology as pilgrimage. *Etnofoor, 1*(2), 66–77.

Dufrechou, J. (2002). Coming home to nature through the body: An intuitive inquiry into experiences of grief, weeping, and other deep emotions in response to nature. *Dissertation Abstracts International, 63*(3), 1549B.

Ellison, M., and Hatcher, T. (2007). *Wilderness solitude and transformational change: Implications for the workplace.* International Conference on Human Resources Development and Practice across Europe. Oxford, England.

Fredrickson, L., and Anderson, D. (1999). A qualitative exploration of the wilderness experience as a source of spiritual inspiration. *Journal of Environmental Psychology, 19*, 21–39.

Gatersleben, B. (2008). Humans and nature; Ten useful findings from environmental psychology research. *Counselling Psychology Review, 23*(2), 24–34.

Ghent, E. (1990). Masochism, submission, surrender: Masochism as a perversion of surrender. *Contemporary Psychoanalysis, 26*(1), 108–136.

Goldfried, M. R., and Davila, J. (2005). The role of relationship and technique in therapeutic change. *Psychotherapy: Theory, Research, Practice, Training, 42*(4), 421.

Grady, B. (2009). *Nature as a transformational space and facilitating environment for psychological growth: A psychodynamic perspective.* Unpublished doctoral dissertation, Massachusetts School of Professional Psychology.

Hammitt, W. E. (1982). Cognitive dimensions of wilderness solitude. *Environment and Behavior, 14*(4), 478–493.

Hammitt, W.E., and Brown, G.F., Jr. (1984). Functions of privacy in wilderness environments. *Leisure Sciences, 6*(2), 151–166.

Hartig, T., Evans, G. W., Jamner, L. D., Davis, D. S., and Gärling, T. (2003). Tracking restoration in natural and urban field settings. *Journal of Environmental Psychology, 23*(2), 109–123.

Held, B. S. (2004). The negative side of positive psychology. *Journal of Humanistic Psychology, 44*(1), 9–46.

Herzog, T., Maguire, C., and Nebel, M. (2003). Assessing the restorative components of environments. *Journal of Environmental Psychology, 23*, 159–170.

Hollander, D. B., and Acevedo, E. O. (2000). Successful English Channel swimming: The peak experience. *Sport Psychologist, 14*(1), 1–16.

Hufford, D. J., Sprengel, M., Ives, J. A., and Jonas, W. (2015). Barriers to the entry of biofield. Healing into 'mainstream' healthcare. *Global Advances in Health and Medicine, 4*(suppl.), 79–88.

Jeka, J. J., and Kelso, J. A. S. (1995). Manipulating symmetry in the coordination dynamics of human movement. *Journal of Experimental Psychology: Human Perception and Performance, 21*(2), 360.

Kaplan, R. (2001). The nature of the view from home psychological benefits. *Environment and Behavior, 33*(4), 507–542.

Kaplan, R., and Kaplan, S. (1989). *The experience of nature: A psychological perspective.* Cambridge: Cambridge University Press.

Kaplan, S. (1983). A model of person–environment compatibility. *Environment and Behavior, 15*, 311–332.

Kaplan, S. (1995). The restorative benefits of nature: Toward an integrative framework. *Journal of Environmental Psychology, 15*(3), 169–182.

Katcher, A.H., and Beck, A.M. (1987). Health and caring for living things. *Anthrozoös, 1*(3), 175–183.

Katcher, A., and Beck, A. (Eds.). (1987). *New perspectives on our lives with companion animals*. Philadelphia: University of Pennsylvania Press.
Kellert, S. R. (2005). Wooing of the earth. *Environmental History, 10*(4), 712–714.
Kellert, S. R., and Wilson, E. O. (1995). *The biophilia hypothesis*. Washington, DC: Island Press.
King, L. A. (2001). The hard road to the good life: The happy, mature person. *Journal of Humanistic Psychology, 41*(1), 51–72.
Korpela, K. M., Hartig, T., Kaiser, F. G., and Fuhrer, U. (2001). Restorative experience and self-regulation in favorite places. *Environment and Behavior, 33*(4), 572–589.
Laski, M. (1961). *Ecstasy in secular and religious experiences*. Los Angeles: Jeremy P. Tarcher.
Linley, P. A., and Joseph, S. (2004). Positive change following trauma and adversity: A review. *Journal of Traumatic Stress, 17*(1), 11–21.
Loder, J. E. (1989). *The transforming moment* (2nd ed.). Colorado Springs, CO: Helmers + Howard.
Lomas, T., and Ivtzan, I. (2015). Second wave positive psychology: Exploring the positive-negative dialectics of wellbeing. *Journal of Happiness Studies*. doi:10.1007/s10902-015-9668-y
Maslow, A.H. (1968). Music education and peak experience. *Music Educators Journal, 54*(6), 72.
Maslow, A. (1971). *The farther reaches of human nature*. New York: Viking Press.
McDonald, B. L., and Schreyer, R. (1991). Spiritual benefits of leisure participation and leisure settings. In B. L. Driver, P. J. Brownand, and G. L. Peterson (Eds.), *Benefits of leisure* (pp. 179–194). State College, PA: Venture.
McDonald, M., Wearing, S., and Ponting, J. (2009). The nature of peak experience in wilderness. *Humanistic Psychologist, 37*(4), 370–385.
Mearns, D., and Thorne, B. (2000). *Person-centered therapy today: New frontiers in theory and practice*. London: Sage.
Mezirow, J. (2003). Transformative learning as discourse. *Journal of Transformative Education, 1*(1), 58–63.
Miller, W. R., and C'de Baca, J. (1994). Quantum change: Toward a psychology of transformation. In T. E. Heatherton and J. L. Weinberger (Eds.), *Can personality change?* (pp. 253–280). Washington, DC: American Psychological Association.
Milner, M. (1969). *The hands of the living God*. London: Hogarth.
Naess, A. (1973). The shallow and the deep, long range ecology movement. A summary. *Inquiry, 16*(1–4), 95–100.
Naor, L. (2014). *Transformational peak experience in nature*. Unpublished master's thesis, Haifa University, Haifa.
Oliver, L. E., and Ostrofsky, R. (2007). The ecological paradigm of mind and its implications for psychotherapy. *Review of General Psychology, 11*(1), 1.
Plotkin, B. (2008). *Nature and the human soul: Cultivating wholeness in a fragmented world*. Novato, CA: New World Library.
Plotkin, B. (2010). *Soulcraft: Crossing into the mysteries of nature and psyche*. Novato, CA: New World Library.
Pretty, J., Peacock, J., Sellens, M., and Griffin, M. (2005). The mental and physical health outcomes of green exercise. *International Journal of Environmental Health Research, 15*(5), 319–337.

Quinn, R. E. (2004). Building the bridge as you walk on it. *Leader to Leader, 34*(1), 21–26.
Roszak, T. (1992). *The voice of the earth: An exploration of ecopsychology*. New York: Simon & Schuster.
Roszak, T. (2009). A psyche as big as the earth. In L. Buzzell and C. Chalquist (Eds.), *Ecotherapy: Healing with nature in mind* (pp. 30–36). San Francisco: Sierra Club Books.
Rust, M., and Totton, N. (2012). *Vital signs: Psychological responses to ecological crisis*, London: Karnac Books.
Ryff, C., and Singer, B. (2003). Ironies of the human condition: Well-being and health on the way to mortality. In L. G. Aspinwall and U. M. Staudinger (Eds.), *A psychology of human strengths* (pp. 271–287). Washington, DC: American Psychological Association.
Searles, H. F. (1960). *The nonhuman environment: In normal development and schizophrenia* (Vol. 5). New York: International Universities Press.
Seed, J., Macy, J., Fleming, P., and Naess, A. (1988). *Thinking like a mountain: Towards a council of all beings*. Philadelphia, PA: New Society.
Seligman, M. (1998). What is the good life. *APA Monitor, 29*(10), 2.
Sevilla, J. C. (2006). *Ecopsychology as ultimate force psychology: A biosemiotic approach to nature estrangement and nature alienation*. Philadelphia: XLibris Random House.
Stilgoe, J. R. (2001). Gone barefoot lately? *American Journal of Preventative Medicine, 20*, 243–244.
Swatton, A. G., and Potter, T. G. (1998). The personal growth of outstanding canoeists resulting from extended solo canoe expeditions. *Pathways: The Ontario Journal of Outdoor Education, 9*(6), 13–16.
Tedeschi, R. G., and Calhoun, L. G. (2004). Posttraumatic growth: Conceptual foundations and empirical evidence. *Psychological Inquiry, 15*(1), 1–18.
Terhaar, T. L. (2005). *Nature, trauma, and the soul: The mystical experience in nature as a wellspring of spiritual values*. Ann Arbor: Proquest. www.il.proquest.com UMI# 3169001.
Terhaar, T. L. (2009). Evolutionary advantages of intense spiritual experience in nature. *Journal for the Study of Religion, Nature and Culture, 3*(3), 303–339.
Thorne, F. C. (1963). The clinical use of peak and nadir experience reports. *Journal of Clinical Psychology, 19*(2), 248–250.
Trace, N. (2003). *Complexity, Buddhism and adventure therapy*. Paper presented at the Third International Adventure Therapy Conference, Victoria, BC, Canada.
Ulrich, R. S. (1993). Biophilia, biophobia, and natural landscapes. In S. R. Kellert and E. O. Wilson (Eds.), *The biophilia hypothesis* (pp. 73–137). Washington, DC: Island Press.
Ulrich, R. S., Simons, R. F., Losito, B. D., Fiorito, E., Miles, M. A., and Zelson, M. (1991). Stress recovery during exposure to natural and urban environments. *Journal of Environmental Psychology, 11*(3), 201–230.
Vieten, C., Schlitz, M., and Amorok, T. (2009). A research-based model of consciousness transformation, *Shift: At the Frontiers of Consciousness, 23*, 32–34.
Williams, D. I., and Irving, J. A. (1996). Personal growth: Rogerian paradoxes. *British Journal of Guidance and Counselling, 24*(2), 165–172.

Williams, K., and Harvey, D. (2001). Transcendent experience in forest environments. *Journal of Environmental Psychology, 21*(3), 249–260.
Wilson, E. O. (1984). *Biophilia*. Cambridge, MA: Harvard University Press.
Wilson, M. (2011). Encounters with nature as a path of self-realisation: A meaning-making framework. *Journal of Transpersonal Research, 3*(1), 11–29.
Wong, P.T.P. (2011). Positive psychology 2.0: Towards a balanced interactive model of the good life. *Canadian Psychology/Psychologie Canadienne, 52*(2), 69–81.
Wood, R. (2010). *Psycho-spiritual transformation experienced by participants of modern wilderness rites of passage quests: An intuitive inquiry*. Unpublished PhD dissertation, Institute of Transpersonal Psychology, Palo Alto, CA.
Yair, G. (2008). Key educational experiences and self-discovery in higher education. *Teaching and Teacher Education, 24*(1), 92–103.
Zimmerman, M. (1997). *Contesting earth's future: Radical ecology and postmodernity*. Berkeley and Los Angeles: University of California Press.

# 11

# DIGGING BONES AND CROSSING THRESHOLDS

## Healing Individuals and Communities Through Nature-Based Expressive Arts, Ceremony and Ritual

*Sally Brucker*

### Introduction

This chapter will outline both the principles and practice of incorporating the use of ceremony and ritual into our work within the broader frame of eco-arts therapies. If we decide to think 'outside the box' of our training, we are going to find ourselves in new terrain. As the field of expressive arts therapies continues to expand globally, evolving methods of eco-arts therapies hold potential for this changing dynamic. For expressive arts therapists versed in the many art forms, which lend themselves to unconscious exploration and insight, adding eco-arts therapies to our repertoire would seem to be a 'natural fit' (Brucker, 2016). From a holistic perspective, working with the psyche, body and spirit automatically includes the natural world. We can see this space as metaphorical, mythical, transpersonal and symbolic. The form that this practice will take will vary according to our own experiences with the natural world, our training, personalities and level of comfort with this model. I would not propose to offer a 'one-fits-all' model of practice within this framework. Indeed, as more expressive arts therapists and others begin to adopt these methods, it will be exciting to see the myriad variations it takes.

### Background

In the book *Green Studio: Nature and the Arts in Therapy* (Brucker, 2016), I wrote of my path to eco-arts therapies from a traditional clinical art therapy and psychodynamic psychotherapy practice. I traced my history of working in the field of psychodynamic psychotherapy in the clinical setting from the individual to group, to the art therapy studio model, and finally to the out-of-doors, over the course of nearly 40 years of clinical practice with adults and children.

Drawing from theoretical underpinnings of Gestalt, Jungian, Transpersonal and Mindful psychotherapies, I was able propose an evolving and dynamic model of eco-arts therapies, which more directly reflected the complexity of both the individual psyche and collective 'container' or the world outside. The addition of the Green Studio (Kopytin, 2016) as a living, organic, reflective space offers new healing potential and possibilities for change.

## Rationale for the Green Studio in the Context of Ceremony

The Green Studio (Kopytin, 2016) concept is concerned with the idea of moving the clinical setting out-of-doors, and to a state of mind, emanating from one's connection to *poiesis* (Levine, 1992). The concept of poiesis, according to Stephen Levine, is that: "art making is . . . an extension and development of the basic capacity of human beings to shape their worlds" (Levine, 1992, p. 23). This capacity to both create and adapt to any situation, which allows for improvisation and creativity, is unique to our work in the field of expressive arts therapies.

According to a recent article in the *Washington Post* (Fears, 2016), the simple act of showing videos of nature to inmates significantly reduced aggressive behavior and recidivism. In fact, when given the choice of viewing nature videos versus watching TV or other activities, 9 out of 10 inmates chose to watch the videos. One staffer stated in the research survey that "the response was amazing because sometimes all it took was 15–20 minutes in the nature imagery area to calm them down and get them back on task."

More than 90 percent of inmates surveyed agreed that "they felt calmer when they watched the nature videos." It was further confirmed that calm state was sustained for hours. Nearly 80 percent agreed that when they felt agitated, they could recall the videos, to calm themselves. A majority also said it improved their relationships with their wardens, and still others reportedly said that it made serving time easier. Others reported that subsequent visits with family members, especially children, were enriched by this experience in that they, themselves, felt calmer and more receptive.

We all might agree that the very act of being in nature slows down our heart rate, which allows us to experience a deeper connection to the environment, our senses and others. Wilderness training weekends challenge the individual to 'push' past fears, reduce stress, improve decision-making and achieve greater interdependence. Activities such as gardening, hiking, camping and watching a sunset or waterfall are experiences that trigger a chain of events that bring us closer to what has been called our 'authentic' selves. Because achieving this 'authentic self' is also the goal of psychotherapy, it would make sense that we, as psychotherapists, would want to 'draw' upon this valuable and free resource. The logistics of how to do this, within the bounds of the 50-minute individual and 90-minute group therapy sessions (usually held indoors and in privacy to maintain trust and confidentiality), might seem insurmountable and even questionable for some.

One simple way we might do this, without changing the paradigm of the clinical psychotherapy session, is by prescription. We could prescribe walking in the woods or watching nature videos to our clients. In these cases it would be as an adjunct to the therapy and would greatly depend on our clients' motivation and capacity to gain from such an experience. As such, it might be seen as temporarily valuable in reducing anxiety and levels of stress. This can also take on the form of a routine or ritual (repeated meaningful actions), sometimes called 'sustenance rituals'. An example of this is seen in the following case vignette.

## *Case Vignette*

Clara,[1] a 60-year-old woman diagnosed with chronic schizophrenia (with paranoid features), reported that her self-prescribed daily walk in the wooded park adjacent to her large apartment complex was a ritual that grounded and quieted her mind. She took photos of birds, squirrels, deer, trees and flowers, often adding original poetry and painted images. To Clara, this daily ritual was a 'quiet refuge' where she could feel 'nearly normal'. This experience of allowing her senses to guide her lowered her anxiety to the point where she could actually perceive herself in an accepting, kind and gentle way, which rarely happened in her encounters on the bus and in her community. It was, as if, her paranoia 'magically' took a back seat. She came to rely on these early morning walks 'to keep me sane'.

Her painting (Figure 11.1) of a black tree 'in the dead of winter' depicts a stark foreground, in contrast to the brilliant colors of the sunrise, in the background. According to Clara, this symbolized her 'desire for peace and solitude' and how she 'gathers energy for her day'. She loves how the light and shadow play off of each other in the painting, likening it to how the 'lights and shadows of my mind' offset each other.

Her unpublished poem further reflects these thoughts:

*The beauty of a tree shall always bring joy to my heart and soul—*
*I have often wondered if trees feel the pain*
*When struck by lightening*
*When they fall in a windstorm*
*And if they feel anguish and dismay when people cut them down*

*I suppose I shall never know*
*If trees feel pain, sadness or despair, as I have often felt myself*
*Perhaps. . . . not knowing what makes them persevere.—*
*The Wonder of it all*
*Adds to their splendor*
*They are indeed*
*Nature's ballerinas*
*Dancing in the wind and rain*
*Making my spirit come alive.*[2]

**Figure 11.1** Clara's tree (acrylic painting, 8″ × 12″)

Printed with permission

## Why Ceremony

Ceremonies have existed across cultures for thousands of years. They offer a fascinating glimpse into our collective unconscious. Ceremonies incorporate myth, story, music, movement and symbolic objects. Ceremonies are inclusive and often transformative. While many of us associate ceremony with the more traditionally religious paradigms, such as weddings, christenings, bar mitzvahs, graduations, and funerals, the use of ceremony has evolved and expanded in meaning over the past decade.

My training in non-denominational ceremony creation and enactment was with the Celebrant Foundation & Institute in Montclair, NJ, established in 2001. "The Celebrant Foundation & Institute believes affirming life's milestones through customized, thoughtful ceremony strengthens the bonds of families, partnerships and communities and deepens the human connection across generations" (Celebrant Foundation and Institute, 2001).

While the focus of this training began with creating more traditional ceremonies such as weddings and funerals, it has branched out considerably in direct response to the changing fabric of our culture and the need of the clients seeking their services. Ceremonies for life transitions might now include adoptions, divorce, new homes, job downsizing, deployment and healing from trauma. While the structure of all ceremonies might be similar, the rituals, stories and intentions are unique to each individual.

My use of ceremony and ritual expands the concept of healing from trauma from the individual or group psychotherapy session to both families and communities, within the Green Studio. Within the global context of our work, the use of ceremony has great potential. Expressive arts therapists are already working within the context of social and global issues, which impact individuals both sociologically and psychologically. Debra Kalmanowitz and Bobbi Lloyd in the former Yugoslavia (Kalmanowitz and Lloyd, 2005), Gloria Simoneaux in Nepal and Kenya (*Harambee Arts Project*), Krupa Devi in south India (*Sankalpa Art Journeys*) and Carrie Herbert and Kit Loring in Cambodia (*Ragamuffin Project*) are just a few of the expressive arts therapists who have made pioneering contributions to the field.

Expressive arts therapists are creating ceremonies with persons suffering from post-traumatic stress disorder (PTSD) as a result of forced migration, abuse, violence, sex trafficking, war, oppression and discrimination and natural and man-made disasters, and those who live with the debilitating complex of symptoms associated with PTSD such as anxiety, flashbacks, uncontrollable rage, nightmares, eating disorders, depression, repressed memories and so on. The threshold ceremony is a useful place to begin understanding how ceremony contributes to healing from an individual to collective level. The threshold ceremony is the type of therapy that is being proposed for expressive arts therapies practice; it is always non-denominational and catered to the specific needs of the client as a co-collaboration between her and the therapist. Threshold ceremonies are designed to usher in a change in status or role of the individual as she passes from one life stage into another, shedding what she no longer needs and acquiring new skills for the path ahead. In a threshold ceremony, one literally steps over or through a constructed or imagined threshold, which symbolizes this change from before, during and after the ceremony.

## Understanding Non-Denominational Threshold Ceremonies in a Contemporary Context

Ceremonies consist of a universal structure that contains story, ritual, music, art and personal vows, in order to assist, affirm and celebrate individuals as they pass through important stages or passages in their lives. The time leading up to the actual ceremony involves a series of stages, which contain both practical and psychological tasks. The outer ceremony then mirrors the inner changes necessary for this life passage that is, in turn, acknowledged by others who serve as 'witnesses'. These 'changes' are thus 'incorporated' into the fabric of the community, which ultimately 'holds' and validates the person within a larger context than he or she could accomplish individually. Within this context, it is important to acknowledge this fundamental role of ceremony and how it exponentially expands the notion of healing for our clients.

While the more familiar life passages (weddings, funerals, etc.) contain socially acceptable rites and rituals with universally held meaning, healing ceremonies, for example, do not. The typical path to healing ceremony is not unlike the 'Hero's Journey' (Campbell, 1949). This begins with a series of impulses that something is wrong or not functional within the prescribed 'roles' in which one is functioning. It is often resisted, which causes stress and suffering. This might be the point where one might seek out a psychotherapist, as a means of alleviating this stress. The 'journey' of psychotherapy may be likened to 'digging up bones', or long hidden or repressed emotions. This in turn might lead to assessing what needs to be released from the past to make room for change.

Assisting in the crossing–over of a threshold from one way of being (role) into another involves a process. This process consists of a series of stages that include:

1. Hearing a 'call'. This time is usually accompanied by feelings of 'unrest', a gnawing sensation that one's way of life is changing. It is often initially met with resistance, followed by relief. It can go unheeded for sometime, often causing physical or psychological distress.
2. Separating physically or psychologically in order to 'sort' out what is happening. This period contain some unknowns and fears and can be navigated alone or with a 'helper', such as an expressive arts therapist. It can take an unspecified amount of continual or interrupted time.
3. Clarification and creating intention for the ceremony. This stage signifies that the process of change is in motion and an action is imminent.
4. Defining the ceremonial space. Because ceremony is often seen as a 'sacred' or out-of-the-ordinary experience, it is important to create a meaningful space. The out-of-doors may not always comply with our

desires, due to the unpredictable forces of nature, but it would be important to consider planning for it regardless. The main purpose for being 'in nature' for ceremony is twofold. First, grounds us to the elements of earth, air, fire and water, which in turn open our senses to a deeper experience. Second, being 'in nature' for ceremony also connects us to the transpersonal realm of life, allowing us to understand our place in the 'grand scheme' of things, however we define it. Any rituals, music and so forth associated to the earth, sun, moon, water, fire, air and planet should be considered.

5. Co-creating rituals and structure of ceremony. This stage involves crafting the elements of the actual ceremony. This might include storytelling, selecting music, creating the 'sacred' space and the 'threshold', creating meaningful rituals such as candle lighting, giving of a symbolic gift for the next phase of life, 'crowning', letting go of something from the past, reciting vows to oneself or others, acknowledging mentors, friends and so on.
6. Enactment of ceremony in front of others. The ceremony is relatively short in length compared to the planning phases that precede it. It may last anywhere from 15 to 40 minutes. It involves a processional and crossing over the threshold, enacting the rituals described earlier; and a recessional where the threshold is crossed again, but in the new phase of life, as enacted through the intentions of the ceremony.
7. Incorporation of the experience through food, drink and celebration. This is an important element of the ceremony in that the imbibing of drink and eating of food and general merriment help to incorporate the experience for the individual within the community. It also reaffirms the community of support available to the individual(s).

Caveats: Ceremonies must never be forced or inflicted upon anyone, however well intentioned. Ceremonies are not indicated if a person has not completed the first stage of isolation and reflection or does not feel ready to cross over this threshold. Ceremonies are not a good idea if one's intentions are superficial or revengeful. In order for ceremonies to succeed it is important to have at least one person of support from one's life.

## A Training Model for Expressive Arts Therapists

This form of creating threshold ceremonies in the natural environment requires time, patience and an in-depth understanding of the power of the natural world to heal, nurture and impact psychological well-being. One of the best ways to train students in eco-arts therapies is to create an outdoor experiential training. One such training was conducted in June 2016, in the Botanical Gardens in Moscow, in co-operation with Varvara Sidorova

PhD, and her students of Expressive Arts Therapies at Moscow University. The students were eager to incorporate this work into their practices. The weather complied with our wishes and we met under a beautiful old tree, bringing picnic lunches, as we planned to be there all day. The process will be described below.

### *Initial Orientation Phase*

We gathered to introduce ourselves by placing an 'object' from nature into our mandala-shaped altar, which served as a visual grounding and collective creation, that we could return to throughout the day, as we processed and shared our questions, concerns, and insights. We could chant, sing, and quiet our minds, mirroring the contemplative practice of Buddhist monks, as they create and dissemble sand mandalas. Although not made of sand, this altar/mandala too represented the intransient time we would spend together, and carried the knowledge that we would need to ritually deconstruct it at the end of the day (Figure 11.2). This Buddhist notion of impermanence is an important transpersonal component of the work, which often serves to intensify the connections and the intention of finding personal meaning for each participant. Students were also instructed to be

**Figure 11.2** Mandala altar—eco-arts therapies training

'silent' for the entire day, except for the time spent planning their ceremony with their small group and the final discussion. This was done intentionally as a ritual, which would allow a much stronger sensorial and psychological experience. It was met with some initial resistance, but quickly dissipated into the norm. The quiet that ensued allowed us to observe the environment to a much greater degree.

Students were next divided into small groups of no more than six persons. An exercise designed to focus them on a particular issue in their lives was given, and they were also instructed to use their five senses as they began to explore the natural environment and collectively select an area in which to work within their small group. We evoked the four elements of wind, air, fire and earth and faced the four directions. These exercises are borrowed from rituals of Native Americans in the United States. They are used respectfully and with acknowledgment of their origin, as a way to 'ground' the participants to the earth. I 'borrow' rituals from other cultures as deemed appropriate and would instruct others to do the same. It is always better if you can experience these rituals through a teacher, rather than just reading about them, but this is not always possible. The structure of the threshold ceremony was outlined in this training, as well as the elements of ceremony and ritual (to be discussed later). The initial orientation took about an hour.

### *Creation Phase*

The students were then asked to disperse throughout the park, and collectively select the site that suited them. They were given 90 minutes to collaborate on creating a threshold space and ritual that would allow them to enact their own rituals and welcome the rest of the class through this space, in a ceremonial intention. They were invited to use both natural, found and 'other' materials (cloth, stones, shells, etc.). It was understood that we were 'guests' of nature and would need both to 'ask' and 'receive' permission to work there, as well as to return the space to the condition in which it was 'found'. All of these intentions were specifically designed to create a 'sacred' or separate-from-ordinary space and to practice the beneficial aspects of collective ritual. Ritual was seen as a collectively agreed upon and prescribed series of actions, which held both personal and transpersonal meaning to the experience, setting it 'apart' from our everyday experience.

It was interesting to observe how others in the park responded by staring, laughing, and so on to our 'alterations' of the natural environment, which included hanging ribbons and cloth and rope, laying things on the ground, making music, etc. One young man, who at first appeared threatening to the group, walked over to a tree where they were 'working', began to grab 'his' tree limb and rather loudly do his exercises, completely ignoring them and their process. He explained that he came to that exact tree every day and that we were interrupting his exercise routine. After this was explained, the students were able to accommodate each other's needs around the tree, despite initial tension. The lesson that came from this was that we could not 'appropriate' the park for our own use!

After this phase of working, we broke for a silent, meditative lunch.

### *Sharing and Enactment Phase*

After lunch, we took turns 'visiting' each of the created sites in order to experience their specific ritual and ceremonial meaning. One of these was a contemplative space, concerned with the aesthetic experience of texture, pattern, color, space, temperature etc. We were invited to sit, observe, listen and be still. Another space invited singing, mimicking sounds in nature and creating music according to one's relationship to animals. There was a childlike, regressive and playful experience in this space (Figure 11.3). In another we were ushered through a maze or labyrinth, up a small hill and into a ritual space. We adorned ourselves with twigs and leaves (Figure 11.4). The complexity and layered meaning of all of these spaces emphasized for me the myriad creative options and psychological

**Figure 11.3** Eco-art therapy training—'tree person'

**Figure 11.4** Eco-art therapy training—one with tree

meanings afforded through interactions with natural elements. It was as if the Green Studio unbound the creator from her own neuroses and collectively allowed a synchronicity of more authentic and 'natural' responses to emerge.

The feedback from students related mainly to pleasure of being outdoors, handling the natural materials of dirt, twigs, flowers, leaves and trees, and spontaneously co-creating, adding cloth and other materials. There was a strong investment in each site by the small group, which made it important to dismantle the space, as a ritual form of closure to the experience. The fact that their hands, bodies and senses were simultaneously engaged served to strengthen the experience as well. Being able to guide others through these spaces, symbolically and creatively, gave them a sense of empowerment and sovereignty, which translated into their outside lives. A long discussion of the entire experience helped to further incorporate this experience before we dismantled our own altar, piece by piece.

### *Reflections on the Experience*

While experiential exercises are an integral part of our training as expressive arts therapists, it is rare that we would spend an entire day out-of-doors with our professors and classmates. On this day in Moscow, I was reminded of a rare experience that I had in 2001, while studying at the EGS Graduate School in Saas-Fe, Switzerland. High up in the Swiss Alps, one could not help but marvel at the physical beauty and grandeur of the mountains, glacial streams, icebergs and mountain walking paths surrounding our school. We hiked, made art out-of-doors and were encouraged to do as much on our own as possible. This contributed greatly to our communal life as students as well as a feeling of being nurtured by nature as well as academia. This memory is particularly poignant for me, as it was during a difficult time in my life.

While I rarely discussed what was going on with me, I participated in all of the outdoor activities and community life, and can say without a doubt that my emotional pain had a strong reprieve during that time. There was a sense of release, freedom, expansiveness and compassion that spilled over into my relationships and work. Had the school been in any other setting, I doubt that I would have benefited as much.

My students, on that glorious June day in the Botanical Gardens of Moscow, seemed to exude a similar sensation.

## Case Example—A Spontaneous Healing Ceremony

Co-creating ceremony and ritual may not be indicated for all of our clients. This work is usually presented to those clients, who have done a considerable amount of self-exploration and are still 'stuck', or unable to reconnect with others or their past. If a connection is seen as important, whether to a person, persons, place or past, we might then explore ceremony. The work is presented as being structured yet malleable enough to shape and create for each individual's specific intention. Clarifying the intention is a crucial aspect of the collaborative work of the therapist and the client.

A recent experience of an unexpected and spontaneous healing ceremony occurred while I was teaching psychology students and art therapists in Moscow. I taught a daylong workshop under the auspices of the Art Therapy Center that dealt with the psychological development of women from a Jungian psychological perspective. We looked at our life-spans as they related to archetypes of maiden, mother, queen and crone, in an attempt to explore our individual and collective psyches and to offer clues to places where we had become stuck in our lives. The purpose of the workshop was to use this knowledge as a way to assist other women with issues of identity, sexuality, and empowerment. As in all of my workshops and classes, which ask that students participate on an experiential and therefore personal level, I initially create a series of checks and balances, agreed upon by the group. These include confidentiality and asking participants to only reveal as much as they are comfortable sharing.

When one of my students, Paula,[3] a woman in her forties, came to the class with many drawings that she wanted to share, I had to make a quick decision. My practice, in situations like this, is to usually allow some time to focus on this, if I think it would be useful for the student and the group, even if it seems to somewhat highly emotionally charged. When Paula spread approximately 15 paintings on the floor, it became obvious that she was relating a story of deep trauma.

She explained that these paintings had occurred rather spontaneously, that she had never done anything quite like this, and that she was a bit overwhelmed, but glad she had done them and showed them to the class. I quickly surmised that this material, along with Paula's issues, would require many hours of psychotherapy, well beyond the scope and framework of our day. My dilemma was how to help Paula with this material, while respecting the needs and focus of the group. We looked at the work with her, listened to her descriptions and acknowledged her bravery and need to process this. Based on some of her story and my perception that she had processed some of this, I made the decision to ask her if she would consider creating a healing ceremony for the future. Our afternoon agenda included creating ceremonies, so she would get some ideas of this. I asked Paula to study this structure along with the class and to co-create a threshold ceremony that would address this issue. Because this was to be a collective ceremony, each student was asked to do the same. Paula agreed and we proceeded to outline the intentions, roles, stages and elements of the ceremony.

At the end of the afternoon, the students enacted a collective healing ceremony, which was both meaningful and powerful. Paula contributed her drawings and spoke about wanting to leave much of her difficult past behind her, but she was unable to create the small ceremony assignment, due to her overwhelming emotions. She was able to contain a great deal of emotion and experience due to the constraints of the group, which greatly impressed me. After the class was finished, she approached me again, saying she was 'ready' to enact her own healing ceremony. I voiced some concerns about the timing and the fact that I could not assist in this due to my work schedule, but she persisted. We exchanged our email addresses and went our ways.

Within several days, Paula contacted me, inviting me to her ceremony. Unfortunately, this was on a day that I could not attend. She also invited several students from the class, who also could not attend. I feared that this would be an overwhelming disappointment for her, while at the same time hoping I could see her again to talk to her about the time that this required. Several days later, she texted me that she would attend another all-day seminar I was teaching in Moscow on SoulCollage (Frost, 2010), and asked if it would be possible to do her healing ceremony at the end of the day. Initially I hesitated, as it was going to be a very long day of teaching. We had no time to plan this, and I wasn't sure if I could use the space or if anyone would come. I decided not to announce it to the class, but did inform several colleagues and students who had been in Paula's other class with me. Not only did they all agree to stay, but they asked me if several psychologists who they knew could attend, as they were very interested in this work. Paula agreed to this and we all agreed to meet after the class was finished. Paula fully participated in the SoulCollage seminar and waited patiently afterwards.

### *Paula's Ceremony*

Approximately 10 people squeezed into a small room, where Paula proceeded to create a long aisle of her drawings down the center (Figure 11.5). The room was then darkened and candles were lit. Within five minutes, this rather drab room was transformed into a sacred space. The group surrounded Paula so closely that it made me think of a womb. There was an unspoken feeling of safety and acceptance, a 'holding environment', as described by Winnicott (2005).

Paula's paintings lined the path. In silence, by candlelight, she then stood at the beginning of her 'path' and slowly made her way, glancing down at her artwork and reading her poetry. When she reached the end, I stood to greet her, as she read out loud a series of vows she had made for herself. At some point, the 'witnesses' spontaneously stood up and collectively raised their hands, surrounding Paula. Many persons voiced their wishes and thoughts in support of Paula, her courage and her journey to this point. She then ate the raspberries and blew a small horn, thus concluding the ceremony.

**Figure 11.5** Paula creating the threshold space

Printed with permission

Here is a description of the ceremony, in Paula's words (adapted and translated from Russian):

**Cranberry, Raspberry and Pomegranate Tears**

*My fear caused me to start painting. My paintings were weird and I did not understand their meaning but this activity helped me to overcome depression. When Sally Brucker came to Russia I went to her seminar devoted to female archetypes and methods of coping with a life trauma. When I completed the first stage I managed to understand the meaning of one of my paintings, which I named 'Pomegranate Tears' (Figure 11.6). I felt related to the archetype Persephone and I understood*

**Figure 11.6** 'Pomegranate Tears'—Paula's original painting

Printed with permission

*for the first time that I had lived, liked her, in the shadow or 'underworld', psychologically. I wished to create a ceremony for myself, in order to have a happier life. But, when it was my turn I failed to go along a symbolic path and step across a symbolic threshold. Physically, this is a very simple act, but psychologically, it was impossible for me on that day. On some level, I felt that I did not deserve happiness and that the path after the threshold, did not belong to me. Sally took my hand to help me, but I still could not do it.*

*The next day I made up my mind that I wanted to complete the ceremony. We were able to arrange it for the following week. Almost instantly, I had a scenario. I chose two Slavic symbols—cranberry (a Russian symbol of foreign lands and woman's burden) and raspberry (a symbol of homeland and a happy life). A cranberry would be at the beginning of my route and a raspberry would be at the end. I took a piece of wallpaper to serve as my symbolic road. The part before the threshold, I colored black and dark blue and the part after the threshold a lighter shade of blue (Figure 11.7). I decided to scatter my paintings along this 'road' and to read my poems about transformation. I bought a basket full of raspberries, to treat everyone after the ceremony. I asked Sally to meet me after I crossed the threshold. I was nervous with many strangers in the room, but I felt their support. They looked at my paintings with interest and asked me about them.*

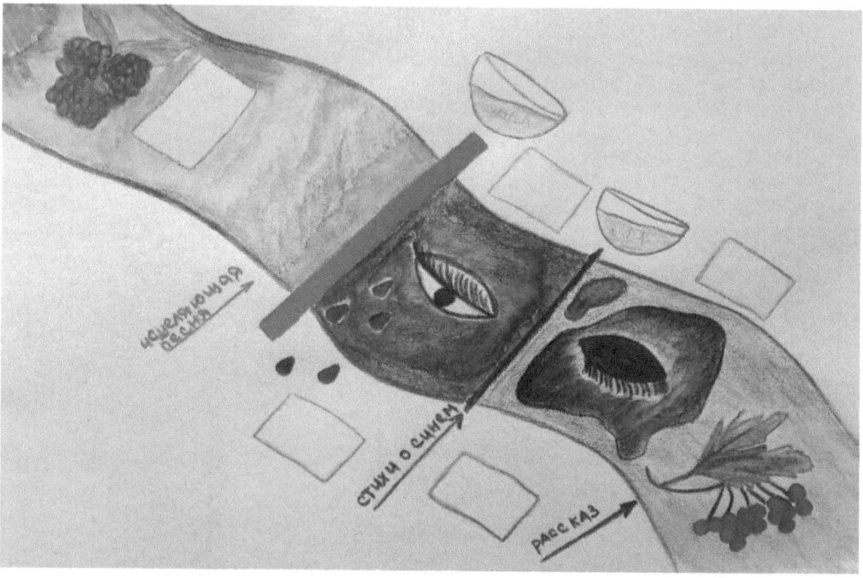


**Figure 11.7** Paula's threshold—detail

Printed with permission

*When the ceremony began, it was emotionally difficult, as I had to remember difficult times in my life. I managed to step across the threshold, where Sally was already waiting for me. She gave me my raspberries. We lit candles and I blew a small pipe. People raised their hands over me, which felt very supportive and afterwards, we drank tea to celebrate the beginning of my new life. It was so important to feel the support of the people who watched my ceremony and to understand that the world is not as dangerous, as I had thought. I believed in myself and I saw that I have everything I need in my life. I just needed to be more attentive to it. This gave me hope.*

This threshold ceremony evolved spontaneously and was highly unusual. It points to the fact that when given the opportunity and once a highly structured 'safe' environment is provided, unexpected healing may occur. In this case, I trusted both myself, Paula and the 'holding environment' of the group, which were crucial ingredients to its success.

The ceremony took place indoors but included elements of the natural world, such as water, fire, earth, fruit and nature imagery.

## Final Thoughts—Implications of Threshold Healing Ceremonies

The field of expressive arts therapies offers highly sensitive and effective approaches to psychotherapy. As expressive arts therapists, we continue to develop, expand and even 'improvise'. My use of threshold healing ceremonies in conjunction with eco-arts therapies evolved from many years of working in the field and efforts to create the 'best' practice, which emanated from the needs of my clients. While this form of work may not appeal to every expressive arts therapist and indeed may not even be appropriate for many clients, it is nevertheless worth studying and considering. As our work evolves from the clinical setting to the refugee camp, for example, it behooves us to adapt new methods and to be open to alternative types of healings that result within this changing context.

The threshold healing ceremony is an example of a cross-cultural form that has universal meaning and can be readily adapted to many situations. Expressive arts therapists can adapt this form in order to co-create artistic and meaningful expressions of inner change, that will outlive the ceremony itself. The healing power of the natural setting and the use of natural elements forge an even richer experience. Further study of ceremony is recommended through reading or online training. It is hoped that many more expressive arts therapists will begin to utilize this form of eco-arts therapy, bringing individuals, families, communities and societies closer to a more accepting way of incorporating everyone's life experience and story into the fabric of their lives. When we are collectively able to acknowledge human suffering among the most vulnerable in our midst, we come closest to our own humanity. We need this on a continual basis and we need to think of this as a very basic human need.

## Notes

1. Name changed to protect identity.
2. Printed with permission.
3. Name changed to protect identity.

## References

Brucker, S. (2016). 'The tonic of wilderness': An evolving eco-arts therapy model: From theory to practice. In A. Kopytin and M. Rugh (Eds.), *'Green Studio': Nature and the arts in therapy* (pp. 137–154). New York: Nova.

Campbell, J. (1949). *The hero with a thousand faces.* Novato, CA: New World Library.

Celebrant Foundation and Institute. (2001). Montclair, NY. Retrieved from www.celebrantinstitute.org

Fears, D. (2016, August 5). Speaking of science. *Washington Post*, Washington, DC.

Frost, S. (2010). *SoulCollage evolving.* Santa Cruz, CA: Handford Mead.

Kalmanowitz, D., and Lloyd, B. (2005). Inside the Portable Studio: Art therapy in the former Yugoslavia, 1994–2002. In D. Kalmanowitz and B. Lloyd (Eds.), *Art therapy and political violence: With art without illusion* (pp. 106–125). New York: Routledge.

Kopytin, A. (2016). Green Studio: Eco-perspective on the therapeutic setting in art therapy. In A. Kopytin and M. Rugh (Eds.), *'Green Studio': Nature and the arts in therapy* (pp. 137–154). New York: Nova.

Kopytin, A., and Rugh, M. (Eds.). (2016). *'Green Studio': Nature and the arts in therapy.* New York: Nova.

Levine, S. K. (1992). *Poiesis: The language of psychology and the speech of the soul.* Toronto: Palmerston Press/Jessica Kingsley.

Winnicott, J. (2005). *Playing and reality.* New York: Routledge.

# 12

# UNTIL DEATH DO US PART

## The Relational Heart of Human-Animal Bonds

*Straja Linder King*

### Introduction: Animals Are Caretakers, Too

*Fragile bones rise again \ Soothing limbs of ancient trees \ Tangled in the stars.*

—Straja Linder King

Since domestication first unfolded between humans, horses, dogs, cats and other furry friends, the role of our companion animals has increasingly evolved in significance. Animals have taken on a variety of roles in people's lives. Animals were our hunting comrades and guardians prior to evolving into sharing our world as family members. Most modern-day two-legged families include at least one four-legged member in the domestic household, and many have two or more.

From feral to family, these animals have bonded to us in a way that still mystifies full comprehension. I say that because the love between a human and non-human animal is often stronger than that of the human-to-human bond. We embrace the adage of 'family is whoever you say', and looking at family disputes in courts demonstrates that our animal companions are close to being fellow citizens. One can pick up any paper and read about families going through divorce and the custody battles entail their animals as well as their children. When families decide not to have children, these animal companions take on an even greater role in the clan. The ensuing bout for custody of the household pet becomes a serious altercation. That is how powerful human–animal bonds have become and continue to grow and blossom exponentially.

Human-animal bonds are instinctive and underscore the basics of attachment theories (on Bowlby and Ainsworth, in Bretherton, 1992). The bare essentials of attachment theory state that we all need love. Added to that are the sense of being known or recognized, essentially understood and a true sense of belonging. Our animal companions deliver all of this and more. A good example is their capacity for unconditional love, attentive listening and forgiveness. Unfortunately, we have been educated out of this natural attachment of human–animal bonding and our deeper ways of knowing, something we refer to as instinct. Animals instinctually deliver all these notions with ease.

The etymology of instinct is from the Latin *instinguere*, 'incite', eventually moving to 'impulse' after the English acquired it (Ayto, 1990). Humans on the other hand have either lost their instincts or overridden their impulses with objectifying thereby masking this deeper knowing with complicated theories. In other words, if the theory overrides our instincts then we lose the passion of reasoning as well. Losing the somatic benefits of trusting our instincts or being aware of this innate knowing often results in minimizing the importance of ceremony and ritual. Ceremony and ritual underscore birth and death rites of passages. The indigenous or First Nations peoples have honored these rites of passage throughout history. They incorporate animals and nature in their ceremonies. Indigenous peoples do not objectify or segregate living forms within nature. This holistic communion can enlighten and provide further insight surrounding three core values: ecology, ethology and evolution.

Indigenous peoples honored the weaving of these three values through their creation myths. Creation stories survived by being passed down through oral tradition. Without these myths our relationship to the natural world becomes disconnected and out of balance. When we drop our rituals and ceremonies surrounding life and death, often fear will take up residency in our thoughts to fill this void. Fear of death can compromise our innate wisdom of knowing that from the moment of birth we are actually in the process of dying.

Animals do not carry this constructed fear around with them simply because they live in the present. In their natural habitat animals are seemingly more comfortable than humans with the death process. Therefore our animal companions make productive assistants for human beings facing death. Animals carry great sensitivity and are known to create rituals surrounding the death of their own. They grieve the loss of life as well. A good example is the filmed death of a young elephant (National Geographic, YouTube, February 23, 2014). The herd of elephants instinctively grieved by shedding tears, stomping their feet, and even trying to bury the deceased. The herd remained at the side of a deceased calf for days. The elephants instinctively created a ceremony and ritual.

Beauty unfolds in witnessing the presence of a therapy dog comforting the client when death is imminent. Therapy dogs are at the utmost a calming agent and known to mitigate the anxiety surrounding death and dying.

Current research and media have shown over and over the beauty and efficacy of engaging therapy animals at the patient's request. The fear mitigates and comfort is increased. Fear continues to be a major factor emotionally for both the palliative patient and surrounding family members comforting them. My working therapy animals have assisted the dying for many years now and as a team we have had the honor of doing celebrant work as well. My therapy dogs have partaken in funerals, memorials, hospital trauma, and hospice work. As working dogs, they are foremost emotional support workers when assisting the dying.

One of my working therapy dogs named Tangus earned the title of *Heart of the Hero Dog* for his grace and guardianship surrounding a memorial service. The service entailed a celebration of life surrounding the death of a young man who was director at a children's camp. Shortly thereafter Tangus, a remarkable therapy dog, once again took the notice of media and hospital officials due to his intelligence and instincts. Tangus alerted the hospital team of professionals present in the emergency's quiet room (a dedicated room for patients when the decision is final to stop all intervention) when the death of this individual was occurring. Tangus literally alerted all present in the quiet room prior to the technology that the life force of the individual was leaving the physical body. Tangus' instincts knew the life went out of this woman's body before the machinery could register the shift. The professionals present stated that if they had not witnessed this incredible experience themselves that they would not have believed it possible. On the other hand, Tangus was simply doing his job in companioning the dying.

Our animal companions bridge life and death with grace and facilitate the shift from this world to the next where often we hope to meet again. After all, we are blessed that animals actually choose to be at our sides. Our animal companions accompany us through the highs and lows of our journey through life. How fortunate for us that human-animal bonds are the strongest known to humankind.

## Death

*Underneath the death \ Of dark pain-filled memories \ Birth of presence dwells.*

—Straja Linder King

Death, lonely as a train whistle, is hauntingly seductive, like a 13th-century Japanese koan full of mystery and paradox. The first time I encountered death without any adult intervention to fast track the experience into a happy ending or euphemism occurred while hiking down the railway line with my best friend from school. With bagged lunches in hand we would challenge ourselves by tightrope walking along the parallel steel bars side by side. Instantaneously, we spotted the dark silhouette of an animal carcass up ahead. Arrested in our tracks we stared at the deceased rodent with a mixture of horror and curiosity. The black squirrel was completely flattened by the unexpected train encounter. I was immediately reminded of how we used to put copper pennies on the rail just prior to the train coming. Most of the time they simply flew off never to be seen again. This was not a penny and this little being was alive once.

I knew a squirrel would have little to no chance of survival against the steam-driven giant. Intrigued, I simply stood and stared at the dust-covered carcass realizing that this little rodent probably expired many moons ago. Oddly, the dehydrated body held its shape perfectly. Mesmerized, the contour reminded me of a template one uses in an elementary class when attempting to render a perfect squirrel. I remember staring without any dialogue in total awe of my proximity to this post-living entity. There was a quiet yet engaging beauty mixed in that ethereal moment where time is meaningless. I was standing with the finality of death. Intrigued, I grabbed my camera from my pack and began taking photos like a forensic detective at the scene of a crime. I had a small 35 mm camera containing one precious roll of film. Back in the days of film-fed cameras there was precious discernment prior to clicking the shutter button. I distinctly remember trying to capture the myriad emotions within the tiny aperture. Above the dark waters of mysteries a bridge of consciousness spanned the horrific to the sublime. When viewing the carcass as pure form the beauty of perfection delivered a stillness that was palpable.

This reminds me of the Japanese aesthetics of the tension found in between time and space (Pilgrim, 1986). The Japanese term *Ma* translates into a negative space beyond meaning and time, and I was definitely suspended in that threshold. Here unfolding in front of me was a stillness that spoke. In other words, the presence of absence heightened my awareness and invited me the opportunity to integrate the two. *Ma* represents this quiet infusion. I tried my best to capture all of these feelings on film. Being outside of time and memory surrounded me in a visceral stillness that remains with me to this day.

A laden day full of unpredicted mysteries or *Ma* allowed my first sliver of enlightenment or conscious awareness to come through the door. Sometimes the most horrific experiences and times of our lives offer up incredible insights, creativity and deep clarity. In other words, I got that rare and raw glimpse through the portal of awareness that lies between the veils. A tiny sliver of light becomes a beacon through the deepest, darkest forest.

*When you walk through a forest that has not been tamed and interfered with by man, you will see not only abundant life all around you, but you will also encounter fallen trees and decaying trunks, rotting*

> *leaves and decomposing matter at every step. Wherever you look, you will find death as well as life . . . Death is not the opposite of life. Life has no opposite. The opposite of death is birth. Life is eternal.*
>
> (Tolle, 2003, p. 101)

Experiencing a dark night of the soul shifts our way of being in the world. I learned foremost that life and death are inseparable. Death feeds life and the circle is endless. Where there is a beginning there will be an end. Walking in any ancient forest attests to this non-dual thinking—the forest where grief roots especially when one of the fallen tree limbs ends up being one of your own. I am gently reminded of Shakespeare's line, 'Nothing is either good or bad but, thinking makes it so'. This is my understanding of grief. It is not possible to grasp life without death. As Eckhart Tolle stated poetically, 'birth not life is the polarity of death.'

Birth and death are much closer than we like to think. And grief is like a rainbow thread that weaves itself throughout our passage here on earth. With each loss endured we add another layer of how the grief impacts our way of being in the world. This grief bundle of living through losses creates a colorful skein that shifts its tones and gradations as it grows. All the unexpected twists and turns produce an intensely hued skein of our experiences that is complex and difficult to unravel. Eventually, consisting of no clear beginning or end. The iridian thread wound throughout this skein weaves a complex path full of mystery. No one is exempt from its needling in our journey especially when faced unexpectedly with death. The string swiftly unravels and binds together without any perceived order or recognized pattern. My emotionally painful initiation into non-dualistic thinking taught me that death does indeed feed life. And witnessing the death of the squirrel in my early childhood was my first helping.

When I got the photos developed of the squirrel on the railway tracks I felt shocked and shamed all mixed together. Viewing the still photographs that held an even more uncomfortable stillness yielded no further answers or clarity. I remember ripping the images up into tiny pieces and yet they remain whole and integrated within me to this day. One can only wonder if this was the prescience to my becoming an art therapist specializing in complicated bereavement. And the philosophy of non-dualism would deepen in later life when invited to assist in the death journey of a loved one, and the gratuitous fact that no one goes through this journey without suffering. Previous to the squirrel encounter, I had processed death as an either/or and not simply as a reality or way of being, especially in my world. Without knowing it at the time, I had learned my first lesson in non-dual thinking. The squirrel story is now a faint memory added to my personal time capsule of living.

Even when taught that nothing lives forever we still find comfort in the eternal moment. However, this healthy denial often shifts when grief unexpectedly rings its ugly alarm. Only then do we wake up to the shock and ravages that life can end without warning. Setting our clocks does little to ensure we see the date change. Hope lives between the hands and digits of its face. Hope is the *Ma* or tension in between the ticking clock hands. Encapsulating this raw awareness provides the certainty that each and every moment passes our way once. Animals seem to have an innate sense of this gospel truth. Animals assist and teach us to realize the infinite power of pure presence. Humans gather and store each and every moment. The collected moments provide the poetic building blocks in the architecture of our memories. Animals know all about the infinite power of raw presence. They are the best teachers, guides and helpers in providing fresh alternatives to the various fears surrounding the mysteries of death.

Animals do not carry the fear of mortality like humans. Animals thrive in presence and therefore do not exhibit this fear. Fear moves in the human psyche when their thoughts deviate from this raw presence. We can broaden our awareness and acquire coping stratagems through simply observing how animals face death or end of life. My first therapy dog named Tangus was remarkable at mitigating this often unconscious fear as well as being able to foster all involved in staying fully present to what was unfolding. The following case study exemplifies how incredible a companion he was when death was imminent. Tangus the therapy dog epitomized the relational heart of human–animal bonds.

## Case Study: Until Death Do Us Part

### *Preamble*

To introduce this case study I must go back a few years prior to becoming an art therapist. While studying fine arts and psychology at university I volunteered at the local hospice. I engaged in art with the residents and staff that inspired me to pursue clinical art therapy at the graduate level. At my side when facilitating weekly art sessions was a long-legged, dark-faced dog named Kuzel, animal companion and best friend. I was unaware at the time that Kuzel would be the inspiring link to future work in animal-assisted therapy (AAT).

Kuzel, a gentle German shepherd, was my co-pilot, teacher and guide. Kuzel was not a registered therapy dog. However, he accompanied me everywhere, happily waiting in my vehicle until work ended. Closely bonded, I took him with me everywhere whether on foot, public transport, or in my vehicle, affectionately referring to it as the 'kennel on wheels'. Together we communicated easily without words. Kuzel understood that he would be rewarded with extended playtime after my classes or work. He had incredible patience and chose to be with me every moment. Always at my side, Kuzel was a loyal and dedicated friend. We made a great team. When I had to leave him in my vehicle, I would give him a couple of cookies and tuck him in his portable bed in the back seat. After a round of warm hugs, I would head off to facilitate the classes that eventually shifted into art therapy sessions after my degrees were completed. I worked in the same seniors complex and adjoining hospice in which I volunteered.

Residents of both the seniors complex and adjacent hospital could be seen gazing out their daily cleaned windows overlooking the compact parking lot. They watched me pull into the parking stall, Kuzel's head out the window smiling at anyone walking toward their cars. The residents witnessed our melodramatic goodbye rituals that we partook of in every visit. Consequently, Kuzel was given an invitation to enter the large welcoming or waiting area of the hospice. Tail wagging, he happily accepted. Kuzel assisted in the 'meet and greet' visits where patients and their loved ones would gather in a large family-like setting. Afterwards, I would put this satiated large black dog back in my truck and I went back in, volunteering my art services in the group room.

Over several months the staff in both the hospice and seniors' residence side came to know Kuzel and would interact with him. A good example was how the kitchen staff spoiled him on numerous visits with leftover meals. Awareness grew knowing there was something truly above and beyond simply having an animal present in this particular milieu. Everyone felt the impact of his presence. The residents, guests, staff and support services all wanted to interact with my canine companion. I noticed that these dog visits produced relaxation, humor, calming and most profoundly the instant sharing among strangers. I did not know then that this human–animal bonding and the communal-type gatherings would unfold and inspire me to pursue a lifelong interest in the power of AAT. You may wonder how Kuzel, a family pet, wound up being the prodigious catalyst for adding AAT to my art therapy profession.

The salient answer is distraction. A dog bearing unconditional love can't be ignored. Reflecting back, the palliative clients along with their loved ones were pleasantly distracted if only momentarily. Grief is inescapable. Any grief is tethered to love in all forms. Interaction with Kuzel activated tiny facial muscles producing smiles on both the grieving faces of patients and visitors. How could this four-legged innocent canine produce such a shift in effect? How could Kuzel manage to break through the darkest barriers of sadness? Distraction. In other words, Kuzel's presence had a way of mitigating anxiety and calming those around him. He was not a legitimate therapy or credentialed dog and he was not allowed into my art therapy sessions. Kuzel was a senior dog who enthusiastically shared his love freely and unconditionally. He had an impact on everyone that crossed his path.

Kuzel died shortly after I began my art therapy profession. His presence remains with me today as he had such an impact on my career path, and became the impetus to my being the recipient of my first pedigreed shepherd from the United States that would attain full credentials as a therapy dog, irrevocably changing my life and work.

### *Between Light and Dark: Last Breath Drawn With Canine Comfort*

For many cultures the month of March represents one of returning light and new beginnings. Quite fitting that the final hours of Regena's life encompassed transitioning from light to dark and into the mystery of both. Concurrently, countries around the world also transitioned between light and dark in celebration of Earth Hour. Earth Hour began in Australia and within a couple of years became a worldwide event honoring conservation of Mother Earth, our planet.

How fitting to be able to be at the bedside of this courageous woman as she transitioned between light and dark facing her own death. March, a month where light and dark meet, encapsulates a non-dualist moment where both elements are in equal measure; the Spring Equinox. Equinox or equilux is a planetary event that means day and night are approximately equal. The Spring Equinox was the penultimate day for what would become the stellar event of Regena's life, the month of her death.

Tangus, my first registered therapy dog, assisted me when I worked with Regena, who attended clinical art therapy sessions weekly. I worked with Regena for many years, and reflecting back I am honored knowing that she called out for Tangus on what would be her final ambulance ride. The hospital contacted me and we drove immediately to the emergency ward. Similar to the proverb surrounding the weather patterns of March, Regena's ambulance roared like a lion into the hospital's entryway. Regena never left that night and exited this world in the quiet room with the gentleness and innocence of a lamb.

Regena and I met during the beginning of my art therapy career. My graduate work was completed outside the country. My first job upon returning to Canada was at a local hospice where I fulfilled the majority of my supervised practicum hours. I met Regena, who resided next door while at this job placement. Regena, a tall slender woman in her sixties, lived in the adjoined seniors' home. The hospice and seniors' buildings looked liked a domino lying on its side. The small-scale windows were blacked out to prevent the glare of afternoon sun. A brief yet spacious corridor connected the hospice to the seniors' residence. The naturally lit passage was wide enough to accommodate those needing wheelchairs. Regena was not one of them. Her ritual as a heavy smoker entailed her having to walk through the second floor corridor that connected the two buildings. The only area that allowed smoking was in the basement of the adjacent hospice or outside of the buildings, weather permitting. Tangus worked alongside me in both buildings. The linking corridor of both buildings would produce an eventual meeting.

The meeting transpired on an overcast day accessorizing Regena's daily smoking ritual. On this windy day steeped in grays she joined the covey of smokers, mostly consisting of hospice staff members, in the designated basement of the hospice. Together they wagged about daily events. Here Regena met the hospice director, also a smoker, who invited Regena to come and experience an art therapy session. I facilitated the bereavement groups along with scheduling individual sessions for palliative patients, family members and staff desiring personal attention. Regena accepted the invitation and attended the next weekly art therapy group.

After the initial session, Regena remained a member of the group until she was moved to a different seniors' complex due to the growth of the hospice. Her new residence was a few miles away. However, Regena kept on attending the group classes and was present the day I added in the animal-assisted therapy (AAT). Here she met Tangus. Even though Regena would move to various locations over the years, she continued to come to her animal-assisted art therapy sessions. I also moved and left the hospice accepting an innovative offer to work in a smaller hospital where I created an open studio approach, a first, in western Canada. With therapy dog Tangus at my side, I ran numerous art therapy groups and worked individually with people of all ages and stages of life. Regena set up a consistent schedule and we met once a week for individual animal-assisted art therapy sessions.

Regena felt more relaxed in the quietude offered in the individual sessions. She also liked the direct and personal attention. During her initial one on one session she disclosed that her cat named Fluffy had died, leaving her bereft and feeling despondent. The actual death of her cat happened prior to her moving to the seniors' residence.

The cat was the only living member left in her immediate family. Regena, predeceased by her spouse and child, was estranged years earlier due to addictions. Both deaths were directly related to addictions. After these deaths Regena had a large, empty home. She decided to invite her elderly mother from outside of the country to move in with her and they would have each other for company. Regena cared for her mother up until her death. After her mother's death she suffered depression, social isolation and deep loneliness due to the complicated bereavement issues. At her darkest hours she rescued a big, fluffy black cat that got its name from this fact. This little ball of fur was just what she needed to instill hope and fill a void. Fluffy was the distraction necessary to help Regena work through the numerous losses.

Rescuing a cat was a healthy distraction that mitigated her loneliness and depression. Fluffy was her family and the bond was solid, deep and safe.

She never felt alone with her loving four-legged feline companion at her side. Fluffy's death left Regena feeling isolated and despondent with a loneliness that defied expression. Shortly afterward she moved into the senior residence, and that is where we met. Regena did not feel safe to disclose this loss in the group. There is still a stigma in sharing the loss of a pet referred to as 'disenfranchised' grief. Regena talked about the other losses in her life but did not mention the pet loss until we worked individually. I attribute this to the presence of therapy dog Tangus in all of our sessions. Regena worked through the pet bereavement with the art therapy, and during her sessions she created a memorial box for Fluffy. This merging of both non-verbal modalities would become the focus of my work. Regena was my first client to experience this merger of AAT and art therapy while attending her individual sessions.

After Regena's death her long-term care residence notified me that the box was waiting for me to come and pick up. Regena stated that she wanted me to have this comfort box always. I still have the embellished memorial to this day. This comfort box held all the memories that Fluffy shared with her prior to her leaving her home and moving into the seniors' complex. And for me all the memories of incorporating animal-assisted therapy into our sessions are encapsulated in this box.

My sense is that Regena would not have opened up so freely if Tangus had not been at her side. He lay beside her chair and attended to her as though he understood each and every word. AAT creates a gate of comfort that facilitates an open invitation to express our feelings safely. Also, Tangus did not talk back and attentively listened with a sacredness that few human therapists possess. Therapy dogs are comfortable with being in long spells of silence. Some sessions consisted of Regena wanting to simply sit in the presence of Tangus, and I would witness a profound communing that was all non-verbal. I would hold this safe space and afterwards observe a shift in both Regena's posture and effect. The efficacy of AAT prevailed through the quiet engagement of Tangus being present to her needs. This is the beauty and power of AAT.

Regena loved Tangus at first sight. She had known my first companion animal Kuzel, who I mentioned earlier, when she resided in the seniors' complex where we initially met. AAT and art therapy merged organically over the years of our working together.

After all those years I found myself at the foot of a hospital bed holding the frail body of Regena in the emergency ward. Regena smiled and thanked me for bringing therapy dog Tangus to be at her side and assist in any way. Tangus happily provided all this and more. His presence impacted all in the emergency room personnel that night. Even the surgeon on triage literally stopped at the sight of Tangus and took off his gloves. He proceeded to squat down next to my therapy dog and petted him in silence. He thanked me, saying that was exactly what he needed and proceeded through the operating doors. Linda, the head nurse on duty that evening, told me that she was actually terrified of big dogs. After witnessing the work of Tangus she said she was forever changed. Years later she still talks about the impact of that particular night and now has a little companion dog of her own. Linda was enamored and fascinated viewing Tangus' work with Regena. Regena looked like a baby robin with the sky blue fading in her soft eyes. As the night grew younger her mouth gasping to catch the slightest stream of air being pumped from intervening machines . . . I was relieved and happy to see the hardware removed from her fine features. Now she was a baby bird mouthing her journey in small strained gasps. Tangus remained loyal and stayed at the foot of Regena's bed. He knew innately that he had the vital role as guardian as she passed from this realm.

This is where Tangus had his first of many experiences comforting and assisting the dying. Tangus and I worked with Regena for over six years until her death in the hospital emergency room in March 2007.

**Figure 12.1** Alberta Hero dog Tangus stands tall after receiving yet another award. Tangus, a Shiloh Shepherd, was nominated for a Leadership Award for 2010 and featured in *Swerve* magazine. At Straja Linder King's side is Tumbra, the pup being trained to carry on with his mentor Tangus' work.

Leah Hennel

## Conclusion

Tangus the therapy dog went on to receive medals and accolades that only touched the surface of his majesty. Tangus had the heart of a hero long before he received that wonderful award. His teachings paved the way for my AAT work that I continue to engage in daily. My current therapy dogs named Twillow and Tala work as a team adding endless joy teaching students the benefits of incorporating and merging AAT with art therapy. Tangus taught me how to be a better human and my work as a clinical art therapist deepened and broadened with our working as a team. Tangus was an extraordinary therapy dog and lived an adventurous life. He died unexpectedly the day before receiving yet another honor for his work in the community.

The untimely death of Tangus was one of the darkest nights of my life. Grief was my payment for his hallowed friendship and endless assistance. Side by side we worked daily for almost a decade. Grief is a broken heart, and the severing of our loving relationship broke mine. I took the time to grieve and invited the joy of knowing that his memory would live forever within me. My fondest memory is that Tangus was a grief counselor held in the highest regard. Animals assist us in understanding that grief is what we pay for love. I loved and trusted Tangus more than words could possibly express. Darcie Sims, a grief specialist, stated, 'May love be what you remember most'. After working through my own grief I focused on remembering our working together and the profound love we shared.

Animals have an uncanny way of reaching us in a way that humans do not. Their playful engagement inspires us to love and trust again. AAT undeniably makes easier the working through processes surrounding the tender and complicated journey of bereavement. Grief is what we pay for love. AAT provides support and unconditional love. Love is built on trust.

Trust is the precursor to love. Trust inspires us to express our feelings and emotions. The etymology of trust stems from the ancient Scandinavian and specifically Norse *traust* (help, confidence, protection and support) and the word *trust* also relates to animals through the hunt. Who on earth would not benefit from this animal relationship? Trust and love are the building blocks to any relationship. Trust makes us feel safe on life's journey. Trust enables us to love again.

Without trust fear has the audacity to take over and rule. AAT softens and often removes these fears. Animals know how to distract and bring us into the moment. One need not interact with animals to benefit. Merely being in the same space as animals produces calmness and mitigates our fears. Animals have an uncanny way of transporting us into being fully present, and they foster the strength to move us into the next moment of being. The everyday playfulness of animals illuminates our hearts at the deepest level. AAT impacts our awareness at a profound level. Their focus on the here and now are necessary nutrients for feeding the darkest nights of our own journeys in life. An animal's trust, confidence, protection, support and unconditional love are catalysts for healing and thriving. These are some of the benefits of including AAT in our counselling practice. Animals are willing helpers.

At my darkest hours in this life when no one could reach me, I turned to animals and our natural world. Here is where trust was reborn through my engagement with our animal companions. Feelings of hope, enchantment, transcendence, humor, joy and wonder are just a few offerings. Animals freely share their gifts of playfulness and unconditional love. Animals provide all the essential nutrients to sustain us between birth and death. AAT adds a dimension of delight enhancing the non-verbal intervention of art therapy.

Animals are true advisors if only we allow them to assist us in everyday living. They help us not only to survive but also thrive. As Grandin and Johnson (2009) stated, 'animals make us human', and I totally agree with that statement. Our relationship with nature is one that *is* nature.

Animals are the honored guests in this remarkable world and increase the beauty of everyday living. Life has no opposite. The opposite of death is birth. Animals teach us that life is eternal and each moment holds eternity.

## References

Ayto, J. (1990). *Dictionary of word origins*. New York: Arcade.

Bretherton, I. (1992). The origins of attachment theory: John Bowlby and Mary Ainsworth. *Developmental Psychology*, *28*(5), 759–775. doi:10.1037/0012-1649.28.5.759

Grandin, T., and Johnson, C. (2009). *Animals make us human*. New York: Houghton Mifflin Harcourt.

It's time to accept that elephants, like us, are empathetic beings. News. (2014, February 23). Retrieved from http://news.nationalgeographic.com/news/2014/02/140221/-elephants-poaching-empathy-grief-extinction-science/

Pilgrim, R. B. (1986). Intervals ('Ma') in space and time: Foundations for a religio-aesthetic paradigm in Japan. *History of Religions*, *25*(3), 255–277.

Tolle, E. (2003). *Stillness speaks*. New York: New World Library.

## Resources

Rowlands, M. (2010). *The philosopher and the wolf: Lessons from the wild on love, death, and happiness*. New York: Pegasus Books.

Sims, D. (1992). *Why are all the casseroles always tuna? A loving look at the lighter side of grief.* Omaha, NE: Centering Corps.

Tolle, E. (2005). *A new earth: Awakening to your life's purpose*. New York: Penguin.

Tzu, G. (2014). *Awakening in the paradox of darkness*. Victoria, BC: Friesen Press.

# ABOUT THE AUTHORS

**Beverley A'Court**, BSc.Soc.Sci. (Joint hons. Phil. & Psych.), Dip. A.T. After a brief research career in Architectural Psychology, Beverley has been practicing art therapy since 1981, initially employed in acute and long term psychiatric services, learning disability, special and adult education, then pioneering holistic eco art therapy via supervision, summer schools and courses for professionals and students. As a long term member of the Findhorn Foundation Community, she has contributed to many international conferences, festivals and programmes, and developed many applications of eco art therapy. She is an advocate for the recognition of poetic language, the body, ecology and cultural traditions in art therapy.

**Ronen Berger** is founder of Nature Therapy, drama therapist, dancer, and ecologist. Founder and head of the Nature Therapy program at Tel Aviv University and the Drama Therapy MA program at the College of Arts and Social, Israel. Ronen has developed national therapeutic programs which took place under the auspices of the Israeli Ministry of Education, including the "Safe Place" program that involved more than 12,000 traumatized children and the "Encounter in nature" program that involved hundreds of children with learning disabilities. He is an active therapist and group facilitator working with various populations. He has published many articles and books and is considered a leading figure in the fields of Nature Therapy.

**Sasha (Sally) Brucker**, MSW, MA, ATR-BC, CAGS, holds three masters degrees; in early childhood special education, art therapy, and clinical social work. She received post-masters training in expressive arts therapies at the European Graduate School in Saas Fee, Switzerland. Ms. Brucker has been practicing art therapy for over 40 years. She has been a visiting professor at Galludet University, Art Therapy Italiana, Hampshire College, Harmony Institute (St. Petersburg, Russia) and Institute for Psychology (Moscow, Russia). She was on the faculty of Montgomery College in Maryland. She founded the Studio Downstairs (www.studiodownstairs.org), a therapeutically-informed arts studio for adults living with mental illness. She is also a certified life-cycle celebrant and SoulCollage facilitator. Ms. Brucker has presented workshops both throughout the United States and internationally. She is also an exhibiting artist. She lives in Takoma Park, Maryland.

**Janet A. Courtney**, PhD, LCSW, RPT-S, is Founder of FirstPlay Therapy® and an Adjunct Professor at Barry University School of Social Work, Miami Shores, FL. She is a Registered Play Therapy-Supervisor, TEDx Speaker, and a StoryPlay® Facilitator. She is past President of the Florida Association for Play Therapy, and is a member of the Association for Play Therapy Ethics Committee. Dr. Courtney is co-editor of the book, *Touch in Child Counseling and Play Therapy: An Ethical and Clinical Guide*, and her research into practitioner experiences of training in touch and Developmental Play Therapy is published in the *American Journal of Art Therapy* and the *International Journal of Play Therapy*, and her co-authored article on Botanical Arranging is published in the *Journal of Therapeutic Horticulture.* She offers a certification in FirstPlay Therapy® (including FirstPlay® Infant Massage Storytelling) and provides training to professionals in the Ethical and Clinical Competencies of Touch, StoryPlay® (an Ericksonian-based model), Expressive Therapies, Gestalt Play Therapy, and Ecopsychology Play Therapy. She has been invited to speak nationally and internationally including the Cayman Islands, England, Ireland, Morocco, Russia and the Ukraine.

**Jean Davis,** MPS, ATR-BC, LCAT, is a licensed, registered and board-certified art therapist with twenty years of experience as a practitioner. She is an Associate Adjunct Professor in Pratt Institute's Graduate Creative Arts Therapy Department, is the Supervisor of the Creative Arts Therapy Department at the League School, is the former Director of the Transitional Living Community, a program of Brooklyn Community Services, and is the former Clinical Director of the Greenwich Village Youth Council. She has postgraduate training in the areas of group therapy, gestalt therapy and applied ecopsychology. She has published several articles on the subject of environmental art therapy and has a private practice in Brooklyn, New York.

**Alexander Kopytin** is a psychiatrist, psychotherapist (Dr. Degrees in Psychiatry and Medical Psychology), Professor, Psychology Department, St. Petersburg Academy of Post-Graduate Pedagogical Education and Psychotherapy Department at North-West Medical I. Mechnokov University. He is a

Programme Leader of Post-Graduate Training in Art Therapy at the Academy of Post-Graduate Pedagogical Education, Chair of Russian Art Therapy Association. He worked with psychiatric outpatients at the day treatment settings in St.-Petersburg for many years, and started to introduce group interactive art psychotherapy since 1996. He wrote and edited many books on art therapy, phototherapy/photo-art therapy.

**Straja Linder King**, MA ATR-BC, Board Certified Registered Clinical Art Therapist. Linder King currently teaches at the University of Lethbridge, Alberta Canada and holds a private practice at the Strawberry Moon Studio. Linder King is a printmaker, published poet and Animal-Assisted (AAT) specialist. Straja has been designing art therapy programs, workshops and presentations both nationally and internationally for over 15 years. Straja holds a Master's degree in Art Therapy and two bachelor degrees both 'With Distinction' in Fine Arts and Art History from the University of Calgary. Ms. Linder King has pioneered art in healing from a spiritual/nature-based perspective in Alberta Canada and does innovative work in health sciences, special education and gerontology. A highly skilled clinician, Straja has taught and supervised for over 10 years at both the graduate and undergraduate levels.

**Lia Naor** is a PhD student in the Department for Counseling and Human Development at the University of Haifa, Israel, researching personal positive transformation, particularly in nature. Lia holds a BA in social work and an MA in drama therapy. She teaches nature therapy, lectures on related topics and has a private practice working with hundreds of clients and groups seeking change. Transformative effects among her clients have propelled her to deepen her knowledge of positive transformation through "Ways of Knowing" – a model for therapeutic quests in nature that she developed. Lia teaches and studies the therapeutic aspects of nature in the context of positive change as a researcher, teacher, and student, and has presented her work in several papers and academic conferences with an international reach.

**Eric Pfeifer**, Prof. Dr., is a music therapist (Dr. and M.A. degrees), teacher and educationalist (BEd degrees), practitioner for psychotherapy, prize-winning composer, musician, author and professor for aesthetics and communication – special emphasis on music at the Catholic University of Applied Sciences in Freiburg, Germany.

**Mary Reynolds Thompson**, CPCC, CAPF, CJF, is a writer, facilitator of poetry and journal therapy, and an eco-coach who teaches and speaks about the transformational power of landscape archetypes. She is core faculty of the Therapeutic Writing Institute, has served on the credentialing board for the National Federation of Biblio/Poetry Therapy and is an instructor for Treesisters, a non-profit working to empower the feminine and reforest the tropics. She is author of *Embrace Your Inner Wild: 52 Reflections for an Eco-Centric World* (2011) and *Reclaiming the Wild Soul: How Earth's Landscapes Restore us to Wholeness* (a 2015 Nautilus Book Award Winner). Born in London, England, she now resides in Marin County, California. www.maryreynoldsthompson.com

**Madeline Rugh**, PhD, ATR-BC, holds a doctorate in adult education, a master's in art education, and a bachelor's in painting and drawing. She is currently an assistant professor at St. Gregory's University in Shawnee, Oklahoma, teaching across disciplines in psychology and visual art. Madeline has facilitated numerous workshops both internationally and in the U.S. on the topic of art therapy with disabled older adults, art therapy and spirituality, and art therapy and ecopsychology. She is an adjunct associate professor for Pratt Institute, the creative therapies graduate program, working as a research/thesis advisor.

**Dina Schapiro**, MPS, ATR-BC, LCAT. Assistant Chair, Director of the Art Therapy Program at Pratt Graduate Creative Arts Therapy Program (NYC). Dina earned her Masters degree in Creative Arts Therapy from Pratt Institute. She began working at Housing Works an institution working with Homeless HIV/AIDS mentally ill chemically addicted population. Within a year Dina became Director of the Creative Arts Therapy department where her interest in creating an inclusive therapeutic environment for her clients was a priority. Dina integrating horticulture therapy with the creative arts therapies. After leaving Housing Works, Dina worked at the Renfrew Center, where she treated women suffering from eating disorders. In 2002 Dina moved to East Hampton and began her private practice specializing in Eating Disorders and addictions. In 2003 Dina was asked to join both Pratt Institute and New School faculty to teach graduate art therapy classes. In 2006 Dina became the practicum coordinator at Pratt while continuing to increase her teaching load. In 2014 Dina took the position of Assistant Chair and Director of the Graduate Art Therapy Department at Pratt she is currently working. In 2013 Dina and her partner, Danielle Epstein, founded the Marble House Project in VT. It is an artists residency program that integrates all the arts with the environment.

**Kate Thompson**, MA, MA, CJT, is a BACP senior accredited Supervisor & Counsellor. She is an existential therapist, a journal therapist and writer. Her first degree was in English Literature at the University of Cambridge. She is core faculty at The Therapeutic Writing Institute and The New School of Psychotherapy & Counselling. She grew up in Yorkshire and now lives in the Rocky Mountains of Boulder, Colorado. Landscape has always been an inspiration for her work, her life and her writing. Her publications include: *Therapeutic Journal Writing: an introduction for professionals* (Jessica Kingsley Publishers, 2011). Co-edited with Kathleen Adams: *Expressive Writing in Counseling and Healthcare* (2015). Co-edited with Gillie Bolton & Victoria Field: *Writing Works: a resource handbook for therapeutic writing workshops and activities* (Jessica Kingsley Publishers, 2006), *Writing Routes: a resource handbook of therapeutic writing* (Jessica Kingsley Publishers, 2010). www.katethompsontherapy.com

# INDEX